American Libraries
before 1876

For B of B.

With very best wishes —
For a real library scholar

Haynes M. M.

American Libraries before 1876

Haynes McMullen

Foreword by Kenneth E. Carpenter

Beta Phi Mu Monograph Series, Number 6

GREENWOOD PRESS
Westport, Connecticut • London

Library of Congress Cataloging-in-Publication Data

McMullen, Haynes, 1915–
    American libraries before 1876 / Haynes McMullen ; foreword by Kenneth E. Carpenter.
        p. cm.—(Beta Phi Mu monograph series, ISSN 1041–2751 ; no. 6)
    Includes bibliographical references and index.
    ISBN 0–313–31277–X (alk. paper)
        1. Libraries—United States—History—19th century.   2. Libraries—United
    States—History—17th century.   3. Libraries—United States—History—18th century.
    I. Title.   II. Beta Phi Mu monograph ; no. 6.
    Z731.M365   2000
    027.073—dc21   99–043164

British Library Cataloguing in Publication Data is available.

Library of Congress Catalog Card Number: 99–043164
ISBN: 0–313–31277–X
ISSN: 1041–2751

First published in 2000

Greenwood Press, 88 Post Road West, Westport, CT 06881
An imprint of Greenwood Publishing Group, Inc.
www.greenwood.com

Printed in the United States of America

The paper used in this book complies with the
Permanent Paper Standard issued by the National
Information Standards Organization (Z39.48–1984).

10 9 8 7 6 5 4 3 2 1

Contents

Illustrations

FIGURES

Foreword

College and university fund raisers believe that it is difficult to raise substantial sums for libraries. The reason, says an acquaintance who has talked with numerous potential donors, is that people have a generic image of a library, which is basically the small, local public library; and consequently they do not understand that a library can need millions of dollars. They do not see the libraries of reality that exist with numerous variations in colleges and universities and in communities all across the country. If contemporaries today tend to subsume libraries in one particular type, how much more likely is it that we do the same for libraries in the past! To be sure, individuals are likely to differ in the image they hold of the library in the past. One person might think that what we today term the public library has always existed; another might believe that elite institutions serving only the wealthy were the predominant library form. Yet another, knowing of Andrew Carnegie, might think that basically there were no libraries until this century. The image would almost certainly not encompass the reality of the past, any more than it does the widespread variation of today's libraries.

Haynes McMullen's *American Libraries before 1876* makes clear the complex reality of the country's library past. His statistical data—and analyses of it—show that Americans sought in a wide variety of ways to have access to reading material through sharing it. Indeed, he covers eighty to eighty-five different kinds of libraries, all of which are also included in a glossary of terms. Here, as an example, is one entry: "*Circulating library.* Originally, any library from which books could be taken home. The term was used to designate two main types: a *Commercial circulating library*, operated for profit, and a *Social library*, operated for the benefit of its users. In recent years, historians have usually limited the term to mean what is called in this study a *Commercial circulating library*." Unfortunately, "usually" is not the same as "always," and it would be well if historians of the book in America always used McMullen's terms, save for very good and explicitly stated reasons.

McMullen provides statistical information about all of these kinds of libraries, which is no surprise to those who know his past work. McMullen has specialized in statistical studies over many decades, and this is the culmination. To identify the libraries that are here recorded statistically has been a gigantic task. To be sure, the "Table of Public Libraries Numbering 300 Volumes and Upwards," published in part 1 of the U.S. Bureau of Education's *Public Libraries in the United States of America* (1876) provides a most handy start. This 131-page list, printed in small type, records 3,647 libraries, and it seems so comprehensive as even to make further research almost unnecessary. The appearance is deceiving. Note that the title of the table implies it contains only libraries in existence in 1876, which in fact it does, but many more libraries had existed. Commonly, a few individuals would form an organization and buy a stock of books that, with occasional additions, would serve its members for several decades, but then as the book stock ceased to be replenished and as the initial tight control over the collection and its use diminished, the membership and the books would both dwindle away. Thus, there had earlier existed many libraries that would not have been recorded in a table of libraries in 1876. Note, moreover, that the 1876 table records only libraries with more than 300 volumes. That made good sense at that time, but a large number of libraries, formed earlier, had fewer than 300 volumes but still termed themselves a library. The table also misses some of the considerable number of libraries held by organizations that were not primarily formed to establish and run libraries, among them churches, YMCA's, literary societies, musical societies, and college student societies, to name only a few. In contrast to the 3,647 libraries of the 1876 report, McMullen identified 10,032 before 1876.

To add to the 1876 table, McMullen drew on some earlier and later published lists; studies of individual kinds of libraries, such as David Kaser's *A Book for a Sixpence: The Circulating Library in America* (1980); theses as well as published studies of libraries in particular areas; catalogs of libraries (catalogs being the sole evidence of a library's existence in more than 300 cases); legislative acts of incorporation; manuscript schedules for tables in the U.S. censuses of 1850, 1860, and 1870; correspondence with librarians; local histories and other printed sources such as almanacs and directories, plus Jesse Shera's cards for individual libraries. These last were used by Shera in writing his *Foundations of the Public Library: The Origins of the Public Library Movement in New England 1629–1855* (1949), and their use by McMullen means that two distinguished library historians have gathered the data for this book for a period of more than fifty years.

Despite all of these sources, McMullen has found it necessary to omit from his statistical treatment three different kinds of libraries: personal libraries, school libraries (including school district libraries), and Sunday school libraries, though he records the available statistical information about these in his final chapter. He cogently argues that these libraries cannot be counted, that estimates of the numbers vary widely, and that, moreover, the number of such libraries is so large as to skew an analysis based on identification of individual libraries. His wise decision is thus not based on importance but rather on practicality and the desire for meaningful statistics in which the institutions have some degree of comparability. All three types of omitted libraries are, however, vitally important. Personal libraries, at the very least up through the first decades of the nineteenth century, were crucial sources of reading material for many Americans besides their owners, as is attested by grateful reminiscences penned by individuals who were permitted by an owner to borrow books. The large numbers of school libraries and Sunday school libraries point up that the institutional forms employed by those who most avidly sought to control reading were also the most widespread types of institutional libraries. They deserve McMullen's kind of analysis as well as study from various other angles. Doing so might, for example, show that Sunday school libraries were an important source of reading for African-Americans.

Surely even more libraries existed than the over 10,000 recorded by McMullen, and he knows better than anyone that he has not found them all, despite the wide variety of printed and manuscript sources he has consulted and the extensive correspondence he has carried on. Alas, if another researcher learns of the existence of a library from an obscure source, it can rarely be determined whether it is among those identified by McMullen. Print virtually precludes a library by library listing, particularly if one were to provide some basic information as well as the source of the data. One can imagine, however, that someday someone will produce a list in electronic form, as Robin Alston has for Britain. But even with a computer and even with data entered into fields, such a list would not render useless what McMullen has done.

In addition to identifying, McMullen has analyzed. Doing so is far from an automatic process. Do the two names represent two libraries or simply variants? Into what category does a library fall? Answering such questions is part of the initial task of analysis, but McMullen has sought to go further, to combine the data on libraries with other kinds of data to produce insight into differences over time and place—and ultimately into the reasons why Americans formed libraries. In time, McMullen goes back to the colonial era, and in addition to showing regional variations, he correlates library founding with population statistics. McMullen demonstrates—incontrovertibly—that the history of libraries in America must take into account differing patterns in various regions, and even in states, some the result of legislative enactment, some stemming from fashion, some from culture, some from population density, and so on. To think that he began the process at a time when edge-notched cards sorted by long needles were the basic tool!

The analysis is by no means purely statistical, for there is extended commentary. The statistics, of course, raise questions, and McMullen often ranges widely in the secondary literature in his search for answers. He also must at times break down the component parts of a number, which makes for consideration of, among many others, Masonic libraries, or Native-American libraries, or African-American libraries, or women's libraries. It is possible, in fact, to see this work as basically statistical tables and graphs, which are then further elucidated in detail in the text.

McMullen's basic analysis should continue to hold up, even if it were possible to increase the number of libraries. The South is not, for example, going to catapult ahead of New England in the number of libraries or the number in terms of population. In only a few cases may the numbers be significantly off. African-American libraries could be an instance, and perhaps the same applies to the sources of shared reading of European immigrant groups. It is also easy to imagine that the more informal types of libraries, for example, those in literary societies are too low, given the ephemeral nature of such societies. Some numbers may be off—or may not be—but the overall patterns have almost certainly been delineated by McMullen.

Historians are interested in many more questions than can be answered statistically, but statistics are always of interest to historians. They are a starting point in that they raise questions and both promote and limit generalization. And the more detailed the statistics are, the more useful they are. Haynes McMullen has brought together an extraordinary amount of detail. All interested in American book history must be delighted that he has persevered to bring this book to completion.

Kenneth E. Carpenter
Assistant Director for Research Resources
Harvard University Library

Preface

Authors of books often tell how a great teacher, a great book, or a great poem caused them to become interested in the topic of their present volume. Many years ago I fell in love with a table—one that has the title, "Table of Public Libraries Numbering 300 Volumes or Upwards" occupying approximately thirty pages in Part 1 of the U.S. Bureau of Education's *Public Libraries in the United States of America*, issued in 1876.

At that time I thought the Bureau's table could show me how many libraries of various kinds existed before the date of its publication. I was wrong. It did not list more than a tenth of the libraries—other than ones belonging to individuals who kept them for their own use—that had existed at one time or another before 1876.

My efforts to learn about early American libraries have resulted in a gradually increasing appreciation of the intense desire that many Americans had to establish and make use of collections of books as they sought to understand and obtain enjoyment from the world they knew. As a person who has been concerned with libraries for most of his life, I have come to feel close to those Americans who lived more than a hundred years ago.

Many persons have helped me in my search for information—some of them knowingly and some unwittingly. I want to mention several groups: First, some years ago, those officials at Indiana University in Bloomington who made it possible for me to have time away from teaching and to obtain research funds. More recently, time and funds have been made available at the University of North Carolina at Chapel Hill through the kindness of Edward G. Holley, who was Dean of the School of Information and Library Science while I was there.

I am particularly grateful to all of those graduate assistants at Indiana and North Carolina who cheerfully did a variety of clerical and intellectual work. Since I have retired I have become fully aware of the magnitude of their accomplishments. In the last few years I have been heavily dependent on two individuals: First, my son David, who has read several drafts, correcting my grammatical slips and helping me to clarify the meaning of some cloudy sentences. Second, Jean Murphy, whose extensive knowledge about the use of computers and whose endless patience about changes in the text have made this book possible in its electronic form. I am grateful to Erica Smith, of the History Department at Old Dominion University, whose carefully critical reading of the text has improved its clarity and accuracy. Earlene Viano and other members of the Reference Department of the Hampton Public Library have cheerfully and skillfully located and borrowed for me many volumes from other libraries.

There are other persons who have helped without meaning to: First, the compilers of lists of early libraries and the authors of numerous articles, theses, and books about the history of libraries and of American life in general before 1876. Second, inventors of several mechanical and electrical devices that continued to make my work easier as I have moved from using edge-notched cards sorted by long needles to the use of a mighty mainframe computer, and, in recent years, to the use of a personal computer, which has made everything easier and more pleasant.

Chapter 1

Introduction

Americans created and used tens of thousands of libraries before 1876, the year that has often been considered the beginning of the modern library movement in the United States.[1] Why did they establish so many? The desire for libraries increased over the years, but, clearly, it was stronger at some times than others, and stronger in some parts of the country than others. And the interest in various kinds of libraries waxed and waned. How were changes in the prevalence of libraries related to changes in other aspects of American life during those years?

At the present time there is an increasing interest in the history of books and reading in America. Scholars who have written about the place of printed materials in American life have sometimes mentioned libraries, often in a fairly general way, as agencies that have been involved in the process by which ideas have moved from the minds of authors into the minds of readers.[2]

The history of American libraries has not been neglected by other scholars; several thousand books and articles on the subject have appeared.[3] However, none of these authors has attempted to examine, in detail, exactly where various kinds of libraries came into existence in the different parts of the country over any extended period of time.[4] This book is primarily a description (or perhaps a narration) of the actions which people took in relation to libraries as they created them and supported them, and as, sometimes, they neglected them, causing them to die or disappear from the records.

To some extent, this book might be considered to be interpretive because it contains speculations about relationships between people's activities concerning libraries on the one hand and, on the other hand, changes that were constantly taking place in other aspects of American life. More specifically, it is about:

1. The times and places people were establishing various kinds of libraries. The founding of a library almost always occurred when a well-defined group of people wanted to derive some kind of benefit for themselves or for others and had the means to do it.

2. The times and places particular kinds of libraries were present. Knowing when and where libraries continued to exist can give us a rough indication of the willingness of people to support and use the collections that they—or others— had decided to establish.

3. So far as can be determined, the reasons why Americans established and used each kind of library. What seem to have been the changes in attitudes and beliefs (what the French have called *mentalités*) or in social, economic, or political conditions that may have affected people's decisions to form and use collections of books.[5]

The main part of this study (in chapters 2 through 11) is about most of the kinds of libraries that existed before 1876—eighty to eighty-five kinds, depending on the way the collections are classified. Information about approximately ten thousand individual libraries was gathered from the sources described later in this chapter, and then this information was analyzed to discover geographic and chronological patterns.

Three kinds of libraries are omitted from the main part of this study: private libraries held for the owners' use, libraries in elementary or secondary schools, and Sunday school libraries. There are two reasons for these omissions: (1) In order to make it as accurate as possible, the main part of this study has been based on the identification of individual libraries; the omitted types of libraries existed in great numbers, and most of our knowledge about them is derived from rough estimates made on a few occasions by contemporaries. The wide variations in these estimates are discussed in chapter 12. Any attempt to provide a count of them now would be almost meaningless. (2) However, it is clear that there were more of these three virtually "uncountable" kinds than all the libraries considered in chapters 2 through 11; the body of libraries analyzed in the main part of the study constituted less than a tenth of all those that existed before 1876. Any attempt to combine the estimates for these three omitted kinds of libraries with the counts of the other kinds would greatly reduce the accuracy of statements about the prevalence of the other kinds of American libraries before 1876. The three kinds omitted from the main study are all discussed in chapter 12.

This study is not concerned with the development of libraries or the origins of kinds that exist today. As will become clear in later chapters, American libraries were not always developing before 1876; various kinds rose and fell in popularity over the years. If we search too hard for progress toward present conditions, we may be in danger of imposing our *mentalités* on people who had a different outlook on life. We need to try to understand how they perceived libraries, and we must be cautious in the use of such words as "inadequate." Collections that seem inadequate to us (or to a few intellectual leaders of the nineteenth century) may have seemed perfectly adequate to most Americans before 1876.

Only a few statements remain that directly report the reasons why Americans, living up to the time of the Civil War and for a few years after that war, established libraries and what they expected to get from those libraries. Authors of periodical articles published before 1876 usually approved of libraries, but several of them pointed out that some European libraries were better or larger than any American ones.[6]

The number of libraries that existed in this country through the year 1875 may be an indication of attitudes. Even if we consider only the ten thousand collections of the kinds that are discussed in chapters 2 through 11, the number is so large that it is reasonable to assume that among their founders were many persons whose experiences in using other collections inclined them to expect value from their new enterprises. Because of the difficulty of transportation, the relatively small number of larger or better libraries were not available to most Americans, and the information and enjoyment obtainable in a small library must have been significant in the minds of the groups of persons who collected the books for it.[7] This study does not place special emphasis on the larger collections.

This study does not place special emphasis on small collections either, but it might be considered to favor them in one way. No minimum size for a library has been established. Some printed lists of libraries have required a certain minimum number of volumes for inclusion, but other sources—particularly the manuscript schedules for the U.S. censuses—included libraries of fewer than a hundred volumes apiece. The word *library* has been used in its traditional sense to mean an organized collection of books that might or might not include such items as magazines and newspapers. However, if an early source listed a small collection of books as a library, no investigation has been undertaken to make sure that it was organized.

This study has not been restrictive in regard to the size of libraries, but it has definite chronological and geographical limits. The year 1876 has been chosen as a cutoff date for the present study for several reasons. In that centennial year of the birth of the nation, many Americans paused to review the past with a measure of pride, to take sober stock of their present condition, to look to the future with optimism and determination, and (some of them) to attend the Centennial Exposition in Philadelphia.[8]

Librarians and the friends of libraries did all of these things in 1876. They set forth in detail what they thought about the past and present status of libraries in the monumental *Public Libraries in the United States of America*, published by the U.S. Bureau of Education in two volumes, the first of which was the largest volume that had ever been published about libraries in this country; nothing that even approached it was to appear for another fifty years.[9] In 1876, the librarians and their friends looked to the future when some of them met in Philadelphia and formed the American Library Association, dedicated to the improvement of libraries. In the same year, the first issue of the *American Library Journal* (later known as the *Library Journal*) was published and became the organ of the association. Mainly because of these events, the year 1876 is often considered to mark the beginning of the modern era in American librarianship.

That year marks, roughly, the end of the period of the geographic expansion of American libraries. By the 1870s, a few existed in every area now occupied by a state, even though some present-day states were still territories. Alaska did not even have territorial status, and Hawaii was not yet a part of the United States.

Another cutoff date might have been the Civil War. For many southern libraries it truly was a stopping place; however, in much of the country it marked not a cessation but rather a temporary diminution in activity. Libraries just after the war were not noticeably different from libraries before the war— there were just more of them and their number was growing faster. And this situation was true of many other aspects of American life. The social, economic, and intellectual life of most of the country in the 1850s was somewhat different from that of earlier years and had much in common with that of the years just after the war. The reasons for considering libraries existing through the end of the Revolutionary period separately from later ones will be mentioned in chapter 2.

As to the geographical limits of this study: The present boundaries of the United States (that is, including the fifty states and the District of Columbia) have been chosen because many people think of them as the United States. If use had been made of the boundaries that existed at the end of the period under study, Hawaii would have been omitted, and Alaska might have been included; in 1876, the latter, not even a territory, was being administered by the War Department. Actually, the inclusion of Hawaii and Alaska is not of much importance in this kind of study because they had so few libraries.

The primary geographical unit on which the study is based is the state (plus, of course, the District of Columbia). The present boundaries of the states are used; to have used boundaries as they existed at various times before 1876 would cause confusion. Virginia, for example, is considered to exclude West Virginia, which became a state in 1863; and Virginia is considered to include Alexandria, which it took from the District of Columbia in 1846.

The use of states as units (as in Table 1.1 and Figure 1.1) seems justified because, in our minds, we so often group libraries according to the states where they exist; the presence of state library agencies and state library associations is an indication of this tendency. We also think of other aspects of American life in terms of states: much political, economic, and social information is presented to us state by state. However, not everyone agrees that states are the most helpful units in the study of America's past life. Geographers and sociologists sometimes remind us that states are not useful units when we consider cultural regions.[10]

Considering states as units and establishing regions by combining states seems to have more advantages than disadvantages in the case of libraries; the scheme that has been used by the U.S. Bureau of the Census since 1910 seems to have the most advantages. It is the basis for the map (Figure 1.1) and for all of the tables in the study. Generally, it presents data for individual states, for nine groups of states (called *sub-regions* in this study), which are combined into four larger groups (called *regions*) each containing two or three sub-regions. This scheme makes it possible, in a study such as this, to see which states are largely responsible for the characteristics of a sub-region, which sub-region is most important in a region, and to what extent each of the four regions is responsible for the characteristics of the country as a whole. Also, using the census scheme makes it easy to compare the prevalence of libraries in any area with the number of people during any of the years when censuses were taken.

One disadvantage of using the regional divisions of the census reports is that

Table 1.1
Number of Libraries in Each State and Region before 1876

Northeast		South		Middle West		Far West		All U.S.
New England		South Atlantic		East North Central		Mountain		
Me.	253	Del.	29	Ohio	572	Mont.	7	
N.H.	419	Md.	204	Ind.	1,277	Idaho	5	
Vt.	133	D.C.	107	Ill.	398	Wyo.	13	
Mass.	1,128	Va.	121	Mich.	856	Colo.	19	
R.I.	255	W.Va.	52	Wis.	120	N.Mex.	11	
Conn.	453	N.C.	94	Total	3,223	Ariz.	12	
Total	2,641	S.C.	114			Utah	53	
		Ga.	66	West North Central		Nev.	9	
Mid-Atlantic		Fla.	14	Minn.	150	Total	129	
N.Y.	693	Total	801	Ia.	144			
N.J.	236			Mo.	132	Pacific		
Pa.	705	East South Central		N.Dak.	4	Wash.	20	
Total	1,634	Ky.	195	S.Dak.	7	Ore.	49	
		Tenn.	229	Nebr.	14	Calif.	262	
		Ala.	32	Kans.	65	Alaska	3	
		Miss.	45	Total	526	Hawaii	11	
		Total	501			Total	345	
		West South Central						
		Ark.	11					
		La.	135					
		Okla.	4					
		Tex.	82					
		Total	232					
Total 4,275		Total 1,534		Total 3,749		Total 474		Total 10,032

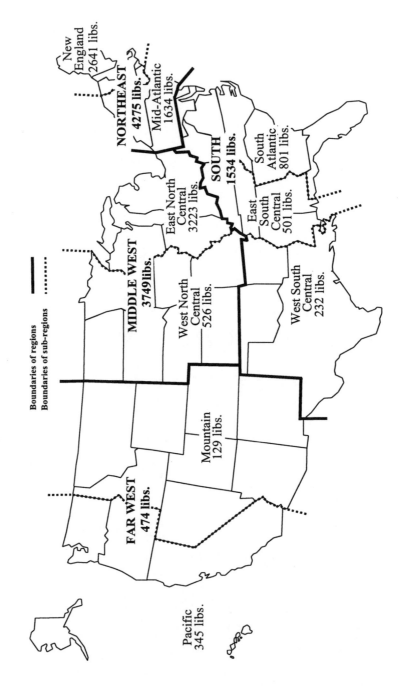

Figure 1.1
Distribution of American Libraries before 1876

Boundaries of regions
Boundaries of sub-regions

NORTHEAST
4275 libs.

New England
2641 libs.

Mid-Atlantic
1634 libs.

SOUTH
1534 libs.

South Atlantic
801 libs.

East North Central
3223 libs.

East South Central
501 libs.

MIDDLE WEST
3749 libs.

West North Central
526 libs.

West South Central
232 libs.

Mountain
129 libs.

FAR WEST
474 libs.

Pacific
345 libs.

a few states on the border of a census region have some characteristics that are similar to those of other states in the region where they have been placed and some characteristics of states in the neighboring region. For example, Texas and Oklahoma are placed in the South but might well have been placed with western states. When situations like these seem to have noteworthy effects on the distribution of libraries, I have mentioned them. The result of moving states from one region or sub-region to another can be seen by rearranging Table 1.1 in any way that seems appropriate.

Although names used in this study for the regions and sub-regions are not always the same as those used by the Census Bureau, there is only the one addition that the Bureau itself has made since 1910: including Hawaii as part of the Pacific sub-region. Almost the only geographic units smaller than states to be mentioned in this study are some of the larger cities, if they contain a significant portion of the libraries in their respective states. One problem is that the boundaries of cities changed more often than the boundaries of states; a few libraries were founded in small towns but lived parts of their lives in the neighboring cities because of annexation.

SOURCES OF INFORMATION

The significance of a study such as this depends in part on whether its sources have provided information on substantially all of the libraries that existed within its geographical and chronological limits. A total of approximately four hundred and fifty printed sources were used; sometimes, when a source contained vague information about a library, it was possible to clarify it with one or more of the other printed sources or through correspondence with a librarian in the town where it had been located. In this part of chapter 1, the different kinds of sources are described; they cannot possibly have listed all of the libraries that were present, so, in discussing several kinds, I have mentioned the possibility of the existence of collections that are not included in the sources.

Lists, Each of Which Contain Information about Several Kinds of Libraries. Perhaps the most helpful of all sources have been a few lists that appeared during the years before 1876 or soon after. The most useful one was the "Table of Public Libraries Numbering 300 Volumes and Upwards" on pages 1012 through 1142 of part 1 of the U.S. Bureau of Education's *Public Libraries in the United States of America*, published in 1876. This list represented a determined effort of its compilers to include all the kinds of libraries considered in the main part of the present study with the exception of those in churches. Libraries of fewer than three hundred volumes were to be excluded, but a few of them were not. And a certain amount of information about libraries having fewer than three hundred volumes is available in some of the chapters by individual authors that precede the table; those authors had access to reports from libraries with small collections. Altogether, some information is available for almost four thousand libraries that were in existence in 1875; some of them belonged to elementary or secondary schools, so they could not be included in the main part of this study.

The U.S. Bureau of Education issued other lists of libraries before and after the one published in 1876. The most useful for this study was the table, "Statistics of Public Libraries Numbering 300 Volumes and Upwards for 1884–85," on pp. 691–782 in the *Report of the Commissioner of Education for the Year 1884–85*, published in 1886. This list contained information about approximately five thousand three hundred libraries, most of which were in existence before 1876. It identified collections that had been too small to be listed in the 1876 table and others that somehow had been missed.

Another source contained information about the history and condition of various kinds of libraries that existed around 1857 to 1859. William J. Rhees's *Manual of Public Libraries, Institutions, and Societies in the United States and British Provinces of North America*, published in Philadelphia by J.B. Lippincott in 1859, provided additional information not available in the lists compiled at the U.S. Bureau of Education.

The volume by Rhees was an extension of an earlier work that was less useful for this study because it contained similar information about a smaller number of libraries: Charles C. Jewett's *Appendix to the Report of the Board of Regents of the Smithsonian Institution, Containing a Report on the Public Libraries of the United States of America, January 1, 1850*. Comparison with other sources indicates that Jewett missed several libraries.

Another list was of great help in regard to several kinds of libraries in an important part of the United States. Not long after Jesse Shera's book, *Foundations of the Public Library: The Origins of the Public Library Movement in New England, 1629–1855*, was published by the University of Chicago Press in 1949, the author very kindly lent me a manuscript list on cards, one library per card, that he had used as he wrote. There were approximately a thousand cards, mostly about three kinds of libraries: social libraries, libraries belonging to other kinds of societies, and public libraries. Each card contained information about the history of the library and included a list of sources, mostly local histories but also other printed works and some manuscripts.

One comprehensive list should be approached with caution. *The American Library Directory* is useful for current information about present-day libraries, but it does not always list correct dates of founding. Through correspondence with the present librarians, I have sometimes learned that the date given was actually for a library whose collection was taken over by the present organization. Sometimes librarians tell me that they do not know why a particular date has been reported for their institution.

Lists of Individual Kinds of Libraries. Lists, each of which is confined to one kind of library, have been the only sources of information about large numbers of obscure collections. Some were contemporary lists and some have been created by twentieth-century historians. Among the most useful has been David Kaser's "Checklist of American Commercial Library Enterprises, 1762–1890" on pp. 127–72 in his volume, *A Book for a Sixpence: The Circulating Library in America*, published in Pittsburgh by the Beta Phi Mu Society in 1980. Two government documents have provided information about many libraries owned by agricultural and horticultural societies: "Societies for Promoting Agriculture,

State Boards, Etc." on pp. 90–213 in the U.S. Patent Office's *Report of the Commissioner of Patents for the Year 1858. Agriculture*, and "Agricultural and Horticultural Societies and Clubs" on pp. 364–403 in the U.S. Commissioner of Agriculture's *Report of the Commissioner of Agriculture for the Year 1867*. Two other federal documents, both from the Surgeon General's Office, mention libraries at some of the military barracks: *A Report on Barracks and Hospitals, with Descriptions of Military Posts*, Circular no. 4, 1870, and *A Report on the Hygiene of the United States Army, with Descriptions of Military Posts*, Circular no. 8, 1875.

Library Histories. Shera's book is perhaps the finest example of historical work about libraries in any particular region in the United States. However, I have been very grateful to many persons who have written books, periodical articles, master's theses, and doctoral dissertations about particular kinds of libraries or about libraries in particular parts of the United States. Several other useful articles have been written about libraries on special subjects—law and medicine, for example—and other studies have been helpful, each of which is about the history of all libraries in a particular state. These histories exist for at least two-thirds of the states and often have mentioned libraries that have not appeared in other sources.

Catalogs of Libraries. The printed catalogs issued by many libraries in the years before 1876 have been useful in two ways: (1) The catalog may be the only evidence of the existence of a library, and (2) the catalog may have an introduction that tells the history of the collection up to the time of printing. By far, the most helpful guide to these catalogs is Robert Singerman's *American Library Book Catalogues, 1801–1875: A National Bibliography*, Occasional Papers, no. 203/04, published by the Graduate School of Library and Information Science in the University of Illinois at Urbana-Champaign in 1996. That volume lists 2,759 catalogs for the kinds of libraries included in the main part of this study. For 303 of Singerman's libraries, the catalogs were the only evidence I have concerning those institutions. For several others, his entries gave helpful information.[11] His bibliography also includes catalogs from 423 Sunday schools, academies, and other schools—kinds of collections that are discussed in chapter 12.

Corporate Charters of Libraries. One kind of source that has sometimes been used by historians as evidence of the presence of a library is the corporate charter issued by a state legislature. Business enterprises and non-profit organizations had been incorporated in the eighteenth century, but most of the library charters seem to have been issued during the first fifty years of the nineteenth century. By 1850, in some states, it was possible to obtain incorporation without a separate legislative act; however, legislatures in some of those same states continued to issue individual charters.[12]

Legislative acts incorporating libraries are readily accessible because they were printed in the volumes of session laws. However, they do not tell much about each library; they usually give permission to a small number of persons to join as a corporation for a particular purpose and to sue and be sued. They may limit the value of property that the corporation is permitted to hold and may limit the length of its life. They do not often report that books have been acquired.

Theoretically, a charter could be issued for a corporation that never came into existence as a library. And, of course, a charter could be issued before or after the library was actually founded. No evidence has come to light that would indicate the failure of a library to materialize; however, for more than two hundred libraries in the study, the incorporation of the library is the only evidence that it existed.

Different sources often give different founding dates for the same library, making it hard to judge how close a date of incorporation is to the actual date of founding. Part of the problem may arise because, for many social libraries, the process of founding—that is, obtaining subscribers, sending away for books, assembling them, and opening the library for use—could easily take two years. However, for many libraries, the various dates reported as founding dates are farther apart than two years.

One way to compare dates of incorporation with dates of founding is simply to notice whether, for the same library, the reported date or dates of founding are earlier than the date of incorporation, are the same, or are later. An examination of dates for fifty-six libraries in four states (Pennsylvania, Kentucky, Ohio, and Indiana) produced thirty-seven libraries where all reported dates of founding were earlier than the date of incorporation, sixteen where they were all the same as the date of incorporation, and only three where all of them were later. For those libraries, incorporation took place at about the same time as founding. Rarely was a library incorporated before it actually opened.[13]

Manuscript Schedules for Tables in the U.S. Censuses of 1850, 1860, and 1870. None of the printed census tables, mentioned earlier in this chapter, contained information about individual libraries, so those tables were of little use in regard to the kinds of collections discussed in chapters 2 through 11. However, some of the information contained in the manuscript schedules sent to Washington by census takers identifies particular libraries, so it has been helpful. The manuscript seldom names a library, but because it tells how many libraries of a particular kind existed at a particular time in a town or census district, its information can sometimes be compared with other information to determine whether a known library was in existence then. However, much of the information in these schedules could not be used because the classification of libraries was broad and terms were not defined: *town libraries* could mean any one of several categories used in this study.[14]

Many—or perhaps all—of the manuscript returns for the 1850, 1860, and 1870 censuses still exist. Microfilm copies of some of them are available for inspection in the National Archives in Washington, where the staff is knowledgeable and helpful. However, at one time the manuscript answers for these three censuses were returned to the governments of the states from which they had come. Correspondence with state archivists has indicated that some of the replies are on paper that is in delicate condition and have never been filmed, necessitating a trip to the state capital if they are to be seen.

Copies of manuscript census replies from only ten states were examined for this study; each of the nine sub-regions of the country except New England is represented.[15] Making use of the records from other states would have required considerable effort and might have produced a relatively small amount of useable information.

Correspondence with Librarians. One source of information deserves special mention, for personal reasons. Several hundred librarians in towns and cities throughout the United States have very kindly answered my requests for information to clarify statements in printed sources and in the manuscript returns sent to Washington by census takers. Those librarians have sometimes had to report that no trace of the ancient collection remained in the memory of persons with whom they have consulted or in the written records that they have been able to examine. However, sometimes they have consulted with experts—semi-official town historians or others—who have provided me with photocopies of printed sources , which I had not known to exist.

Other Sources. At least five other kinds of sources exist, but I have used them only for a few states that I have studied intensively. For some other states, I have benefited indirectly from these by depending on the work of library historians.

Among the more useful sources were these: For larger towns and cities, there were city directories or almanacs that mention libraries. For example, in Louisville, Kentucky, information about libraries was provided in at least eleven directories published between 1832 and 1870. A large number of county histories have been published; they often mention libraries. Guides for immigrants in the years before 1876 sometimes mention libraries in their descriptions of towns. Travel accounts cite libraries, but usually only the larger or better-known ones. Newspapers regularly carried notices about libraries in the towns where they were published, but periodicals (magazines) rarely mentioned any except the larger and better-known ones. Their editors ordinarily furnished information that would be of interest to a wide audience.[16]

This chapter has presented a general overview of the geographical and chronological framework that will be used in the rest of the book and has generally described the sources that have provided the information to be examined within this framework. Chapter 2 will use this framework to examine the prevalence of libraries during the colonial and revolutionary years, and chapter 3 will move on through the remaining years up to 1876. Chapters 4 through 11 will consider in detail the times and places individual kinds of libraries existed. Finally, chapter 12 will consider briefly the three kinds of libraries omitted in the main part of the study.

NOTES

1. Two indications of the significance of that year: (1) Articles and books written about the history of modern American libraries often begin with that year, and (2) a group of librarians gathered at a special occasion in 1976 in order to celebrate its centennial. Papers presented at that meeting have been published with the title *Milestones to the Present: Papers from Library History Seminar V*, ed. Harold Goldstein and John

Goudeau (Syracuse, N.Y.: Gaylord Professional Publications, 1978).

2. For example, *Cultures of Print: Essays in the History of the Book* by David D. Hall (Amherst, Mass.: University of Massachusetts Press, 1996), contains a thoughtful treatment of the history of books and reading in America; it includes several references to libraries. *Knowledge is Power: The Diffusion of Information in Early America, 1700–1865* by Richard D. Brown (New York: Oxford University Press, 1989) considers all means for the transfer of ideas—oral, written, and printed. It, too, mentions libraries.

3. *American Library History: A Comprehensive Guide to the Literature* by Donald G. Davis, Jr. and John Mark Tucker (Santa Barbara, Calif.: ABC-CLIO, 1989) lists more than seven thousand books and articles.

4. Jesse H. Shera, in *Foundations of the Public Library: The Origins of the Public Library Movement in New England, 1629–1855* (Chicago: University of Chicago Press, 1949), used records for more libraries than anyone else. His book is described, with other sources, later in this chapter.

5. Two discussions of the concept of *mentalités* are to be found in Robert Darnton's, *The Great Cat Massacre, and Other Episodes in French Cultural History* (New York: Basic Books, 1984) and "The Fate of the History of Mentalités in the Annales" by André Burguière, *Comparative Studies in Society and History* 24 (July 1982): 424–37. Brown's book, *Knowledge is Power*, helps greatly in the understanding of changes in American attitudes up to the time of the Civil War.

6. "The Treatment of Libraries in Periodicals Published in the United States before 1876," by Haynes McMullen and Larry J. Barr, in *Journal of Library History* 21 (Fall 1986): 657 and *Libraries in American Periodicals Before 1876, A Bibliography with Abstracts and an Index*, compiled by Larry J. Barr, Haynes McMullen, and Steven G. Leach (Jefferson, N.C.: McFarland & Co., 1983), 7–33.

7. By applying the modern theory of "reader response" to Americans living before 1876, it becomes easy to believe that they were capable of using a small library, perhaps consisting of some standard classics and a few religious texts, and combining what those volumes supplied with what they already knew or believed in order to produce a satisfactory reading experience.

8. Dee Brown, in *The Year of the Century: 1876* (New York: Charles Scribner's Sons, 1966), discusses the conditions and attitudes that brought about the events of that year.

9. U.S. Bureau of Education, *Public Libraries in the United States of America: Special Report*, 2 vols. (Washington, D.C.: Government Printing Office, 1876).

10. The complexity of the problem of defining regions in the United States is evident in such works as these: Raymond D. Gastil, *Cultural Regions of the United States* (Seattle: University of Washington Press, 1975); Ann Markuson, *Regions: The Economics and Politics of Territory* (Totowa, N.J.: Rowman & Littlefield, 1987); and Michael Bradshaw, *Regions and Regionalism in the United States* (Jackson, Miss.: University Press of Mississippi, 1988).

11. A similar guide, *A Descriptive Checklist of Book Catalogues Separately Printed in America, 1693–1800* by Robert B. Winans (Worcester, Mass.: American Antiquarian Society, 1981), was of only a little help because, before I saw it, I already had the kind of information I needed about almost all of the libraries represented there.

12. Some state legislatures were not enthusiastic about issuing charters. Their reasons are discussed in *The Organization of American Culture, 1700–1900: Private Institutions, Elites, and the Origins of American Nationality* by Peter Dobkin Hall (New York: New York University Press, 1982), 96–124.

13. The figures given do not include two other groups of libraries for which incorporation dates were known: (1) Twenty-nine libraries for each of which the date of

incorporation was within the range from the earliest to the latest founding date, (2) 268 libraries for which the only records concerning their early lives were the dates of incorporation. For this latter group, the date of incorporation was accepted (perhaps incautiously) as the founding date.

14. In the book, *The American Census: A Social History* by Margo J. Anderson (New Haven, Conn.: Yale University Press, 1988), it is explained why the schedules for the 1850, 1860, and 1870 censuses were somewhat different from each other. In those days, the taking of each census was a separate enterprise, planned and executed by temporary employees.

15. The ten states are: from the Middle Atlantic sub-region, Pennsylvania; from the South Atlantic, Virginia and West Virginia; from the East South Central, Tennessee; from the West South Central, Louisiana and Texas; from the East North Central, Michigan; from the West North Central, Kansas; from the Mountain states, Colorado; and from the Pacific states, Washington. New England is the only sub-region that is not represented; it is fairly well covered in other sources.

16. McMullen and Barr, "The Treatment of Libraries in Periodicals," 665, 669.

Chapter 2

Libraries in the Colonial and Revolutionary Periods

In the area now occupied by the United States of America, libraries appeared on the Atlantic coast and in the Far West at about the same time. The first clear records of an organized collection of books on the East Coast concern the Harvard College Library, formed in 1638. In New Mexico, a variety of books were in private hands as early as 1640. At least two missions had libraries there before the Pueblo Indian Revolt of 1680 drove the Spanish out of the area; after the reconquest in 1692, missions again built collections.[1] The settlement of Florida had begun long before, but many records were destroyed during the bloody struggle between Spain and her rivals. There are references to a private library in existence in 1680 and to a library belonging to a convent in St. Augustine around the year 1700.[2] No definite record has come to my attention of the existence of any library before the year 1800 in areas occupied by the French.[3]

The year 1785 has been chosen, somewhat arbitrarily, as the ending date for this chapter. There have been three reasons for this choice: (1) In this book, the establishment of libraries is often compared with the number of people present at various times and places. The United States Census, which began in 1790, gives a more accurate indication of population than the various estimates for earlier years, and it is convenient to compare the number of libraries founded during a ten-year period centered approximately on a census year—for example, libraries founded from 1786 through 1795—to the population in the decennial year 1790. (2) Stopping at that point instead of a few years earlier (before or during the Revolution) makes it possible to show, in this chapter, the extent of disruption to colonial libraries that was caused by the events during the war (from approximately 1775 through 1781) and the effect of the nation's recovery after the war. (3) In most of the area now occupied by the United States, there were no libraries before about 1790, so that is a convenient beginning date for consideration of libraries outside of the eastern states.

Also, something should be said about the geographic divisions used in this chapter. Because most of the libraries in existence before 1786 were established in the British colonies and the states that grew out of them, those libraries will be considered first. They were all in three of the sub-regions that appear on Table 1.1 and Figure 1.1—New England, the Middle-Atlantic states, and the South Atlantic states—so those divisions are used (see Table 2.1). With the exception of the one library in Florida eligible for inclusion in this study, all of the libraries in the Spanish areas were in the Pacific sub-region.

Table 2.1 shows the number of libraries existing at some time before 1786 in the parts of the country mentioned above. It accurately shows the distribution of libraries, but it has these limitations: (1) When there are only a few libraries known for a state, the number may change noticeably as records of other libraries are found in the future. (2) It does not necessarily indicate the amount of interest in founding libraries that was shown by the people who lived in each colony because quite a few libraries were organized and financed by persons living in Britain.

IN THE BRITISH AREA

The Founding of Libraries, 1638–1785

In chapter 1 it was mentioned that the founding of a library almost always occurred when a well-defined group of people wanted it. During the seventeenth and eighteenth centuries, the kind of society that existed in Britain and its American colonies permitted individuals and groups to exercise a considerable amount of freedom. In Britain, people were often successful in achieving their purposes—religious, economic, or whatever—by voluntarily forming associations.[4] Most of the libraries in the colonies were established by voluntary groups, some of which were in England and some in America. A few were founded by individuals; governments were seldom directly involved.

In thinking about the attitudes of Americans toward their libraries, it is necessary to pay particular attention to the dates when libraries were being established. For any library formed by a voluntary association, the date of founding is likely to have been the date when interest in the library was most intense. After that year there might be a decrease in enthusiasm, and after some years the library might pass out of existence without anyone being able to say exactly why enthusiasm diminished or exactly when the library ceased to function

The pattern of founding that is shown in Table 2.2 gives a general idea as to when and where libraries were being established in the British colonies in the years before the Revolutionary period and, after the war, in the states formed from those colonies. Times and places where the table is most likely to be inaccurate will be mentioned later in this chapter. The table includes only libraries for which a year of founding could be discovered. If sources disagreed,

Table 2.1
Number of Libraries in the American Colonies and the Corresponding States before 1786[a]

New England		South Atlantic		Mountain	
Maine	6[b]	Delaware	2	New Mexico	2
New Hampshire	3	Maryland	41		
Vermont	1	Virginia	13		
				Pacific	
Mass.	43	N. Carolina	15		
				California	4
Rhode Island	9	S. Carolina	24		
Connecticut	58	Georgia	3		
		Florida	1		
Total	120			All Colonies &	
		Total	99	States	308
Mid-Atlantic					
New York	21				
New Jersey	21				
Pennsylvania	41				
Total	83				

[a] In Florida, New Mexico, and California, the libraries existed during Spanish Rule; for all other states, the colonies were British.
[b] Maine was not a state until 1820; its area was part of Massachusetts before that date.

the date given by the most reliable source was used.[5] If the only information was "in existence before the Revolution" or "no longer in existence after 1780," the library was omitted.

Particular kinds of libraries will be considered later in this chapter, but one kind must be mentioned now because it was responsible for a major part of the general trend shown in Table 2.2. Founding dates for a relatively high proportion of church libraries are available; as we shall see, most of them were located in the southern colonies. Some of these church libraries, collections assembled by the Reverend Thomas Bray, an Anglican clergyman, were responsible for the sudden increase in the number of foundings around 1700.[6]

Table 2.2
Libraries Founded in the British Colonies and the Corresponding States before 1786

	New England	Mid-Atlantic	South Atlantic	Entire Area
Before 1691	4	0	0	4
1691-95	0	0	1	1
1696-1700	5	4	38	47
1701-05	1	4	6	11
1706-10	0	0	3	3
1711-15	0	1	1	2
1716-20	1	0	0	1
1721-25	3	1	2	6
1726-30	0	1	0	1
1731-35	2	1	2	5
1736-40	5	1	0	6
1741-45	3	6	0	9
1746-50	3	3	1	7
1751-55	4	6	2	12
1756-60	5	10	3	18
1761-65	7	10	6	23
1766-70	11	6	1	18
1771-75	14	4	3	21
1776-80	3	1	2	6
1781-85	19	3	7	29
Total	90	62	78	230

During the rest of the first half of the eighteenth century, the number of libraries being founded was so small that differences are probably insignificant. During the last half of the century, numbers were higher except for the period from 1776 through 1780. The decrease in the number of foundings in all sections of the country around that time was undoubtedly the result of disturbances caused by the Revolutionary War. If a table were made to show the number of libraries founded in each of the years just before, during, and after the war, the numbers would not show a sudden drop when war broke out in 1775 and a smooth increase after the fighting ended in 1781. However, the numbers were noticeably lower from about 1776 through 1780 than they were in the years just before the war and were much lower than in the years just after the war. The enthusiasm for libraries that appeared soon after the war was to continue into the early years of the republic. It may have been at least partly the result of two beliefs that were prevalent during the decades just after the war: that the Revolution had freed American society and culture to develop rapidly and that, in a republic, books and learning should be widely available.[7]

The totals for the numbers of foundings in the three regions shown in Table 2.2 require comment. It is not surprising that New England had the most, considering the reputation that its colonists had for bookishness. The authorities in the Massachusetts Bay Colony, for example, began to emphasize education, at least beginning in the 1640s.[8] However, the ability to read did not ensure the establishment of libraries; very few of the kinds of collections considered in this study began to appear in that colony—or elsewhere—before the middle of the eighteenth century.

The good showing of the southern colonies in regard to the establishment of libraries was caused by the large number of collections sent there by Thomas Bray and his associates. At least thirty-three collections arrived in Maryland alone in the years just before and after 1700.

THE FOUNDING OF LIBRARIES AND THE GROWTH OF POPULATION

The American colonists were establishing libraries in a geographic area where population was increasing at a fairly steady rate; the increase in the number of libraries being founded might have been related to the increase in the number of people living there. In the next part of this chapter, these two increases will be examined, and possible reasons for changes in the ratios of library foundings to population will be considered. These ratios are shown in Table 2.3, which begins with 1740 because the founding of most libraries before the 1740s was a result of voluntarism that was more often present among benevolently inclined persons in the mother country and less often evident in the attitudes of the American colonists. From the 1740s on, the founding of most of the libraries were the result of the colonists' desires.

The purpose of comparing the rate of founding of libraries with the size of the population is not to determine a *normal* ratio but to look for variations in this ratio at different times and in different places. One tendency that might keep the ratio from changing very much is this: In a country where most libraries served people in small towns and where transportation was limited, it would be difficult for an existing library to serve nearby areas that were just being settled. New settlers might be expected to establish a library in their area. As we will see in chapter 4, even in cities, the number of libraries increased rapidly as the population increased because of the special interests of small groups of citizens. Whether it is *normal* for the ratio of the founding of libraries to population to be constant or not, this ratio is a helpful measure to use as a very rough indication of the interest Americans had in establishing libraries. Whenever this ratio changes, we can try to find some reason for the increase or decrease of the growth in the number of libraries founded. The same ratio is helpful in comparing the founding of libraries in one part of the country with another; we can try to discover the reasons for geographic differences in the ratios.

In using ratios of the founding of libraries to population, at least four conditions must be considered: (1) These ratios include only about two out of every three libraries in the study because I have discovered the exact year date of founding for only approximately two-thirds (67.4 percent) of the libraries. For the British area during the years before 1786, a comparison of Table 2.2 with Table 2.1 indicates that the dates were found for 76.2 percent. (2) There is no ideal ratio. In reporting that the ratio of library foundings to population at one date or period of time (or in one region) was twice as great as at another date or period (or in another region), we are simply saying that, considering the number of people present, libraries were being founded twice as frequently at one date or period of time (or in one region). (3) The founding of libraries may not represent the will of any large part of the population. In this study, when a noticeable proportion of the libraries have been founded with the help of a single philanthropist or, as in the nineteenth century, by a state government, the effect of these gifts will be mentioned. (4) The method used in this study for establishing a ratio by comparing the number of libraries founded during a ten-year period with the population during one of the two years nearest to the center of the ten-year period is not completely satisfactory. However, a decision to count only the libraries founded during the decennial year would have been less satisfactory for these two reasons: (a) That would have made use of only approximately a tenth of all libraries founded. (b) Because the number of libraries sometimes fluctuated considerably, the number for a single year might not have been typical of those founded during the decade. For the years before the first U.S. Census in 1790, the only continuing series of numbers for the individual colonies' population or states are estimates at ten-year intervals.[9]

In all three regions, population grew steadily in the years from 1740 to 1780. Because the purpose of all of the libraries during these years, so far as we know, was to serve white persons, we may be more interested in the columns for the white population in Table 2.3. For the entire area of British settlement, the number of whites in 1780 was almost three times the number in 1740 (an increase of 191.8 percent). The slowest growth occurred in New England (148.4 percent), and the most rapid in the Middle-Atlantic states (244.4 percent). The rate of increase in the South Atlantic states (200.4 percent) was just a little above the average, given above, for the entire area of British settlement. By 1780, approximately 868,000 white persons lived in the South Atlantic states; New England and the Middle-Atlantic area each had fewer: about 698,000 in New England and about 638,000 in the Middle-Atlantic states.

Table 2.3 clearly shows that the founding of libraries did not increase at the same steady rate as the population in the years before 1786. Perhaps the most

Table 2.3
Ratio of Libraries Founded in the British Colonies and the Corresponding States to Population, 1740–1780

	New England		Mid- Atlantic		South Atlantic		Entire Area	
	w.p.	t.p.	w.p.	t.p.	w.p.	t.p.	w.p.	t.p.
1740	.28	.28	.38	.35	—	—	.20	.17
1750	.20	.17	.36	.34	.09	.06	.20	.16
1760	.27	.27	.54	.51	.19	.12	.32	.26
1770	.44	.43	.21	.19	.06	.04	.23	.18
1780	.32	.31	.06	.06	.10	.06	.16	.13

Note: Number of libraries founded per 10,000 white population = w.p.; number of libraries founded per 10,000 total population = t.p. Each number represents the libraries founded in the ten-year period that includes the four years before the decennial year, the decennial year itself, and the five years after it. (The first row of figures is for 1736–45, etc.).

obvious difference in the numbers in Table 2.3 is the presence of lower ratios for the South throughout the forty-year time span. The reasons may have been various. Perhaps they were related to the pattern of settlement there—widely scattered population with fewer towns and cities. And perhaps they were related to the situation in much of the area where political and social leadership was in the hands of a few men who often owned private libraries—a kind of library omitted in this study. A reputed preference of southerners for the outdoor life may have had an effect. Also, the less affluent whites may have had to devote more time to agricultural work than did the less affluent northerners because the shorter southern winters provided less time for reading and using the libraries. Certainly the southern climate would have encouraged outdoor activities; the effect of the climate on southern life is taken seriously by some scholars.[10]

Philanthropy has already been mentioned as a major factor in the founding of colonial libraries. However, it had little effect on the pattern shown in Table 2.3 for these reasons: Most of the libraries founded through gifts were the parish libraries established by Bray and his colleagues. (135 out of the 145 church libraries shown later on Table 2.6 were from this source.) Of the 145 church libraries, only 26 are in Table 2.3; the others were either established too early or were ones for which founding dates were lacking in the available records.

The libraries sent to the colonies by Thomas Bray and the organizations he founded were by far the most significant expressions of philanthropy in the years before 1786. Most of them were libraries sent to Anglican churches; Bray made it quite clear that the purpose of these collections was to improve the spiritual life of the ministers and their congregations and, thereby, to help the churches compete with other Protestant churches and with Catholics. In addition to these parish libraries, he established or helped to establish several libraries intended for more general use. He was personally responsible for founding most of the libraries that appear on Table 2.2 around the year 1700. He also formed organizations that began to send libraries before his death in 1730; those groups did not cease their work until the time of the Revolution. Either Bray or his colleagues provided at least one library for each colony outside of New England and at least one library for each of several New England colonies. Maryland was most favored; the records available for this study include thirty-four libraries there.

Thomas Bray and the members of his organizations were not the only generous persons to help in the founding of libraries in the American colonies. At least three of the five libraries shown in Table 2.2 as having been founded before 1696 were based on gifts: Harvard's, in 1638, on books from John Harvard; a public library in Boston, in 1656, on books from Robert Keayne; and, in the same year, a gift to the town of New Haven, Connecticut, on some books from the library of Samuel Eaton. The details are less clear concerning the founding the other two, a town library in Concord, Massachusetts, sometimes dated from 1676, and the library of the College of William and Mary, dating from 1693; it is clear, however, that gifts of books figured very early in the history of those libraries. In the seventeenth century and early eighteenth century, philanthropy was the accepted means of founding colonial libraries.[11]

The colonists apparently did not begin to band together to provide libraries for themselves until Benjamin Franklin and his friends set an example by forming the Library Company of Philadelphia in 1731.[12] This library was the first of a type that is often called a social library. Some that were to follow were called library companies; others were called library associations or subscription libraries.[13] The social library was a collection owned by a society or association (these two terms are used interchangeably in this study) formed to obtain reading matter for its members and their families. In those days of patriarchy, the founders were almost without exception men. In the present study, the term *strict* social library is used when membership in the society had no overt limitation as to age, ethnic origin, or occupation, and the subject matter of the collection was general. Kinds of libraries formed for the use of particular groups—women or young men, for example—or on particular subjects—such as religion or agriculture—are considered separately from the strict social libraries because libraries of each kind, although they were formed by library societies, had a particular purpose; each kind had its own history before 1876.

In the years through 1785, almost all of the social libraries were general, or strict. The number of these slowly increased; from the latter half of the 1740s until the coming of the Revolution, these libraries accounted for approximately half of all the collections founded in the British colonies on known dates (fifty-one out of ninety-nine of the libraries in 1746 through 1775). However, the

Society for the Propagation of the Gospel in Foreign Parts (one of the Bray organizations) was actively sending parochial libraries during these years, and the exact dates for many of its libraries are not known, so the proportion of social libraries is almost certainly less than half of the actual total. The strict social libraries and the church libraries were the two groups that existed in large numbers before 1786; therefore, they are likely to have had the most influence on the patterns shown in Tables 2.2 and 2.3.

One set of numbers in Table 2.3 may be misleading. The ratios for 1780 represent two very different periods—the troubled war years from 1776 through about 1781, and the first years of the proud and vigorous new republic from about 1782 through 1785. If the ratio for the war years could be figured separately it would be considerably less, and the ratio for the later years would be considerably more, than the figures in Table 2.3. The histories of several colonial libraries tell that they ceased to exist during the Revolution or were in abeyance and had to be reorganized after the war. Table 2.3 shows a temporary decrease in the founding of libraries that was apparently caused by wartime disruption.

Economic conditions can sometimes be seen to have a connection with the founding of libraries; for example, Jesse Shera noted that New England social libraries tended to be founded more frequently during periods of prosperity in the years before 1855.[14] Historians agree that economic conditions in the American colonies were quite satisfactory during the eighteenth century. Edwin J. Perkins, in the second edition of his *Economy of Colonial America*, after considering the situation in detail, concludes, "Indeed, by the mid-eighteenth century, if not earlier, the typical white household in the mainland colonies was almost certainly enjoying the highest standard of living anywhere around the globe."[15]

Everywhere, this prosperity was based on the ability to export products desired in Europe and elsewhere, but different colonies sent different exports. Fertile land made possible the production of tobacco, rice, and indigo in the South and grain in the Middle-Atlantic states. In New England the land was less productive, but ship building, ocean shipping, and other activities brought good incomes.

One noticeable economic difference among the regions existed: There was greater per capita wealth among white southerners.[16] The numbers in Table 2.3 indicate that this definitely did not result in a greater tendency toward the founding of libraries in the South. Apparently, southern lifestyles, mentioned earlier, had more effect.

Taken as a whole, the figures in Table 2.3 are low when compared with the figures in Table 3.2 for later years (in chapter 3). The libraries surrounding only one decennial point (1760) in one area (the Mid-Atlantic colonies) reached as high as .50, a rate equivalent to the establishment of one library within the ten-year period for every 20,000 inhabitants. For whatever reasons, the act of founding libraries of the kinds included in this study was not occurring as frequently among colonial Americans as it was to occur later.

Libraries in Existence, 1690–1780

As pointed out in chapter 1, even though the founding of libraries indicates an interest in them, it could happen that in certain regions, or at certain times, while libraries were being founded as frequently as elsewhere or at other times, the average life of a library was shorter, with the result that fewer were in existence at any one time. In effect, Table 2.4 presents one kind of measure of the results of the activity shown in Table 2.2.

The method of determining the number of libraries in existence has been to take a census of libraries for each tenth year beginning with 1690. By the use of years ending in zero, comparisons can easily be made with the estimates of population mentioned earlier in this chapter.

Table 2.4 includes a few libraries that are not included in Table 2.2 because their founding dates could not be discovered. But any library (whether or not its founding date is known) has been omitted from Table 2.4 if its life began after one decennial year and if there is no indication that it still existed during the next decennial year.

The pattern of libraries in existence at ten-year intervals in Table 2.4 is similar to the pattern of founding shown in Table 2.2, but there are some noticeable differences. For the entire area, both show a general increase from early to late; and for the South, Table 2.4 shows the results of the rapid founding of libraries around 1700. The main difference between the pattern for founding libraries and the pattern for the number in existence is caused by the apparently shorter lives of many southern libraries, particularly the Bray parish libraries. For most of the Bray libraries, the only available date is the founding date. Contemporary accounts remark on the tendency of these church libraries to disappear quickly, but undoubtedly, some continued to exist after they had disappeared from the available records.[17] Records for the social libraries, which were much more common in the North, indicate longer lives. Percentages help to illustrate the difference between the North and the South in this respect: The South Atlantic region had almost exactly a third of all of the libraries in the British colonies before 1786 (in Table 2.1) but had only 5.4 percent of those in existence in 1770 and 6.8 percent of those in existence in 1780.

An important question still remains about the number of libraries in existence at different times in the three parts of the British settlements. Could the differences among the three be mainly related to the number of people in the regions? Table 2.5 answers this question by comparing the number of libraries in existence at ten-year intervals with the same estimates of population that were used for Table 2.3. Again, the table begins with 1740.

Generally, Table 2.5 shows that in New England and the Middle-Atlantic states, the ratio of libraries in existence to population was increasing—although, in the Middle-Atlantic region, perhaps because of the disruption caused by the Revolutionary War, this was not the situation between 1770 and 1780. Whatever caused the ratio in the Middle-Atlantic states to drop between 1770 and 1780 was sufficiently serious to cause the ratio for the entire region of the British settlement to decrease slightly between 1770 and 1780.

In the South, whether we consider the total population or only the white

Table 2.4
Libraries in Existence in the British Colonies and the Corresponding States, 1690–1780

	New England	Mid-Atlantic	South Atlantic	Entire Area
1690	2	1	0	3
1700	7	3	12	22
1710	5	1	4	10
1720	6	1	2	9
1730	6	2	2	10
1740	9	4	2	15
1750	12	14	3	29
1760	18	27	4	49
1770	34	36	4	74
1780	49	33	6	88

population, the ratio of libraries to population remained quite low during all of the years from 1740 through 1780—years after most of the church libraries had disappeared from available records. Whatever the causes—attitudes of the population, lack of large towns, or other—as we have seen, they do not include a lack of attraction for new settlers. In connection with the reasons for the founding of libraries, we saw that the population of the South Atlantic colonies grew as rapidly as the population in the northern colonies and that the total number of white persons in the South was larger than the total in either of the other two areas.

Kinds of Libraries

In addition to the strict social libraries and the church libraries, mentioned earlier in this chapter, several other kinds deserve attention. Following the order of their appearance in Table 2.6, the five social libraries with mainly religious content are first. If everything were known about more of the colonial library societies, it is possible that one or more libraries would be added to this religious

Table 2.5
Ratio of Libraries in Existence to Population in the British Colonies and the Corresponding States, 1740–1780

	New England		Mid-Atlantic		South Atlantic		Entire Area	
	w.p.	t.p.	w.p.	t.p.	w.p.	t.p.	w.p.	t.p.
1740	.32	.31	.22	.20	.07	.05	.20	.17
1750	.34	.33	.56	.52	.09	.06	.31	.25
1760	.41	.40	.74	.68	.09	.05	.39	.31
1770	.60	.59	.74	.69	.06	.04	.44	.34
1780	.70	.69	.52	.49	.07	.04	.40	.32

Note: Number of libraries in existence per 10,000 white population = w.p.; number of libraries in existence per 10,000 total population = t.p.

group and would be subtracted from the strict group. It may be significant that the religious libraries were the only social libraries to depart from the strict pattern before 1786. In the early decades of the nineteenth century many other kinds of specialized social libraries were to be established—either with collections on special subjects or collections intended for particular groups such as women or children.

Closely related to the subject-specialized social libraries were the collections belonging to societies that maintained libraries as only a part of their activities. Table 2.6 shows that a few of these had begun to appear before 1786. The eight organizations represented included three that were considered to be "scientific," a term that may have been used more freely than now. The other five were two masonic groups, a literary society, a merchants' exchange, and a "Franklin Society" whose purpose is not clear. It may be significant that the three scientific societies were located in Philadelphia, a recognized center of social and intellectual activity.

Following the order in Table 2.6, church libraries are next. They have been discussed earlier in this chapter, but the members of the group that follows them, the libraries owned by towns, were probably not much different. Although information about most of the collections is scanty, it is clear that some of them had a preponderance of religious material. Three of the six in New England were founded in the seventeenth century, a time when civil authorities would have been disposed to provide religious material; one in New York was intended for the use of the clergy and "gentlemen," and the two in the South were acquired at the end of the 1600s through the generosity of Thomas Bray.[18] Only one of these eight libraries was founded after 1730, and there are no available records concerning any library with a high proportion of religious material owned by a town at any time between 1786 and 1876. This situation could have been the result of the sentiment favoring the separation of church and state, which grew in the late eighteenth century and remained strong in the nineteenth. Apparently, the town libraries of colonial days were not related to the public libraries that began to appear in the nineteenth century.

The next kind of library in Table 2.6, the commercial circulating library, was one that ordinarily contained very little religious material. These collections, owned by individuals who lent the books for a fee, were modeled on ones that had been in existence in the British Isles from the latter part of the 1600s. The earliest in the American colonies seems to have been a short-lived one established in Annapolis, Maryland in 1762.[19] There are records of eleven that were founded through 1774; none from 1775 through 1781 (the war years); and then six from 1782 through 1785. The exact year dates for four others could not be determined. All but one of the entrepreneurs who attempted to establish this kind of business were located in larger towns or cities; Swedesboro, New Jersey was the only small town mentioned in the records used for this study.

Libraries in colleges and professional schools were very different from the commercial circulating libraries. Fourteen of the eighteen were in liberal arts colleges, institutions that typically had, as one of their purposes, the preparation of Protestant ministers. In colonial times, about half of the books in these libraries were on religion and about half on a variety of other subjects.[20] The four libraries that were not in liberal arts colleges were in these professional schools: two in medical schools, one in a law school, and one in a theological seminary.

Libraries appeared early in the lives of these institutions, usually at their opening or within a year or two after. In at least one case, the library was older than the college. The institution that later became Washington and Lee University started as a secondary school, an "academy," but began to offer college-level work in 1776. Its library was older than the college because the collection had been formed during the academy period.[21]

These collections owned by institutions of higher education were unusually longlived. All eighteen were still in existence in 1786, and all but one (in a law school at Litchfield, Connecticut) held on through the years before 1876[22]; most are very much alive today. This tendency to live long supports the notion that a library has a better chance of survival if it is attached to some other social agency.[23]

These libraries in colleges and professional schools were well distributed among the three parts of the British area. By the time of the Revolution they were to be found in eight colonies, and by 1785 two more collections had been established in a state that had none in colonial days. In Maryland, Washington College at Chestertown formed a collection in 1783, and St. John's College at Annapolis acquired one of the Bray libraries in 1784. Apparently, libraries held by student societies were not as common as they were to become later.

Table 2.6
Kinds of Libraries in the British Colonies and the Corresponding States before 1786

	New England	Mid-Atlantic	South Atlantic	Entire Area
All libraries	120	83	98	301
Social libraries				
In the strict sense	50	28	6	84
With religious content	4	1	0	5
Libraries belonging to associations not formed to establish libraries	2	3	2	7
Libraries belonging to churches	43	29	73	145
Libraries belonging to local governments (public libraries)	6	1	2	9
Commercial circulating libraries.	5	9	6	20
Libraries belonging to institutions of higher education				
Colleges & professional schools	6	7	5	18
Student societies	4	2	0	6
All others libraries	0	3	4	7

Available sources mention only six of them during the years before 1786: two at Harvard, two at Yale, and two at Princeton.[24]

The libraries that appear as "all others" in Table 2.6 were varied. Two of them were established in small South Carolina towns for the benefit of sailors. Philadelphia had two hospital libraries. Another Philadelphia collection was called the Assembly Library, which later moved to Harrisburg and, together with other collections, became the Pennsylvania State Library. A very early library existed at a garrison in Baltimore County, Maryland. Finally, there was a "trust" library in Georgia, around the 1750s, which may have been similar to the later state libraries except that it contained mainly religious books.[25]

We may be able to get a rough idea as to how many of all the kinds of libraries in the study got their start in the years before 1786. The nine categories listed in Table 2.6 include nineteen kinds. In the entire study there were approximately eighty kinds, each of which had at least one library with a known founding date. It seems clear that the greatest variation in kinds was to come after 1785.

The total number of *first* or *precursor* libraries before 1786 seems to have been so small that only the broadest generalizations are possible when the libraries are arranged chronologically or geographically. Generally, new kinds first appeared at times when Americans were most actively founding other libraries; a few more appeared in the early 1760s and in the early 1780s than in other five-year periods. Geographically, no region predominated: Five *firsts* appeared in New England, six in the Mid-Atlantic states, and six in the South Atlantic region. All of the kinds that appeared before 1786 would continue to be founded throughout the years before 1876, but as in the case of kinds that appeared later, enthusiasm for individual kinds of libraries waxed and waned over the years.

IN THE SPANISH AREA

Although libraries appeared quite early in the Spanish possessions that were to become part of the United States, they did not multiply as quickly as the ones in the British colonies. There is clear evidence of the existence of only seven in Spanish colonies before 1786. All seven were in convents or missions: one in Florida, two in New Mexico, and four in California. It is likely that there were several more; for example, I have been unable to identify any of the group of missions that are said to have rebuilt their libraries after the very destructive Pueblo revolt of 1680. The missions at Santa Fe and Santo Domingo Pueblo both had collections before that date. The Franciscan convent at St. Augustine in Florida, whose library was destroyed by Governor Moore of South Carolina in 1701, may not have been the only one there, and it is likely that more than four missions in California had libraries before 1786. The library at Mission San Carlos de Monterey was founded in 1770, and three others were mentioned as existing during the 1770s: Mission San Antonio, Mission San Diego, and Mission San Luis Obispo.[26]

The paucity of Spanish American libraries in this study may be partly caused by the destruction visited upon the missions, but a good part of the reason is undoubtedly related to the attitudes of the colonizers. In the first place, the civil authorities did not manage to attract many settlers from Europe or from other parts of the New World. And, apparently, most of the settlers who did come were from environments where books and reading were unimportant.[27] Furthermore, the religious authorities were unhappy with how a few settlers used the books they had.[28] In New Mexico, the churchmen discouraged the use of religious texts by laymen because they felt the owners were misinterpreting what they read. Later, in California, mission authorities discouraged the reading of books that were not under their control or were not approved by them.[29]

NOTES

1. The history of books and libraries in early New Mexico is told in two articles, "Books in New Mexico, 1598–1680" by Eleanor B. Adams and France V. Scholes, in *New Mexico Historical Review* 17 (July 1942): 226–70, and "A History of Libraries in

New Mexico—Spanish Origins to Statehood" by Rosalind Z. Rock, in *Journal of Library History* 14 (Summer 1979): 253–73.

2. The private library that belonged to a military officer is described by Luis R. Arana in an article, "A Private Library in St. Augustine, 1680," *El Escribano* 8 (Oct. 1971): 158–71, and the convent library is mentioned by Wilbert H. Siebert in an article, "Some Church History of St. Augustine During the Spanish Regime," *Florida Historical Quarterly* 9 (Oct. 1930): 121.

3. W. H. Venable, in his *Beginnings of Literary Culture in the Ohio Valley: Historical and Biographical Sketches* (Cincinnati: Robert Clarke, 1891), 256, mentions an eighteenth century church library in Vincennes, Indiana, but he apparently misinterpreted some early records concerning the church.

4. For some time now, social historians have been aware of the significance of voluntarism in British and American life during the eighteenth and nineteenth centuries. Several theories about it are described in *Voluntary Associations; Perspectives on the Literature* by Constance Smith and Anne Freeman (Cambridge, Mass.: Harvard University Press, 1972). The extent of the tendency to form associations just after the colonial period is described in "A Society of Societies: Associations and Volunteerism in Early Nineteenth-Century Salem," by Anne Farnam in *Essex Institute Historical Collections* 113 (July 1977): 181–90. I am not aware of any general history of voluntarism in the American colonies and the United States in the eighteenth and nineteenth centuries.

5. Sources frequently disagree as to the founding date of a single library. For a discussion of the problems caused by these disagreements, see pp. 32–33 of my chapter, "Primary Sources in Library Research," in *Research Methods in Librarianship: Historical and Bibliographical Methods in Library Science*, ed. Rolland E. Stevens (Urbana, Ill.: University of Illinois Graduate School of Library Science, 1971).

6. The fullest account of the libraries established by Bray and his organizations is given in Charles T. Laugher's, *Thomas Bray's Grand Design: Libraries of the Church of England in America, 1695–1785* (Chicago: American Library Association, 1973).

7. Several historians have mentioned these beliefs: among them, Joseph J. Ellis in *After the Revolution: Profiles of Early American Culture* (New York: W.W. Norton, 1979), and Richard D. Brown in *Knowledge is Power: The Diffusion of Information in Early America, 1700–1865* (New York: Oxford University Press, 1989), especially on pages 242 and 290–91.

8. The Massachusetts General Court (the legislature) in 1647 passed a famous law that has been called "The Old Deluder Satan Act," the first law in the colonies to require universal education. Its main purpose was to insure that children could read the scriptures in order to defeat the Devil.

9. U.S. Bureau of the Census, *Historical Statistics of the United States, Colonial Times to 1970* (Washington, D.C.: Government Printing Office, 1975), part 2, 1168.

10. 196–98, discusses possible reasons for the lower literacy rate in the South in the early nineteenth century, and A. Cash Koeniger writes about possible effects of the southern climate on life in general in "Climate and Southern Distinctiveness," *Journal of Southern History* 54 (Feb. 1988): 21–44. Most of what both authors say could be applied to the South in the eighteenth century.

11. Jesse H. Shera discusses all of these early libraries except the one at William and Mary in *Foundations of the Public Library: the Origins of the Public Library Movement in New England, 1629–1855* (Chicago: University of Chicago Press, 1949), 18–26.

12. In Great Britain, clubs for the exchange of books, commercial circulating libraries, and religious libraries for the use of the subscribers existed before the establishment of the Library Company in 1731, but the Leadhills Library in Scotland, "the first fully-fledged secular subscription library," was not established until 1741;

Thomas Kelly, *Early Public Libraries: A History of Public Libraries in Great Britain Before 1850* (London: Library Association, 1966), 121–23.

13. For a discussion of the use of terms for various kinds of libraries, see the glossary at the end of this book.

14. Shera, *Foundations of the Public Library*, 80–81.

15. Edwin J. Perkins, *The Economy of Colonial America*, 2d ed. (New York: Columbia University Press, 1988), 14.

16. Alice Hanson Jones, *Wealth of a Nation to Be: The American Colonies on the Eve of the Revolution* (New York: Columbia University Press, 1980), 308–11. Her figures are for the year 1774.

17. Laugher, *Thomas Bray's Grand Design*, 77–78.

18. An example: "The Beginnings of the Library in Charles Town, South Carolina" by Edgar Legare Pennington, *Proceedings of the American Antiquarian Society* 44 (Apr. 1934): 159–87, includes a transcript of an early catalog showing a heavy emphasis on religion.

19. David Kaser, *A Book for a Sixpence: The Circulating Library in America* (Pittsburgh, Pa.: Beta Phi Mu, 1980), 19–23.

20. Joe W. Kraus, "The Book Collections of Early American College Libraries," *Library Quarterly* 43 (Apr. 1973): 142–59.

21. Betty Ruth Kondayan, "The Library of Liberty Hall Academy," *Virginia Magazine of History and Biography* 86 (Oct. 1978): 432–46.

22. The Litchfield library is described in *Tapping Reeve and the Litchfield Law School* by Marian C. McKenna (New York: Oceana Publications, 1986), 111–17.

23. Being connected with another agency could not always ensure a long life. In the nineteenth century, school libraries provided by state governments often died out if local officials and other individuals lacked the desire or means to maintain them.

24. Libraries owned by student societies in colonial colleges are briefly mentioned in Thomas S. Harding's *College Literary Societies: Their Contribution to Higher Education in the United States, 1815–1876* (New York: Pageant Press International, 1971), 26.

25. Jiles Berry Fleming, "199 Years of Augusta's Library: a Chronology," *Georgia Historical Quarterly* 33 (June 1949): 128–30.

26. J. N. Bowman, "Libraries in Provincial California," *Historical Society of Southern California Quarterly* 43 (Dec. 1961): 426–39.

27. David Lavender makes the reasons for the reluctance of people to settle in California clear in his succinct treatment of that state's colonial years in *California, a Bicentennial History* (New York: W. W. Norton, 1976). Thomas D. Hall's *Social Change in the Southwest, 1350–1880* (Lawrence, Kans.: University Press of Kansas, 1989) contains an analysis of conditions in other Spanish colonies that makes it seem unlikely that settlers would have had much interest in founding libraries.

28. Adams and Scholes, "Books in New Mexico, 1598–1680," and Rock, "A History of Libraries in New Mexico—Spanish Origins to Statehood."

29. Doyce B. Nunis, Jr., *Books in Their Sea Chests: Reading Along the Early California Coast*, California Library Association Keepsake no. 6 (n.p.: California Library Association, 1964), 3–4, 8–9.

Chapter 3

Libraries from the End of the Revolutionary Period through 1875

The libraries that existed during the colonial and revolutionary periods made up only a small fraction of all of those identified for this study as having been in existence before 1876. Even in the areas that had the most libraries before 1786, this condition held true: in New England, only 4.6 percent first appeared in the available records before that year; in the Middle Atlantic states, 5.1 percent; and in the South Atlantic states, 12.4. Of course, a few libraries founded before 1786 continued to exist during part or all of the later years: sixty-four libraries in New England, thirty-six in the Middle-Atlantic states, seven in the South Atlantic, and four in the Pacific.

In the areas that had few or no libraries before 1786 (that is, almost everywhere except the eastern seaboard) the differences in the number of libraries established in the various regions before 1876 indicate areas that were settled first usually had the most libraries (in Table 1.1). Americans from the Northeast and the old South first settled the Middle West, and people from the old South moved into the South Central states; then, toward the end of the period in this study, Americans from the East, the South, and the Central West were beginning to join the small number of Mexicans who were already in the Far West. Events that affected the general pattern for the distribution of libraries—the panic of 1837, the gold rush, the Mormon settlement in Utah, and the Civil War, to name a few—will be mentioned later in this chapter.

THE FOUNDING OF LIBRARIES, 1786–1875

Chapter 2 mentioned the difficulties in establishing the founding dates of some libraries. In chapter 3 the decisions given in chapter 2 will be followed: For each library, the year date given by what seems to be the most reliable source will be used. Table 3.1 and Figure 3.1 omit any libraries for which sources do not give year dates or are vague about them: "in the early 1820s" or "a few years before the Civil War."

It is impossible to be certain whether knowing the founding dates of libraries that now have unknown dates would produce, for all libraries, a chronological pattern closely resembling the one in Table 3.1 and Figure 3.1. There was considerable variation among regions in regard to the availability of founding dates, apparently because, in some regions, there was a higher proportion of small libraries—the ones from sources that most often lacked founding dates. The West South Central region and the Mountain states had high proportions of libraries without known founding dates; in each of those regions, dates are lacking for at least half of the libraries. Also, the presence of certain kinds of small libraries in the records used for this study had an effect. For example, most of the information about libraries owned by frontier military garrisons has been derived from contemporary surveys that almost never gave dates of founding.

The relative lack of founding dates for the West South Central and Mountain regions did not have much effect on the proportion with dates in the entire country because there were fewer libraries in those two areas than elsewhere; the combined number of libraries in those areas was only 3.6 percent of the ones in the entire study. Other parts of the country were mainly responsible for the numbers in Table 3.1 and Figure 3.1. Those numbers show a general increase in the number of libraries being founded in the United States, an increase that might be expected in a country with a rapidly growing population. But the lines in the graph are not nearly as smooth as the increase in population. (The relationship between the number of libraries being founded at different times and the number of persons in the region at those times is shown later in this chapter in Table 3.2.)

The most pronounced irregularity in Figure 3.1 and Table 3.1 is the sharp peak that occurred during the 1850s. Actually, this peak was caused by the large number of township libraries founded in Indiana during three years: 597 in 1854, 197 in 1855, and 138 in 1856.

Michigan also established a large number of township libraries, beginning in the 1830s; a total of 620 were identified for this study. However, founding dates were discovered for only forty-five of them, so they had little effect on the numbers in Table 3.1 and Figure 3.1. Township libraries are discussed in more detail in chapter 8.

There seem to have been three periods when the founding of American libraries was failing to keep pace with the steadily increasing population: Table 3.1 and Figure 3.1 show a relatively low rate of founding between about 1800 and 1820, a brief drop in the early 1840s, and a sharp drop in the early 1860s. These will be examined in chronological order.

Tables 2.2 and 3.1, combined, show that from the 1760s into the 1830s, most American libraries were being founded in the Northeast; and most of the ones in that region were in New England. Figures that formed the basis for Table 3.1 show that in seven of the eleven five-year periods between 1786 and 1840, the number of libraries founded in Massachusetts was greater than in any other state; Connecticut led in two of the periods and New Hampshire in two. In New England, the social library (defined as in chapter 2, in the strict sense) was the favorite type; from the 1760s into the second decade of the nineteenth century,

Table 3.1
Libraries Founded in the United States, 1786–1875

	Northeast	South	Middle West	Far West	All U.S.
1786-90	56	10	0	1	67
1791-95	146	11	0	0	157
1796-1800	160	16	1	0	177
1801-05	124	13	6	0	143
1806-10	120	30	6	1	157
1811-15	99	35	18	0	152
1816-20	102	43	22	0	167
1821-25	145	51	25	1	222
1826-30	154	37	72	0	263
1831-35	157	40	86	3	286
1836-40	133	80	96	0	309
1841-45	100	69	87	4	260
1846-50	175	79	104	16	374
1851-55	236	103	945	34	1,318
1856-60	211	90	369	44	714
1861-65	158	32	111	43	344
1866-70	363	97	296	56	812
1871-75	371	105	310	52	838
Total	3,010	941	2,554	255	6,760

Figure 3.1
Libraries Founded in the United States, 1786–1875

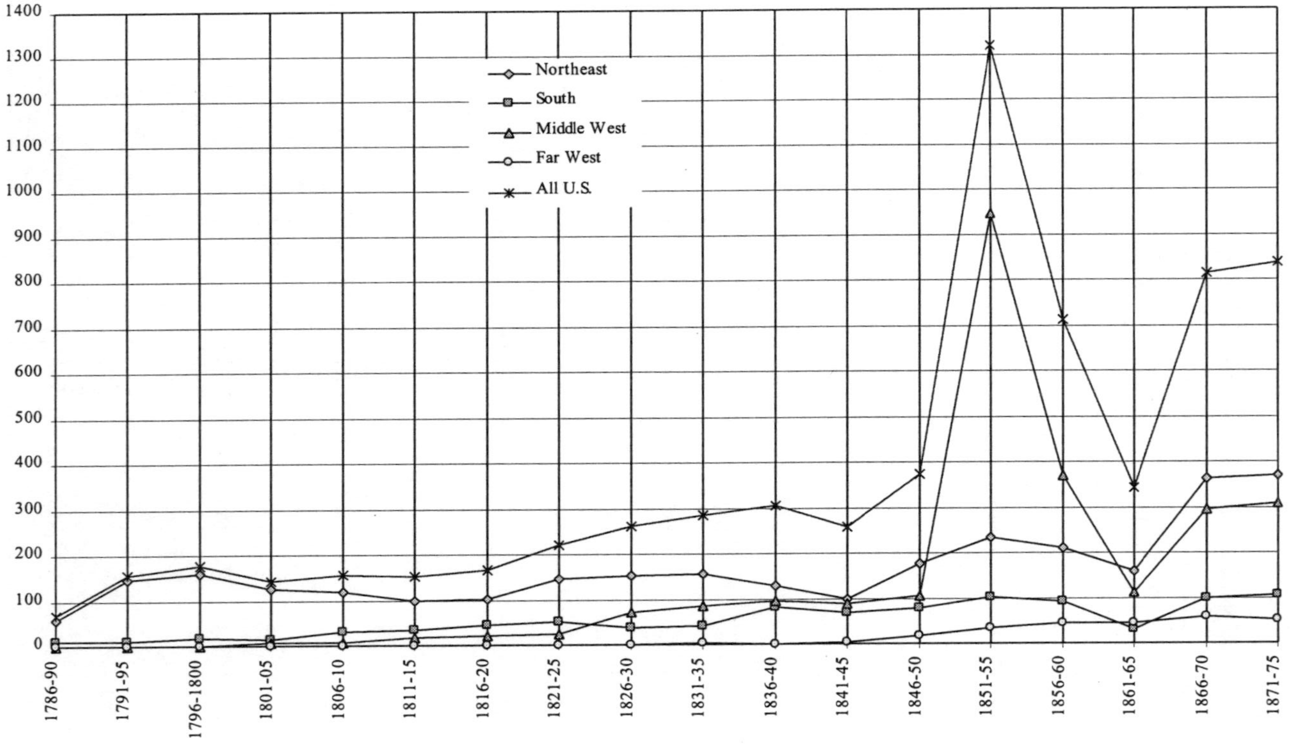

social libraries made up well over half of all the libraries being established there. So the little "hill" for the 1790s in Figure 3.1 was primarily caused by the tremendous enthusiasm for a single type of library in only one of the nine divisions of the country; never again did a small part of the country demonstrate such a strong preference for any one kind. However, as we shall see in chapter 5, considering all the years before 1876, the strict social library was more popular than any other kind.

To understand each of the later two dips in the lines in Figure 3.1, we must consider the founding of several kinds of libraries in several parts of the country. The reasons for the apparent "valley" from about 1800 to 1820 are not entirely clear; there was a marked decrease in the rate of founding of social libraries in New England, possibly because only a few more were needed. Figures that form the basis for Table 3.1 indicate that the rate of founding in the Middle-Atlantic states had not increased sufficiently to make up for the lack of enthusiasm in New England.

During the first half of the nineteenth century, almost all the kinds of libraries in this study belonged to people who either voluntarily formed associations for the purpose of establishing the libraries or who formed organizations (such as bar associations) whose members felt the need for a library. Individual members of the association had to be willing to contribute financially for its support, so we might expect that in periods of economic depression fewer libraries would be established. As was mentioned in chapter 2, Jesse Shera found that there was sometimes a tendency for New England social libraries to be founded less frequently during economic depressions in the years before 1855.[1] Could an unfavorable economic climate have been related to the comparatively low rate of founding of libraries during the years from about 1800 to 1820? While trying to find the answer to that question, we must consider some of the characteristics of American depressions during the nineteenth century. First, they had different effects in different parts of the country; second, they had different effects on different elements in the economy—banking, manufacturing, agriculture, and so on;[2] third, some economic elements or parts of the country recovered before others; and fourth, depressions had a greater or lesser effect on different classes in society. Scholars still disagree abut the concept of "class" in nineteenth century America, but a few careful studies have indicated that, at least in larger cities, families with large fortunes were little affected by downturns in the economy. Members of these families were often much involved in the management of libraries and the organizations that owned libraries.[3]

The result of all of this is that it is difficult to know exactly when and how a depression might affect the founding of libraries. Between 1800 and 1820, at least two minor depressions have been recognized: a brief one around 1808 and a somewhat deeper one centering around 1819 and 1820. The year-to-year rate of founding of libraries does not reveal any decrease at those times; more libraries than usual were being established in each of the two years 1820 and 1821.

Wars clearly have caused disruption in the formation and continued existence of libraries. We have noticed the effect of the Revolution and will easily see the effect of the Civil War. However, it is difficult to see any variation in the rate of founding of libraries that might have been caused by the War of 1812. If there were a graph showing the year-to-year changes in the number of libraries being founded just before, during, and after that war it would show no evidence of a decrease in the rate during the war, although the number fails to increase from about 1813 to 1817 as one might expect, considering the pattern just before and after those years.

Returning to the more general trends shown in Table 3.1 and Figure 3.1, the next decrease occurs in the numbers for 1841 to 1845—some of the years when the country had not entirely recovered from the long depression following the panic of 1837. Economists give varying dates for the end of that depression, from the mid 1840s to about 1850. Some of them mention a brief period of normal conditions in 1839, quickly followed by a return to hard times.[4] Because this was a major depression and because the five-year periods used in this study do not fit well with its onset or disappearance, the year-to-year record of foundings is helpful. This record does not present the picture that might be expected; instead, the numbers might seem appropriate for a depression that followed a panic in 1840 or 1841; there is a steady increase from 1836 to 1840, and then a steady decrease through 1844. Could the temporary economic improvement around 1839 have had an effect? The figures for the Northeast, the South, and the Middle West are not closely similar, but they produce a smooth pattern for the entire United States.

It is always possible that a pattern of founding such as the one that showed a peak in 1840 was caused by Americans' interest in a single kind of library or in only a few kinds. One naturally thinks of the social library. In the first decade of the nineteenth century, approximately two out of every three libraries founded were social libraries in the strict sense. By 1840 only about one out of every three libraries was a social library, but this type was still more popular than any other. More strict social libraries were founded in 1840 than in any other year from 1836 through 1845, and 1839 had the second-largest number.

Other kinds of libraries showed a somewhat similar pattern. Libraries in colleges and professional schools had high points in 1839 and 1844. For libraries formed by the societies that primarily had other purposes (bar associations, medical societies, and others), 1839 saw more collections being started than any year before 1843. For several other kinds, 1839 or 1840 was a popular year. Apparently, changes in economic conditions were not responsible for the increase in the years just before 1840 and the decrease after that year. However, the apparent reluctance to found libraries of several kinds in several parts of the country during the years from 1841 through 1845 is consistent with the slow movement out of the depression that took place. The Mexican War seems to have had no appreciable effect on the founding of libraries around the time it took place (1846 to 1848).

The early 1850s were good years for business and for the founding of libraries. The panic of 1857 caused economic disruption in all parts of the country, although southerners felt that their region was not being damaged as much as the rest of the country.[5] The country had not fully recovered from the effect of the panic before the Civil War began. The founding of libraries could have been generally responsive to economic conditions during this period: the yearly totals on which Table 3.1 and Figure 3.1 are based show a marked decline from 1856 to 1857, then a smaller decline from 1857 to 1858, and little change before another sharp drop from 1860 to 1861.

The general effect of the Civil War on the founding of libraries is shown in Table 3.1 and Figure 3.1. Neither in the North nor the South did the onset of the war put a complete stop to the founding of libraries. However, the decrease in this kind of activity took place throughout the country except the Rocky Mountain area, and the rate of founding increased everywhere at about the time the war ended. For the whole United States, the number of libraries established in the five-year period, 1861–65, was 48.2 percent of the number founded in 1856 through 1860; if the Indiana township libraries are omitted from the 1856–60 figures, the wartime number was 60 percent of the number for the five preceding years. The number for the peacetime years, 1866–70, was 236 percent of the number for 1861 through 1865.

When the founding of libraries during the war is compared with that kind of activity before the war, the different parts of the country show quite different patterns. As might be expected, the South saw a severe drop in activity during the war; the number of libraries founded there from 1861 through 1865 was only about a third (35.6 percent) of the number founded from 1856 through 1860. The figures for the Middle West show a somewhat greater decrease to 30.1 percent of the 1856–1860 Figure, but if the Indiana township libraries are not considered, the number established from 1861 through 1865 is close to half (48.5 percent) of the number established during the five preceding years. The war caused less of a decrease in the Northeast; 1861 through 1865 saw 75.2 percent as many foundings as occurred from 1856 through 1860.

Americans in two regions were founding many more libraries than Americans in the other two regions during the Civil War. The figures for the years from 1861 through 1865 in Table 3.1 for the Northeast and the Middle West combined are 78.2 percent of the total for the country. This high percentage is partly related to population differences: these two regions had 62.6 percent of the total population of the United States in 1860 and 71.8 percent of the white population in that year. (The relation of library founding to population is examined in more detail in the next section of this chapter.) However, two other conditions may have affected the number of libraries being founded during the war: economic conditions in these two more populous regions in the North and attitudes there toward the war itself.

The pattern of library founding year by year during the war (not shown in Table 3.1) is generally consistent with the notion that libraries are more frequently established during prosperous times. In the South, the rate continued low throughout the war because life was always difficult for almost everyone. In the industrialized Northeast and Midwest, the wartime needs for such things as arms and uniforms brought prosperity for the people who could produce them. Also, the loss of workers to the army encouraged mechanization on farms and in factories.[6] For the country as a whole, there was a marked increase in the number of libraries being founded from 1861 through 1865. It is quite possible that this increase was related to the generally favorable economic conditions in the North. However, it is also possibly related to the attitudes of many northerners who, in the later years of the war, began to feel that a Union victory was inevitable; they may have wanted to return to peacetime pursuits, including the more rapid establishment of libraries.[7]

The Mountain sub-region in the West provides the greatest wartime variation from the pattern for the whole country, but the numbers are so small that they should be interpreted with caution. Apparently, more libraries were founded there during the five war years than during the preceding five-year period, and the rate of founding did not change much during the war. It is tempting to attribute what seems to be a "business as usual" library situation to the attitude of people in Utah (then a territory) because the Latter-day Saints (Mormons) were inclined to stand aloof from the conflict; they may not have been affected by whatever forces caused decreases in foundings elsewhere.[8] But the population of Utah was only about a fourth of that in the Mountain sub-region (23 percent in 1860 and 27.5 percent in 1870). That state provided only five of the twelve libraries known to have been founded in the Mountain sub-region from 1861 through 1865.

In the Pacific states, California had most of the population around the time of the Civil War (85.6 percent in 1860 and 83 percent in 1870). Californians were not indifferent to the war. Before and during the conflict, some people in that state favored the Confederacy, but most were loyal to the federal government, and the state contributed sixteen thousand volunteers to the Union army.[9] Around the time of the war, California had more libraries with founding dates available for this study than any other state in the Far West. The total of twenty-two for 1861 through 1865 was noticeably fewer than in the previous five-year period, but the number founded from year to year during the war did not change significantly. Again, numbers were too small to justify solid conclusions.

The first few years after the war were generally good for the country—at least for the North—and for the founding of libraries. In most parts of the United States, more libraries were founded during the ten-year period from 1866 through 1875 than during any earlier ten-year period. This was not the case in the East North Central region because of the large number of township libraries distributed in the 1850s by the state government in Indiana. If those libraries are not considered, in each of the four major regions, more libraries were established from 1866 through 1875 than in any other ten-year period. However, in one sub-region this was not the situation: in the South Atlantic area, a few more were founded during the 1850s than in the ten years after the war.

The depression following the panic of 1873 has been considered a major economic disturbance. However, any adverse results for the founding of libraries through 1875 cannot be detected; the annual figures on which Table 3.1 is based show that in both 1874 and 1875 more libraries were being founded than in most of the years from 1866 through 1873.

This section of the study had been concerned with the effects—or lack of effects—of economic depressions and wars on the rate of founding of libraries. It has sometimes been necessary to mention the growth of the American population between 1786 and 1875; the next section will contain a more detailed consideration of the relationships between the number of libraries being founded and the number of people in the areas where the libraries were appearing.

THE FOUNDING OF LIBRARIES AND THE GROWTH OF POPULATION, 1790–1870

Chapter 2 described the reasons for comparing the rate of founding of libraries with the number of people who were present close to the time of founding. This section of chapter 3 is, in effect, a continuation of the part of chapter 2 that was concerned with that comparison; Table 3.2 is a continuation of Table 2.3, with the additions of the regions that had few or no libraries before 1786.

Table 3.2 and Figure 3.2, like Table 2.3, contain different ratios for the total population and for the white population so that the reader may consider race. The ratios for the white population are more significant if the intentions of the founders are to be considered because very few libraries were established for the use of other races. The scarcity of Afro-Americans in the Northeast and in the East North Central region has caused the differences in the two ratios to be slight there; of course, the presence of large numbers of blacks in the South caused the greater differences there.[10]

Of all the libraries considered in the main part of this study, only twenty-nine (less than half of one percent) were clearly intended for Afro-Americans. Twenty-three of these were located in the Northeast, usually in cities; Philadelphia had eleven, more than in any other place. All of the libraries for blacks appeared from the 1820s through the 1850s, except for three that were established at Howard University in Washington, D.C. after the Civil War. For the most part, the collections were formed by voluntary organizations: literary societies, lyceums, churches, and others. Northern cities had many such organizations for blacks, so it is possible that many more libraries existed.[11]

Unfortunately, Table 3.2 does not properly take into account the presence of Native Americans because the Constitution called for the enumeration, at ten-year intervals, of everyone "excluding Indians not taxed." This rule, in effect, excluded those who were on reservations or were nomadic. The officials in charge of the censuses from 1850 through 1870 excluded these untaxed Indians from their census tables but obtained figures (often estimates) from other agencies and printed them in separate tables within the census volumes.[12] If the small numbers of Indians living within the general population are added to the much larger numbers of those who lived on reservations or were nomadic, the totals were still small in the United States as a whole—never more than 2 percent of the total population.

In the Far West, the percentage of "civilized" Native Americans (that is, counted in the censuses) was negligible in 1850, only 1.8 in 1860, and 1.1 in 1870. However, the percentages of Indians who were nomadic or on reservations were higher in the Far West than elsewhere. It would be almost useless to calculate the difference that the recognition of Indians would make in the 1850 figures because the ratio for the Mountain states is based on only four libraries and because the number of Indians reported for California is

Table 3.2
Ratio of Libraries Founded in the United States to Population, 1790–1870

		Northeast	South	Middle West	Far West	All U.S
1790	w.p.	1.06	.17	—	—	.71
	t.p.	1.03	.11	—	—	.57
1800	w.p.	1.11	.17	1.40	—	.74
	t.p.	1.08	.11	1.37	—	.60
1810	w.p.	.65	.30	.84	—	.53
	t.p.	.63	.19	.82	—	.43
1820	w.p.	.58	.34	.56	—	.49
	t.p.	.57	.21	.55	—	.40
1830	w.p.	.57	.22	1.01	—	.52
	t.p.	.56	.13	.98	—	.43
1840	w.p.	.35	.35	.56	—	.40
	t.p.	.34	.21	.55	—	.33
1850	w.p.	.48	.32	1.99	2.81	.87
	t.p.	.48	.20	1.94	2.79	.73
1860	w.p.	.35	.17	.54	1.58	.39
	t.p.	.35	.11	.53	1.41	.34
1870	w.p.	.61	.23	.48	1.19	.48
	t.p.	.60	.15	.47	1.09	.41

Note: w.p. = ratio to 10,000 white population.; t.p. = ratio to 10,000 total population. Each number represents the libraries founded in the ten-year period that includes the four years before the decennial year, the decennial year itself, and the five years after it. (The first row of figures is for 1786–95, etc.)

suspiciously high and round—100,000 out of a total of 400,764 for the entire United States. If the estimates of Indians omitted in the 1860 census had been included, the number of libraries founded per 10,000 population for the Far West would have been 1.12 instead of 1.41. In 1870 the inclusion of the population estimates for the nomadic Indians and those on reservations would have reduced the ratio for the Far West from 1.09 to .88. Clearly, if these Indians had been considered, the ratio of libraries founded to population would have been noticeably lower.

Of the kinds of libraries included in this study, only two collections for Native Americans could be identified: the National Library of the Cherokees at

Figure 3.2
Ratio of Libraries Founded in the United States to Total Population, 1790–1870
(Ratio of libraries founded to 10,000 total population)

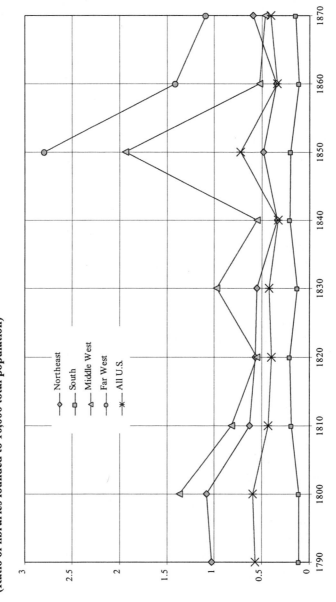

Tahlequah (now in Oklahoma) and an asylum for orphans and destitute Indian children in Collins, New York. The library for the Cherokees was established by the 1860s (sources disagree about the date of founding), and the one in New York was opened in 1872. A few educational institutions for Indians existed before 1876, but no libraries could be discovered that belonged to any that offered college-level work.

The Chinese were the only other non-white group of any significant size to be included in the census; they appear only in the figures for 1860 and 1870.[13] In 1860 they were reported in only one state, California, where there were 34,933. If they had been excluded from consideration, the ratio in the Far West (including Indians not in the census) would have been 1.07 instead of 1.12 libraries per 10,000 population, not a great difference. At the time of the 1870 census, almost all (99.4 percent) of the Chinese were still in the Far West. If they had been omitted in calculating the ratio of foundings to population (including Indians not in the census), the ratio would have increased from .88 to .93, again not a very great difference. No libraries for the Chinese were identified for this study.

In chapter 2 and earlier in this chapter, several conditions were mentioned that should be considered as we discuss the founding of libraries. Two more conditions apply to the relationship between the founding of libraries and the growth of population during the years after 1785. The first is that a few libraries must be omitted in this part of the study because no census had been taken at the time when they were established. There was a total of fewer than forty of these, about half of them in the Pacific region. All of the Hawaiian libraries with known founding dates had to be omitted, as did a few that were started in Texas before its first federal census in 1850.

Another situation can be deceiving in parts of Table 3.2. Sometimes very few libraries had been founded during the ten-year period centering on the first census for a region; the discovery of only a few more libraries would cause a marked change in the ratio. The parts of Table 3.2 that are based on small numbers of libraries can easily be discovered by comparing that table with Table 3.1.

Figure 3.2 and Table 3.2 give an indication of the tendency of Americans in various places and at various times to establish libraries. Numbers that form the basis for the early parts of this figure and table show that the large number of social libraries founded by New Englanders was not just the result of the large number of persons living there, but was, in addition, the result of their enthusiasm for this kind of library. The good showing for the Middle West just before and after 1800 is not significant because it is based on such a small number of libraries (only seven). But after that, its ratios should be taken seriously. The decrease in activity in the Northeast and the Middle West in the years just before and after 1840 may have been at least partly caused by the depression following the panic of 1837. In the country as a whole, the figure and table showing ratios of foundings to population indicate that, except for the variations already noted, and except for the sudden bestowal of township libraries by the Indiana state government in the 1850s, the ratio of foundings to population remained about the same before 1876. There was no clear indication of a tendency to slack off, which might have taken place if libraries already established were able to supply the need of Americans, and no indication of any sudden increase in the desire for new libraries.

For several parts of the country, Table 3.2 fails to show some marked differences that existed. Within the Northeast, New England continued to produce new libraries at a rapid pace—fast enough to assure a respectable ratio for that major region despite a lower rate in the Middle Atlantic states. Sometimes, for the whole population (whites, blacks, and a few others) at least, the rate of founding in the Middle-Atlantic states was lower than in the South Atlantic states. However, the South, as a whole, remained low even when only the white population is taken into consideration.

The parts of the United States where settlement before 1786 was slight show patterns that were somewhat different from those in the East and the Old South, but the patterns in the West were clearly influenced by attitudes and habits that existed in the East. Always, part of the western population had been born (and perhaps had grown up) farther east. There have been many studies of the sometimes complex movement of Americans as the central and western parts of the country were settled. However, scholars agree that usually, settlers moved straight west; they less frequently moved northwest or southwest.[14] In the years before 1850, the eastern parts of the Middle West were mainly settled by people from New England and the Middle Atlantic states. In at least three states—Ohio, Indiana, and Illinois during the years before 1850—more social and public libraries were being founded in areas settled by New Englanders (especially in the Western Reserve part of Ohio) than in other areas.[15]

During the later years included in the present study, immigrants from Europe joined the Americans in settling several parts of the country; after the Civil War, certain states made special efforts to attract Europeans.[16] However, the number of libraries that were founded by immigrants, mainly Germans, was not large; these libraries will be discussed in later chapters of this study.

Figures not shown in Table 3.2 indicate that during most of the time from about the beginning of the nineteenth century until about 1850, the ratio of library foundings to population was greater in New England than in any other sub-region. However, when each of the four major regions is considered as a whole, the ratio in the Middle West was highest during most of those years. Then, beginning at about 1850, people in the Far West showed much more interest in founding libraries, as measured by the ratio of foundings to population.

Why were settlers in the Far West in a much greater hurry to establish libraries than were residents of any other part of the country during the later years included in this study? We may be inclined to think of the years of the gold rush and the years just after it as ones when the whites on the Pacific coast and in the Rockies were busily seeking their fortunes by mining or by selling products to the miners at high prices. Why would they be establishing libraries—an activity with little apparent relation to mining—at a rate higher than the rate in any other part of the country then or previously? A little more than half of the western population was in California at the time of the censuses for 1850 through 1870; in 1880 that state still had 48 percent. However, figures used as a basis for Table 3.2 show that the enthusiasm for libraries existed in the Rockies as well as on the Pacific slope.

The reasons for the intensity of this form of library activity in the Far West are not clear, but they may be related to several western conditions and attitudes. In the first place, mining, the chief occupation in the Far West, was more lucrative than agriculture, the chief support in much of the United States. The earliest available estimate of per capita income puts the figure for the Mountain states at 168 percent of the U.S. average in 1880, and for the Pacific states at 204 percent.[17] Miners may have had more money to spend on libraries.

Another situation could have had an effect. The ratio of workers to dependents was higher in the Far West because many miners either left their families in the East or had no families. The lack of dependents in the Far West is consistent with its gender ratios. In each of the other large regions of the country (the Northeast, the South, and the Middle West) the percentages of females in the population ranged between 47.9 and 50.6 in the censuses from 1850 through 1880, whereas in the Far West, the percentage in 1850 was only 26.3, and it had risen to only 38.8 by 1880.[18] We might expect that the founding of libraries would become more frequent (in relation to population) after western society had become more like that in the East, but such was not the case. Could the abnormally low numbers of women have caused western men to turn to libraries?

Could the rapid establishment of libraries in the West have been part of an effort to quickly catch up with the East? Social historians have reported that, in the decades just after 1850, people in the Far West were making other efforts to transform western society into a more stable and comfortable society like that of the East.[19]

The rapid rate of library founding in the Far West indicates that libraries are not necessarily founded more rapidly in areas where population density is greater. In other parts of the country the rate of founding was sometimes greater where there were more inhabitants per square mile. However, statistics concerning the density of population are not very useful in studying libraries. Theoretically, libraries are more likely to be found in densely populated areas such as cities, but again theoretically, in a city a single library might be able to serve a larger number of people because more persons could easily reach it. Two studies have attempted to examine American libraries existing before 1875 in relation to population density or location in cities as compared with other places. Each of them is concerned with several states but, together, they are too limited to be helpful in discovering a relationship between the founding of libraries and the density of population in the country as a whole before 1876.[20]

Any statement about the density of population in the various regions must remain very general for two reasons: (1) Each of the four major regions at one time or another included areas of scattered population along with areas of denser settlement. (2) Within most of the regions the land area increased occasionally as the United States acquired new territory, causing what seemed to be a sudden decrease in density. Here are some generalizations that may be safe: in every major region, the density of population increased during each decade from 1790 through 1870. However, population was always much more dense in the

Northeast than elsewhere. In 1790, about twelve inhabitants per square mile lived there, and about eight per square mile lived in the South Atlantic area, three of whom were whites; very few people had gone into the East South Central area by that time. By 1870, the density in the Northeast had reached about seventy-six per square mile, and for the entire South, there were about fourteen per square mile, nine of whom were whites. In the Midwest the ratio was nearly seventeen per square mile, and in the Far West, less than one per square mile. The density of population could have been related to the rate of founding of libraries, but Table 3.2 and Figure 3.2 show that density was not the dominant factor: For example, frequently the rate of founding was greater in the Midwest than in the Northeast.

The next section of this chapter is concerned with some of the results of Americans' activities that have just been described—where and when the libraries existed.

LIBRARIES IN EXISTENCE, 1790–1875

Chapter 2 showed that the number of libraries in existence increased in the years through 1780 but that there was considerable variation in the rate of increase over the years and considerable variation among the three areas that had most of the libraries. From 1790 through 1875, the number continued to increase, but with similar variations over time and among different parts of the country.

The extent of these variations is shown in Table 3.3 and Figure 3.3, which indicate that, except in 1855 when the Indiana state government had suddenly established many township libraries, the Northeast always had more libraries than did any other major region. If numbers for the two sub-regions in the Northeast were shown separately, it would become clear that New England always had more libraries than did the Middle-Atlantic states. The number of libraries in the South increased during every decade before the Civil War, but at all times the South Atlantic states had more libraries than the other two parts of the South combined. The Middle West did not surpass the South until the 1850s; as in the South, the eastern part of the Middle West always had more libraries than did the western part. In the Far West, there is evidence of only a few libraries before the region was settled by people coming mainly from east of the Rockies. The rapid rate of founding of libraries in the Far West starting about 1850 did not produce enough libraries to bring the total close to the total for any other region by 1875.

The conditions mentioned earlier in this chapter that may have affected the rate of founding of libraries probably also affected the numbers of libraries in existence at various times and places. However, there seems to have been an important difference in the two sets of numbers. A graph can be constructed that shows the percent of increase or decrease in the number of libraries existing in the United States from one of the five-year intervals that are used in Table 3.3 to the next interval. Such a graph will show considerably less variation at different times from 1790 through 1875 than will a similar graph based on Table 3.1,

Table 3.3
Libraries in Existence in the United States, 1790–1875

	Northeast	South	Middle West	Far West	All U.S.
1790	131	20	0	6	157
1795	252	28	0	6	286
1800	365	41	1	6	413
1805	416	45	5	6	472
1810	448	71	12	7	538
1815	479	88	16	7	590
1820	500	100	26	7	633
1825	585	110	40	8	743
1830	628	124	69	8	829
1835	666	152	100	18	936
1840	737	213	144	14	1,108
1845	752	248	196	16	1,212
1850	869	322	273	25	1,489
1855	1,027	378	1,578	48	3,031
1860	1,078	372	695	66	2,211
1865	1,158	366	623	90	2,237
1870	1,470	630	898	146	3,144
1875	1,814	555	1,128	181	3,678

Figure 3.3
Libraries in Existence in the United States, 1790–1875

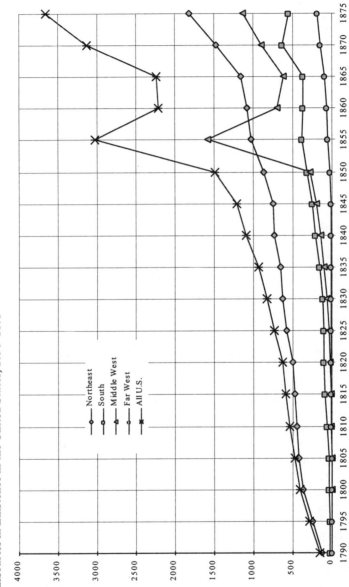

showing the percentage of variation in the number of libraries being founded. The average amount of change in the number of existing libraries from one measuring point to the next point, five years later, would be 26.7 percent, and the average amount of change for foundings would be 34.4 percent. And the only decrease in the number of existing libraries was from 1855 to 1860, whereas there were seven out of seventeen times when there were fewer libraries founded than in the previous five-year period.

The reason for this relatively steady increase in the number of existing libraries despite noticeably greater changes in the rate of founding seems to be that some of the libraries that appeared during each five-year period lasted a short while, some lasted a few years longer, and some much longer. So the results of a period of rapid founding might be spread over several decades. Similar situations occurred, of course, for libraries founded when activity was less than average; the lack of founding reduced the growth in the number of libraries for several years. At any point in time, some libraries had probably come into existence when founding was rapid and some when it was slower; the net result was a tendency to maintain a fairly constant rate of increase. The libraries with long lives seem to have made the greatest contribution to the relative stability in the rate of increase of the number of existing libraries.

LIBRARIES IN EXISTENCE AND THE GROWTH OF POPULATION, 1790–1870

Chapter 2 examined the ratio of libraries in existence to population for the colonial and revolutionary periods, and explained the plan for showing this ratio. The same system is used in Table 3.4 and Figure 3.4, so the relationships of the libraries' presence and the number of people during the earlier years can easily be compared with the same relationships after 1785.

Table 3.4 and Figure 3.4, like Table 3.2 and Figure 3.2, do not include a small number of libraries that existed before federal censuses were taken in the most thinly populated parts of the country and in those areas that were not yet a part of the United States. For Table 3.4 and Figure 3.4, the libraries that had to be omitted were in the Far West or in one of three states adjoining that region: Texas, Oklahoma, or Kansas. There were fewer than seventy instances where a library existed during a census year but could not be included, about half of them in California. (A library that existed during four census years before a census was taken in its state was considered to be providing four instances.)

The ratios in Table 3.4 show a definite improvement for the United States after the Revolution. Ratios were always higher than those for 1740 through 1780 in the column for the entire area covered by Table 2.5. However, there is no significant improvement after 1800; the ratio of libraries to population from 1820 through 1860 remained at a relatively low level, and the 1870 figure is almost the same as the one for 1800. It is difficult to be sure about the reasons why the ratio changed so little during the ninety-year period. The lines for the ratios in the four major regions in Figure 3.4 show that the almost unchanging national ratio from 1820 to 1860 was not characteristic of any single region. People in the Northeast continued to be well supplied with libraries, even though

Table 3.4
Ratio of Libraries in Existence in the United States to Population, 1790–1870

		Northeast	South	Middle West	Far West	All U.S.
1790	w.p.	.69	.16	—	—	.49
	t.p.	.67	.10	—	—	.40
1800	w.p.	1.43	.24	.20	—	.96
	t.p.	1.38	.16	.20	—	.78
1810	w.p.	1.32	.32	.42	—	.92
	t.p.	1.28	.21	.41	—	.74
1820	w.p.	1.18	.36	.31	—	.80
	t.p.	1.15	.23	.30	—	.66
1830	w.p.	1.16	.35	.44	—	.79
	t.p.	1.13	.22	.43	—	.64
1840	w.p.	1.11	.49	.44	—	.78
	t.p.	1.09	.31	.43	—	.65
1850	w.p.	1.03	.57	.52	1.40	.76
	t.p.	1.01	.36	.51	1.40	.64
1860	w.p.	1.03	.53	.78	1.20	.82
	t.p.	1.02	.33	.76	1.07	.70
1870	w.p.	1.21	.64	.71	1.60	.92
	t.p.	1.19	.41	.69	1.47	.80

Note: w.p. = ratio to 10,000 white population.; t.p. = ratio to 10,000 total population.

the ratio for that region declined during five decades. The situation in the South and Middle West improved enough to counteract the downward movement in the Northeast; there were so few people in the Far West that its phenomenally high ratio of libraries to population had little effect on the ratio for the entire country.

The pattern exhibited by the numbers in Table 3.4 is shown in Figure 3.4: increases in all major regions from 1790 to 1800, a decline from 1800 to 1820 in the Northeast, then a slower decline in density until 1860, offset by increases that occurred most often in the Middle West and South. If the graph showed the ratio for the white population, the ratio for the South would have been as good as the ratio for the Middle West. From 1860 to 1870, this measure of availability of libraries shows an increase everywhere, but most noticeably in the Far West.

Figure 3.4
Ratio of Libraries in Existence in the United States to Total Population, 1790–1870
(Ratio of libraries in existence to 10,000 total population)

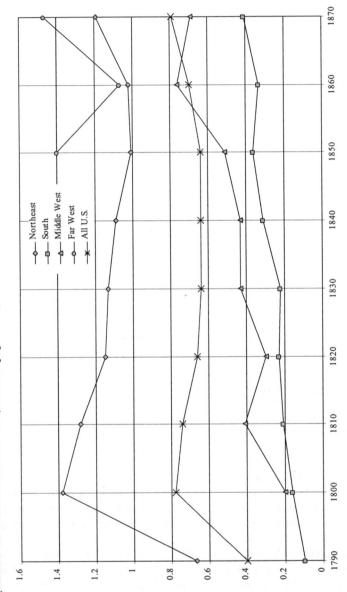

The situation within each of the different major regions is not shown; more detailed figures would indicate that the rapid rate of founding in New England always produced a ratio of libraries to population that was considerably higher than in the Middle-Atlantic states. In the rest of the country, the number of inhabitants and the number of libraries in some of the sub-regions was often low, so chance is more likely to have caused some of the apparent relationships. In the South there were more times when the South Atlantic states led both in the ratio of foundings to population and in the ratio of libraries in existence to population, but each of the other two sub-regions occasionally led in one or the other ratio. In the Middle West, the situation was somewhat the same: at several times the East North Central led; the West North Central less often led. In the Far West, the Pacific states always led in the ratios.

In this chapter, the different kinds of libraries have all been considered together unless those of one kind were so numerous that they made up a significant portion of the libraries in one or more areas. In chapters 4 through 11, most of the kinds in the study will be considered separately—where and when they flourished. Some attention will be given to the apparent reasons for the increase—or, less frequently, the decrease—in the popularity of each kind over the years.

NOTES

1. Jesse H. Shera, *Foundations of the Public Library: The Origins of the Public Library Movement in New England, 1629–1855* (Chicago: University of Chicago Press, 1949), 80–81.

2. The bad effects of depressions on libraries could have been mitigated in either or both of these ways: (1) Publishers sometimes had to lower their prices, thus making the formation of libraries easier, or (2) the purchase of books could become too difficult for some individuals, so they may have turned to libraries because reading library books was more economical. However, I am not certain that American libraries were affected by either of these situations before 1876.

3. Edward Pessen, in his book, *Riches, Class, and Power Before the Civil War* (Lexington, Mass.: D.C. Heath, 1973), on p. 148, tells how the very rich were not hurt by the panic of 1837, and on pp. 251–78, gives details about the urban rich's part in voluntary associations management before the Civil War.

4. For example, Peter Temin in his book, *The Jacksonian Economy* (New York: W. W. Norton, 1969): 151–57.

5. James L. Huston, *The Panic of 1857 and the Coming of the Civil War* (Baton Rouge, La.: Louisiana State University Press, 1987): 60–65.

6. Northern agriculture and industry during the Civil War are discussed in several sources. Among them are Phillip Shaw Paludan's *"A People's Contest," the Union and the Civil War, 1861–1865* (New York: Harper and Row, 1988), and Richard H. Sewell's *A House Divided: Sectionalism and Civil War, 1848–1865* (Baltimore: The Johns Hopkins University Press, 1988).

7. The attitude about the end of the war is mentioned by Frederic S. Klein in "Life in the North . . ." *Civil War Times Illustrated* 8 (Feb. 1970): 34.

8. The attitudes of the Mormons are examined in detail in Everette B. Long, *The Saints and the Union: Utah Territory During the Civil War* (Urbana: University of Illinois Press, 1981).

9. The attitudes of Californians toward the Civil War are discussed in several sources, including James F. Carson, "California: Gold to Help Finance the War," *Journal of the West* 14 (Jan. 1975): 25–41.

10. One state in the North Central region had more Afro-Americans than did other states there: Missouri, which was a slave state until the time of the Civil War. At the time of its first census, in 1810, approximately 20 percent of its population was Afro-American, but by 1870 the percentage had gone down to about 7. The percentage for the North Central region was never above 3 at any time, and the percentage for the Northeast was never above 4 from 1790 through 1870. In the South the percentage was between 35 and 38 during those years.

11. Two sources of information about Afro-American library societies and related organizations are "The Organized Activities of Negro Literary Societies, 1828–1846" by Dorothy B. Porter in *Journal of Negro Education* 5 (Oct. 1936): 555–79 and "The Founding & Prevalence of African-American Social Libraries & Historical Societies, 1828–1918" by Rosie L. Albritton in *Untold Stories: Civil Rights, Libraries, and Black Librarianship* ed. John Mark Tucker (Champaign, Ill.: Graduate School of Library and Information Science, 1998): 23–46.

12. U.S. Superintendent of the Census, *The Seventh Census of the United States: 1850* (Washington, D.C.: Robert Armstrong, Public Printer, 1853), p. xciv (figures are for 1853); *Population of the United States in 1860* (Washington, D.C.: Government Printing Office, 1864), pp. 596–97, 605; and *Ninth Census, vol. 1, The Statistics of the Population of the United States, 1870* (Washington, D.C.: Government Printing Office, 1872), pp. xvi–xvii, 8.

13. Statistics for the Chinese population in 1860 and 1870 are given in volume 1 of the *Ninth Census*, pp. xvii, 8.

14. This general east-to-west movement had many exceptions. They are discussed in such works as these: Raymond D. Gastil, *Cultural Regions of the United States* (Seattle, Wash.: University of Washington Press, 1976); James W. Oberly, "Westward Who? Estimates of Native White Interstate Migration After the War of 1812," *Journal of Economic History* 46 (June 1986): 431–40; John C. Hudson, "North American Origins of Middlewestern Frontier Populations," *Annals of the Association of American Geographers* 78 (Sept. 1988): 395–413; and Robert P. Swierenga, "The Settlement of the Old Northwest: Ethnic Pluralism in a Featureless Plain," *Journal of the Early Republic* 9 (Spring 1989): 73–105.

15. Haynes McMullen, "The Founding of Social and Public Libraries in Ohio, Indiana, and Illinois through 1850," *University of Illinois Library School Occasional Papers*, no. 51 (Mar. 1958): 9–10.

16. John Higham, *Strangers in the Land: Patterns of American Nativism, 1860–1925* (New Brunswick, N.J.: Rutgers University Press, 1955), 17–18.

17. Richard A. Easterlin, "Regional Income Trends, 1840–1950," in Seymour E. Harris (ed.), *American Economic History* (New York: McGraw Hill, 1961), table on p. 528. But see also the discussion of the limitations of his data on pp. 533–534.

18. Percentages are based on numbers in U.S. Bureau of the Census, *Historical Statistics of the United States, Colonial Times to 1970* (Washington, D.C.: Government Printing Office, 1975), pt. 1, p. 22.

19. Several social historians have told about the ways in which westerners imitated eastern customs and imported eastern institutions. Three who mention the establishment of libraries or reading rooms are Elliott West, in *The Saloon on the Rocky Mountain Mining Frontier* (Lincoln: University of Nebraska Press, 1979), pp. 134, 146; Robert V. Hine, in *Community on the American Frontier: Separate But Not Alone* (Norman: University of Oklahoma Press, 1980), 80; and David Fridtjof Halaas, in *Boom Town Newspapers: Journalism on the Rocky Mountain Mining Frontier, 1859–1881*

(Albuquerque: University of New Mexico Press, 1981), 97.

20. Haynes McMullen, "The Founding of Social and Public Libraries in Ohio, Indiana, and Illinois through 1850," examines the relationships between the founding of libraries and the density of population; my "Prevalence of Libraries in the Northeastern States before 1876," *Journal of Library History* 22 (Summer 1987): 330–33 compares the presence of libraries in three large cities with their presence in the rest of the Northeast.

Chapter 4

Kinds of Libraries in Existence before 1876

In order to understand how and why libraries spread across the territory now occupied by the United States, it is helpful to consider the individual kinds that appeared in different regions at different times before 1875. Chapter 1 explained why the very numerous school and Sunday school libraries are omitted from chapters 2 through 11; they are discussed briefly in chapter 12. Chapter 2 mentioned the kinds of libraries that existed before 1786; they will not be excluded from the present chapter, but because the emphasis is on the times and places when each type was more popular, references to libraries in colonial days and the revolutionary years will be infrequent.

Chapters 5 through 10 discuss each kind of library separately. Usually, its general characteristics will be mentioned first; then, the reasons why anyone wanted this kind; then, when and where the kind was to be found—in what parts of the country it was most prevalent and the times when it was most popular. If changes in the attitudes and interests of Americans or in economic conditions seem to have been related to the prevalence of a particular kind of library, those changes will be mentioned.

The method for dividing libraries into kinds has been to consider four aspects of the libraries that existed before 1876: (1) What kind of agency was responsible for them: an association, a government, a commercial firm, or, in very rare cases, an individual? (2) If an association or government was responsible, was the library intended for persons within the organization or for others (e.g., apprentices or hospital patients)? (3) If a library belonged to some kind of association, was the formation and use of the library the primary purpose of the association? (4) Was the library's collection general or specialized in content? Or did it contain both a general and a specialized section? State libraries, for example, frequently contained a law division and a miscellaneous division.

By considering these four aspects it is easier to understand the purpose and function of each individual kind, and it is possible, as well, to group several kinds in order to look at libraries more broadly. For example, it is possible to notice the slow increase in the part that federal or state governments played in the founding of libraries or to consider as a group all libraries that contained mainly law books, no matter what their sponsorships.

INDIVIDUAL KINDS OF LIBRARIES

One way to examine the great variety of kinds of libraries that existed is to divide them into five large groups that, to some extent, indicate the kinds of motives or attitudes that Americans had when they decided to form libraries. The five groups are shown in Table 4.1 and Figure 4.1.

The first group of libraries in Table 4.1 and Figure 4.1 is comprised of those created by organizations that were formed for the purpose of establishing libraries. These libraries may be considered as the most direct result of the desire to use book collections. They are usually called *social* libraries because they were created by library societies.

A second group of libraries illustrate a less intense interest in the collection and use of books: libraries formed by societies or other voluntary organizations that were established for some other purpose but whose members perceived a need for the information (and perhaps the pleasure) to be found in books: churches and many kinds of societies, including bar associations, medical societies, fraternal organizations, and even fire companies. These make up the second group in Table 4.1 and Figure 4.1.

Americans have always enjoyed political activity, setting up various kinds of governments and assigning duties to government officials. Sometimes governments of one kind or another have formed institutions with the same purposes as the institutions that had previously been established by voluntary organizations. The third group of libraries in Table 4.1 and Figure 4.1 consists of ones owned by such organizations. Both voluntary organizations and units of government have established and operated three main types of institutions, all of which had libraries: colleges and professional schools, hospitals, and asylums for the care of persons with disabilities.

The fourth group of libraries were those that almost always belonged to governments. When government officials have established these libraries, they have had either of two motives: to aid in the work of unit members (a motive similar to that of members of many societies in the second group above) or to benefit the citizens of the geographical area governed by the unit. Most of the libraries intended for the general citizenry were the free public libraries operated by local governments, with collections that were sometimes bought with local funds and sometimes with state funds.

Libraries in the fifth section of Table 4.1 and Figure 4.1 were all owned by business organizations or individuals. Most of these were operated for profit as commercial circulating libraries, but a few were intended for employee use and a very few were free libraries for public use.

Sometimes a library clearly belongs among those mentioned above, but the

Table 4.1
Kinds of Organizations that Had Libraries before 1876

	Northeast	South	Middle West	Far West	All U.S.
Societies formed with the primary purpose of establishing libraries (social libraries, in chapter 5)	1,895	368	883	150	3,296
Organizations not formed with the primary purpose of establishing libraries (churches and various societies, in chapter 6)	1,065	488	588	185	2,327
Institutions, some of which were operated by private organizations and some of which were operated by governmental units (colleges, hospitals, and asylums, in chapter 7)	401	282	354	44	1,081
Governmental and quasi-governmental units (local, state, or federal governments and military posts, in chapter 8)	449	151	1,754	69	2,423
Businesses (firms and individuals; commercial circulating libraries and others, in chapter 9)	455	88	96	24	663
Libraries whose exact kinds of organizations could not be determined ("law libraries," "town libraries," and others, in chapter 10)	10	157	73	2	242
Total	4,275	1,534	3,749	474	10,032

small amount of information available about it does not justify placing it in any particular category. For example, in 1860 a census taker may have reported a "town library" in some village. Social libraries were often considered "public libraries" or "town libraries," but this one may have been established by a local government as a free public library. All libraries that could not be classified have been gathered in a sixth group in Table 4.1.

In chapters 5 through 9, the same two indicators of popularity will be used for individual kinds of libraries that were used in chapters 2 and 3: the number of libraries that were being founded at various times and the number in existence at various times. As in chapter 3, five-year intervals will be considered: the number founded from 1786 through 1790, 1791 through 1795, and so on, as well as the number in existence in 1790, 1795, and so on. Because of some rapid variations in annual totals, those figures seldom help in understanding trends.

Figure 4.1
Ownership of Libraries before 1876
(Not including private, school, and Sunday school libraries)

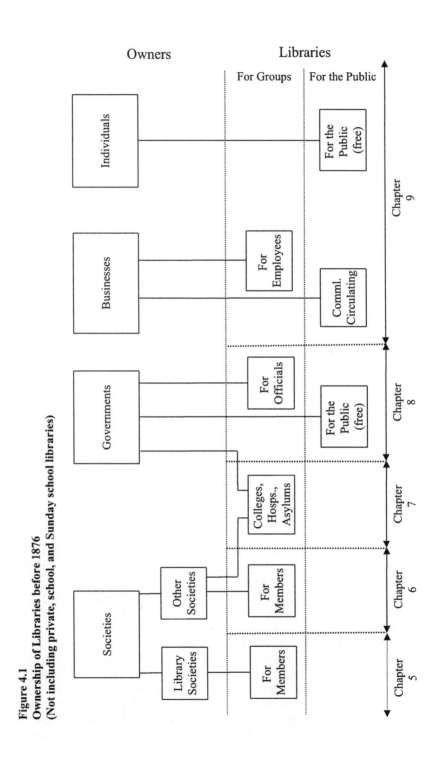

One way in which the prevalence of an individual kind of library will sometimes be compared with the prevalence of all libraries in the study is in reference to geographical distribution. As in chapters 2 and 3, the distribution of libraries among the four major regions and the nine sub-regions may be mentioned. If the distribution for a particular kind varies noticeably from the distribution of all libraries in the study, that variation will be noted, also. And, if a particular state made a significant contribution to the total number of libraries of a single kind, it will be named and an attempt will be made to discover the reason for the prominence of that kind in that state.

Various groups of Americans felt free to establish libraries for any purpose; when their exercise of this freedom produced collections that do not fit neatly into the scheme used in this chapter, the nature of their variation will be mentioned. One student of the relation between reading and economic conditions in the United States before the Civil War has referred to the "bewildering variety" of types of libraries in existence.[1] Because Americans had a variety of interests and because many of them wanted to have books at hand, their libraries existed in what a present-day historian might easily consider a bewildering variety.

THE FOUNDING OF NEW KINDS OF LIBRARIES

Chapter 2 mentioned the dates when various kinds of libraries first appeared in the colonies and the United States through 1785. The appearance of each new kind of library had little significance in itself because sometimes it was several years—or even several decades—before that kind became popular. However, because the act of starting a new kind does indicate a wish to innovate, it may be the result of a change in American society that will have consequences for library history.

Chapter 2 mentioned that Americans' interest in starting new varieties of libraries increased markedly just after the Revolution; that interest continued strong in the decade just before 1800 and in the first decade of the new century. By about 1810, half of all the varieties that were to appear before 1875 had come into existence. New ones started rather frequently until about 1830, then less frequently until the end of the period.

Why did Americans lose some of their interest in starting new kinds of libraries after about 1830? By that time, had they just established enough different kinds to take care of most of their needs? That may have been one reason, but another reason may be related to the general differences in the kinds being favored at different times. In the years before about 1815, the predominant varieties were libraries founded by associations for the use of their own members. Groups of Americans were banding together to obtain easier access to information and entertainment.

Around 1820, the situation changed. Apparently, by that time members of voluntary associations had all of the types of libraries they needed. But the 1820s saw several new kinds established by members of associations for the benefit of less fortunate persons—for apprentices, patients in hospitals, and so on. These were years when reformers were active, particularly in northern cities—whether altruistically concerned for the welfare of disadvantaged persons or, perhaps selfishly, concerned about maintaining a stable and peaceful society.[2]

Then, by about 1830, there seem to have been enough varieties to serve the needs of organizations with philanthropic aims. After that date, very few new kinds were started by societies; the federal, state, and local governments were establishing new kinds, but at a much slower rate than did associations in the earlier years.

Where were the new kinds of libraries appearing in the years before 1875? Were they being established in the older parts of the country where population was denser and the prevalence of cities might encourage the development of specialized collections? Or did people in the newer sections start innovative types of libraries without regard to kinds back east? The answer is clear: Americans in the older parts of the country continued to introduce new kinds of libraries through most of the years, and people in the newer states made little or no contribution to the variety of libraries that were available. From 1786 through 1875, approximately seven out of every ten new kinds were started in the Northeast (fairly evenly divided between New England and the Middle Atlantic states). If the ones in the South Atlantic states are added, about nine out of ten kinds originated in the eastern states. The other one-tenth were all in the East North Central sub-region. Apparently, the founders of libraries in all of the other five sub-regions were content to use established forms of organization. As might be expected, eastern cities provided an environment that encouraged the establishment of new kinds of libraries; three out of every ten new kinds of libraries appeared first in one of these three cities: Boston, Philadelphia, or Washington, D.C.

NOTES

1. Ronald John Zboray, *A Fictive People: Antebellum Economic Development and the American Reading Public* (New York: Oxford University Press, 1993), 106.

2. Individual reformers may have had mixed motives; some historians have not hesitated to attribute particular motives to them. What seems to me to be a reasonable attitude is expressed by Lawrence Frederick Kohl in "The Concept of Social Control and the History of Jacksonian America," *Journal of the Early Republic* 5 (Spring 1985): 21–34.

Chapter 5

Social Libraries

The terms "social libraries," "library societies," "library associations," and "library companies" were used by Americans in the eighteenth and nineteenth centuries to refer to societies whose main purpose was to establish libraries that would be used by members of the society or by some other group. Twentieth century historians have sometimes used the term "social libraries" to include, as well, libraries belonging to societies with some other main purpose, such as historical societies. In this chapter, the earlier definition will be used: the term "social library" will be used to refer to a collection owned by a society that had the formation and maintenance of a library as its main object. The kinds of social libraries are shown in Table 5.1. Libraries owned by societies that had some other purpose will be considered in chapters 6 and 7.[1]

"STRICT" SOCIAL LIBRARIES

Of all the kinds of libraries that existed in the American colonies and the United States before 1876, the social library was the one in which its organizers and users most clearly demonstrated an attachment for books and reading. In its earliest and purest form (called in this study, the *strict* form) the social library was organized and used by a group of people whose main purpose was to gather and read a general or miscellaneous collection of books. It was almost always founded by men but was used by men, women, and sometimes children, an arrangement that was appropriate for a time when *patriarchy* was the established pattern for families and when men dominated the worlds of politics and business.[2]

The strict form of social library was the most popular of any of the kinds of libraries considered in the main part of this study. These *pure* social libraries were exceeded in number only by the school libraries and Sunday school libraries, considered in chapter 12. The strict social libraries in Table 5.1

Table 5.1
Social Libraries

	Northeast	South	Middle West	Far West	All U.S.
"Strict" social libraries	1,531	268	541	123	2,463
Libraries on particular subjects					
Religion	77	12	22	7	118
Law	25	10	15	2	52
Agriculture	32	4	4	0	40
Other subjects	14	1	1	0	16
Total	148	27	42	9	226
Libraries for persons of a particular age or gender					
Women's library societies	39	2	58	5	104
Young men's library societies	16	7	27	1	51
Juvenile social libraries	27	5	3	1	36
Total	82	14	88	7	191
Apprentices', mechanics', and workingmens' libraries					
Apprentices' libraries	19	6	2	0	27
Mechanics' libraries	45	23	13	6	87
Workingmens' libraries (Maclure libraries and others)	2	1	146	0	149
Total	66	30	161	6	263
Mercantile libraries	13	11	8	3	35
Atheneums	45	15	12	2	74
Foreign language social libraries	3	3	14	0	20
Social libraries aided by govts.	7	0	17	0	24
Total	1,895	368	883	150	3,296

constitute almost exactly a fourth (24.6 percent) of all of the libraries considered in chapters 4 through 11. However, so little is known about a very few of them that they could have been specialized.

The strict form of the social library was coming into favor by the time of the Revolution. The reasons for its popularity in the years between the Revolution and 1876 occasionally varied, but some of them seem to have been generally influential: (1) Many Americans believed that the acquisition of general knowledge contributed to "self-culture," something that had value in itself and that would be of value to a professional person or businessman. (2) Except in the Northeast, a formal education at the secondary or college level was difficult to obtain. Considering the limited curriculum in the typical college, reading books from a well-selected library may have provided an education that was as helpful as that obtained in a college. (3) As fiction increased in popularity in the early nineteenth century, these libraries became better able to meet the emotional needs of their users. In most social libraries, novels seems to have made up only a small part of the collection; however, some records indicate that fiction circulated heavily.[3]

Although the number of strict social libraries being founded varied from year to year and from decade to decade, there were some definite long-term trends. By the 1790s, the number was averaging about twenty-five per year. A slow decline followed, but by the late 1820s the frequency of founding was again around twenty-five. Another decline followed until the average number in the 1840s reached sixteen. Then the number increased until the late 1850s when it was again close to twenty-five per year. After a drop during the Civil War, a surprising thing happened: despite the increasing popularity of the free government-supported public library, the number of strict social libraries being founded rose to new heights. At least thirty-nine per year were established from 1866 through 1870, and at least forty-nine per year from 1871 through 1875, mainly because of enthusiasm for this kind in the East North Central states. Even though half of these libraries had been founded by the early 1830s, the later interest in them is indicated by the figures for the number in existence at five-year intervals; considerably more existed in 1875 than at any earlier date.[4]

Many new kinds of libraries were gaining favor before 1876; perhaps changes in the rate of founding of strict social libraries should be considered in relation to the rate for all kinds. The strict social libraries made their greatest contribution just before 1800 and in the early part of the century. They made up 70 to 80 percent of all new libraries from the middle of the 1780s to about 1810. If the number being founded in each five-year period is counted, the highest point was in 1791–95 when the strict social libraries provided about 82 percent of all founding dates. After that, the percentage declined steadily in each five-year period through the first half of the nineteenth century except in the one for 1826 through 1830 when, for some reason, there was a small increase. In the 1830s approximately one in three of the new libraries was of this type; after that decade these libraries never exceeded the ratio of one in four until the early 1870s when about 29 percent of all new libraries were of this type.

As might be expected, the strict social libraries were to be found in most parts of the country. At least one library of this kind existed in every state and territory (and the District of Columbia) except in the areas now occupied by Oklahoma, North Dakota, and Arizona. Only one kind of library was to be found in more states and territories. Everywhere except in Alaska, there was a library for the use of state or territorial officials by 1875. Considering all of the years before 1876, six of the nine sub-regions had more pure social libraries than libraries of any other kind.

Even though these libraries were widely distributed, the numbers that form the basis for Table 5.1 show that almost half of them (47.5 percent) were to be found in New England. Massachusetts had more than any other state (354 libraries) and that state, together with Connecticut and New Hampshire, provided at least a third (36.9 percent) of all American libraries of this type. Some of the reasons mentioned above for Americans' favorable attitude toward these libraries may have applied most strongly in New England. Jesse Shera, in his study of all kinds of social libraries in that part of the country before about 1855, considered the library environment in New England in detail. He found that, generally, more libraries were being founded in periods of economic prosperity, but he felt that other conditions were related to the growth in the desire for libraries. He cited the increasing habit of reading in the early nineteenth century and the acceptance of the rather vague theory that American society should make some kind of progress.[5]

In the years following those in Shera's study, the enthusiasm for social libraries in New England was not as great as before, but was still considerable. The number being established around the time of the Civil War was low but at least in the ten-year period, 1866 through 1875, ninety-five strict library societies were founded there, considerably fewer than the 226 libraries founded during the ten-year period from 1791 through 1800, but more than during most ten-year periods before the Civil War. As in the other eight sub-regions of the United States, more of these pure social libraries were in existence in 1875 than at any earlier five-year benchmark.

We have already seen that a small town often provided a favorable environment for a strict social library. Actually, a small town might have had two or more such libraries before 1876, often because interest in the first one declined and a new one was organized later. In each of at least thirty smaller towns in Massachusetts, three social libraries existed before 1875. Towns in southern and mid-western states seldom had more than two, but even in California, half a dozen small towns had at least that many.

SOCIAL LIBRARIES ON PARTICULAR SUBJECTS

Before 1876, only a few societies were formed for the explicit purpose of establishing libraries on particular subjects. The total number of collections on special subjects in Table 5.1 is only 6.9 percent of the libraries in that table. Members of special vocational groups such as mechanics and businessmen sometimes claimed, perhaps sincerely, that their libraries were intended to help them succeed in their occupations, but they actually bought and read mostly books of history, biography, travel, and belles lettres. For whatever reasons, they wanted to read books like those in other social libraries. Most of the libraries on special subjects were established either by associations—whose main purpose was not to maintain libraries—or by governmental units. Those libraries will be discussed in later chapters.

The subject-specialized social libraries were more frequently found in the Northeast than in any other region (148 out of the total of 226), and New England had more than any other sub-region (ninety-five). For the entire United States, well over half (118) were religious libraries. Of the library societies with special subject emphasis, the second most common were those formed to supply law books (fifty-two), and the third most common were the agricultural or horticultural libraries (forty). Five other kinds of subject-specialized social libraries existed: societies formed to collect in the fields of medicine, military affairs, history, science or technology, and art. However, no more than six libraries in any one of those fields were discovered. Of the six libraries that are considered in this study to have been military libraries, four, all in Massachusetts, were called "military libraries"; the other two, one in Philadelphia and one in Raleigh, North Carolina, were reading rooms for soldiers, and perhaps were general in content. The libraries organized at military garrisons for the soldiers' use are treated in chapter 8 of this study; they were, apparently without exception, general in content.

The subject-specialized social libraries present no definite overall pattern when their dates of founding are considered. In fact, there is no discernible long-term trend for either of the two most popular types. The rate of founding of the library societies that collected religious books rose and fell over the years, but more were founded in the ten years from 1866 through 1875 than in any other ten-year period. Very few law library societies existed before the 1830s; from then on, several were formed during each decade.

SOCIAL LIBRARIES FOR PERSONS OF A PARTICULAR AGE OR GENDER

Three main kinds of associations were formed to provide reading matter for persons of a particular age or gender before 1876: women's library associations, young men's library associations, and associations formed to provide libraries for children. In the records used for this study, the ones for women were the most numerous (a total of 104); there were fewer for young men (fifty-one), and fewest for children (thirty-six). The young men's libraries considered here are those that, so far as the records show, were not intended for young men in particular occupations or with special interests: the mechanics' and apprentices' libraries and the mercantile libraries are discussed later in this chapter; the libraries owned by the Young Men's Christian Associations are considered in the next chapter.

Women's Library Societies. During the first three-quarters of the nineteenth century, many American women were engaged in movements that had as their aim the amelioration of social conditions—particularly, the temperance movement, the anti-slavery movement, and the improvement of conditions in prisons, hospitals, and asylums.[6] Women took part in the management and use of libraries connected with the agencies engaged in charitable and philanthropic works, to be discussed in chapter 7. But there was one kind of library that was established by and for women and that was not intended for the use of any group that was less fortunate than the members of the society that formed the collection: the kind owned by a "ladies' library association." Sometimes these libraries were deliberately intended as expressions of independence from the rule of men in social and cultural affairs. This is clear in the case of several of the ladies' libraries in Michigan, where, in 1875, a representative from each of fourteen of the associations wrote a historical sketch of her library that was included in a printed volume intended to be presented to the Women's Department at the Centennial Exhibition in Philadelphia the next year.[7]

The authors of the reports in the Michigan volume wrote with pride but also with humor. At Battle Creek a rival men's library, founded in the same year as the Ladies' Library Association, expired, whereas the women's organization continued. The reporter from that city allowed herself to record that the men's library "went out, altogether ingloriously." The reporter from Feltonville wrote that in two days' time "we had obtained about $130.00, a fair list of books, and a good many opinions of our ultimate success or failure." Women in that town succeeded for a while, but within a few years they lost most of their four hundred volumes in a fire.

Of 104 women's social libraries recorded for this study, a single state, Michigan, had thirty-five, a number that was almost exactly three times as many as were to be found in any other state. Why was enthusiasm for this type of library so much greater in that Midwestern state? There is no clear answer to that question, but at least three conditions were favorable there. In the first place, many of the settlers who came to Michigan were from New England or New York, and the ancestors of many of the ones from New York had come there from New England. The women's social libraries first appeared in Michigan in the early 1850s; of the twenty-three that had clearly existed elsewhere, seventeen were in New England towns. Also, other kinds of women's organizations were common in Michigan. And, finally, the historical sketches mentioned above indicate that, sometimes, a group of women in a town decided to form a library when they learned of one in a neighboring town. The idea seems to have spread rapidly in the years just after the Civil War.

Considering the country as a whole, the chronological pattern for the establishment of these libraries is not much different from the pattern for several other kinds of libraries. The first, apparently, was a "female library" that got started at Candia, New Hampshire, around 1795. Very few were established before the 1820s. In that decade and in the 1830s and 1840s they averaged fewer than one per year. At least sixteen came into being during the 1850s, and only eight during the war years. But the ten-year span from 1866 through 1875 saw at least forty-eight, mostly in the part of the Middle West that is east of the Mississippi. For the entire country, more were in existence in 1870 (fifty-one) and in 1875 (seventy-two) than in the earlier years when counts were made.

In the parts of the East North Central states outside of Michigan, seventeen social libraries for women had been established by 1875. Thirty-six libraries had existed in New England by that time, at least one library in each of the nine states. At least one collection had existed in each of twenty states or territories, but only three of these states were outside of New England or the Middle West.

Another kind of women's association, one that owned and operated a library as only one of its activities, may have, in actual practice, been quite similar to the ladies' library associations. These other associations are discussed later in chapter 6, together with various other kinds of organizations that owned libraries.

Young Men's Library Societies. During the nineteenth century, young men in a few towns and cities formed associations with the establishment of libraries as their main purpose. The reasons for the founding of these libraries have not been mentioned in the records available for this study. It is possible that the young men felt the need for reading matter not available to them in the social libraries that were controlled by older men. There is no indication that the books in the young men's libraries were unlike those in the other social libraries.

Of the fifty-one young men's libraries in the study, twelve were in New England, four in the Middle-Atlantic states, only seven in all of the South, twenty-one in the East North Central area, and only seven elsewhere, a distribution that is not significantly different from that of other social libraries. No one state had more than eight. These libraries first appeared in the Northeast. Information about the earliest ones is vague; one may have been founded in a small town in Maine around 1814;[8] two more were established around 1820, one of them in a small town in Massachusetts and the other in a small town in Connecticut. Very few existed outside of the Northeast before the 1840s; after the Civil War, when about half of them had been founded, few were being established outside of the Middle West. In 1875, at least nine existed in the Northeast, ten in the Middle West, and only three elsewhere.[9]

Juvenile Social Libraries. A small number of libraries were organized for children. These libraries were most commonly called "juvenile libraries," but the term "youths' libraries" or others were used for some of them. For most of the libraries, the available records do not show whether adults or children were responsible for starting them; for seven, adults were involved and for six others, the children organized them. Possibly, the situation in a Kentucky library may not have been unique. The Lexington Juvenile Library was organized in 1812 by a group of boys and continued successfully until 1816 when at the invitation of members of the Lexington (social) Library the boys' collection was "blended" with the collection of the adult society, and several of the boys were asked to sit on the board of the grown-ups' organization.[10] Perhaps a juvenile library in Deerfield, Massachusetts, was more typical than the one in Kentucky. It was the result of a project started by a clergyman in 1827 to supply boys and girls with good reading; its collection later became the basis for a Sunday school library.[11]

Juvenile libraries present a geographical and chronological pattern that is quite different from those of women's libraries or young men's libraries. Of the thirty-six libraries that could be discovered, twenty-four were in New England; no other sub-region had more than four. The juvenile social library was one of the few kinds that did not grow in number during the middle years of the nineteenth century. The earliest children's library society identified for this study was at Harwinton, Connecticut, founded in 1797. Half of them had been established by about 1825, and only two had founding dates after the 1830s; however, at least six were still in existence in 1875.

During the nineteenth century, the increasingly popular Sunday school libraries, usually owned and operated by churches, may have enjoyed a more stable financial basis than did the independent juvenile library associations. The public school libraries also could have replaced them, but those libraries were quite unevenly distributed among the states, and were often unsuccessful, lasting only a few years.[12]

APPRENTICES', MECHANICS', AND WORKINGMEN'S LIBRARIES

The system of apprenticing a boy to a master craftsman began in Europe in the Middle Ages and was to be found in the American colonies in the seventeenth and eighteenth centuries. It continued in the nineteenth century, but decreased in importance soon after the Revolution, partly because the scarcity of labor tempted the boys to run away[13] and partly because the rise of the factory system made the one-to-one relationship between master and apprentice less common. Most factory workers performed specialized tasks and did not need several years of preparation.[14]

In the early nineteenth century, the term "mechanics" was used much more broadly than at present. It included such groups as skilled workers in factories, carpenters, printers, and bakers—in fact, any skilled workers; however, it did not include unskilled workers or clerks.[15] The term "workingmen" had come into use by the middle of the nineteenth century to include both skilled and unskilled workers who did physical labor, although the mechanics continued to be recognized as a separate group of workers.

The decrease in the use of the apprenticeship system was not accompanied by a decrease in the importance of mechanics. "Mechanics' institutes" in Britain had existed in the late eighteenth century, often having the maintenance of a library as one of their functions, along with the presentation of lectures. In the Unites States, there were very few libraries intended primarily for the use of apprentices, mechanics, or workingmen before 1820.[16] In that year, four apprentices' libraries were founded and four mechanics' libraries; by 1825, at least eleven apprentices' libraries and seven mechanics' libraries existed. Of the libraries identified for this study, only four were founded expressly for apprentices after that year. Of the twenty-seven libraries for apprentices that could be identified as existing in the United States before 1876, only four were still alive in 1875.

As the years passed the mechanics' libraries had difficulty in competing with other kinds of libraries. The interest in founding mechanics' libraries continued longer than the interest in libraries for apprentices, but had almost disappeared by 1875. Of the seventy-six libraries with known founding dates, almost all were established from the 1820s through the 1850s; only five were founded after the Civil War. As might be expected, the more industrialized part of the country (the Northeast) was the home of more than any other region—forty-five in all—but in the South, twenty-three existed for the benefit of skilled artisans; the Middle West had almost all of the rest. By 1875, the records used for this study show fourteen still existing in the Northeast and eleven elsewhere.

Both the libraries for apprentices and the libraries for mechanics were often established by businessmen for the benefit of workers; however, so little is known about the management of most of them that it is impossible to generalize on that subject. At least two of the apprentices' libraries were founded by associations of mechanics.[17] Whatever the amount of direction and financial support from businessmen, both the libraries intended for apprentices and those intended for mechanics had collections that seem to have been general in nature, with few if any technical books.

Some of the libraries became more widely available over the years, perhaps in order to compete with other kinds of libraries. The Apprentices' Library of Philadelphia, for example, was opened for apprentices in June of 1820, to other young men under the age of twenty-one in May of the next year, to girls about 1841 (after much debate), and to people over twenty-one (if approved by the managers—the board of trustees) around the year 1869.[18]

The term *workingmen's library* is almost synonymous with the term *Maclure library* because only a few libraries intended for both mechanics and other workingmen existed before a group of libraries in Indiana and Illinois were established with money left by the philanthropist Samuel Maclure. He directed that $500 should be given to any organization formed by men "who labor with their hands" if they would assemble a library of at least a hundred volumes and would "establish a reading and lecture room."[19] At least 146 Maclure libraries were founded in Indiana and sixteen were said to exist in Illinois. (These sixteen could not be included in my records because I could not identify individual ones.) A few mechanics' libraries received Maclure funds and presumably became, in effect, workingmen's libraries; they are not included in the figures for mechanics' libraries, given above.

For the present study, the locations of 143 of the Indiana Maclure libraries could be determined, although the names of fewer than forty were found; most of the Indiana libraries started around 1855, the year in which the funds became available. In some cases, the organization gathered books, including government documents, of little value, but others assembled useful collections in order to qualify.

These Maclure libraries suffered the same fate as so many others for which the main incentive came from philanthropists; most of them did not last long. When the Civil War broke out, many association members went off to war, and the collections were unused. However, the libraries did not completely disappear; by 1875 at least nineteen Maclure libraries still existed.

MERCANTILE LIBRARIES

Mercantile libraries were collections of books intended for young men in the business world—bookkeepers and others. Almost without exception, they were managed by the young men themselves, not by older businessmen. Most of them were intended to provide a general education useful for members of the business community, with little emphasis on technical aspects of commerce or economics.[20] Typically, they provided fiction, not because of any presumed educational value, but because members wanted to read it.[21] Often, the public could use them by paying an annual fee. Like other varieties of social libraries, they often sponsored lecture series, partly because lectures were an accepted method of disseminating knowledge but partly for the same reasons that other organizations did, because they could make money if they paid speakers less than the amount they received from ticket sales.[22]

The mercantile libraries were among the best-known of any kind that existed in the United States before 1876; some of the larger ones, located in cities, were the most accessible libraries in their communities. More than a hundred periodical articles about these libraries published before 1876 give us a clear picture of the ways in which they were managed and used.[23] Even though some of these libraries were large and heavily used, the total number in the United States was very small; only thirty-five could be identified for this study. Thirteen were in the Northeast; eleven in the South, and eight in the Middle West; the only ones in the Far West were the three in California.

The chronological pattern for the establishment of mercantile libraries was different from the pattern for most kinds of libraries; the first was opened in Boston in 1820; New York and Philadelphia had theirs in operation by the next year. In the East, there was no great rush to found others; they appeared at intervals into the 1860s. In other parts of the country there were only a few before the 1840s, and there was a decrease in the number being founded after the 1850s: only six were started during the eleven years from 1865 through 1875.

A few mercantile libraries were among the largest libraries of any kind in the country: the New York and Philadelphia collections each had more than a hundred thousand volumes by 1875. But there was clearly a lack of interest in mercantile libraries in most towns. Perhaps, in some towns and cities, competition with other kinds of libraries may have been a factor. Apprentices' and mechanics' libraries began to appear at about the same time as the mercantile libraries and were often available to the general public. In the 1830s, two other kinds of libraries began to find favor, some that were operated by young men's library associations and others that were owned by young men's associations that had the maintenance of a library as only one of their purposes. Then, in the 1850s, the Young Men's Christian Associations began to open libraries that met some of the needs because they were deliberately planned to contain secular as well as religious material. This competition may have held the number of mercantile libraries down, but the ones that did exist were relatively long-lived. Of the thirty-five identified for this study, at least fifteen still existed in 1875.

ATHENEUMS

The main difference between atheneums and most social libraries was that the collections in the atheneums tended to favor current reading material. Even the Boston Athenaeum, to become famous for its book collection, at first emphasized its reading room in its promotional literature, as well as the books it owned.[24] When Henry Clay strolled around his hometown of Lexington, Kentucky, with the prospective president of Transylvania University, Horace Holley, in the spring of 1818, he took Holley to see the Athenaeum. His visitor noticed that it was "an institution not yet furnished with many books, but well supplied with newspapers, and the best periodicals."[25] If he had visited other atheneums (to use the more recent spelling) he might have made the same remark.

Atheneums, apparently, have never been studied intensively. They seem to have made no distinctive contribution to American cultural life and are best described by using vaguely comparative terms: they were sometimes, like lyceums, organized with a few non-library purposes, but these purposes were more social and less high-minded than those of the lyceums. Like both the lyceums and the strict social libraries, they gathered general libraries, but, apparently, with more emphasis on journals and newspapers. If they appealed to any particular class or occupation, they may have attracted the same moneyed or professional people as did some of the "strict" social libraries. They were often incorporated as stock companies, but people who did not own stock were permitted to use their collections in about the same way as in other library associations.

Atheneums were most popular in the Northeast; of the seventy-four located for this study, thirty-four were in New England and eleven in the Middle-Atlantic states. Each of the three other major regions had some: the South, fifteen; the Middle-West, twelve; and the Far West, two, one of them in California and one in Hawaii. The first with a known founding date was the Boston Athenaeum, organized in 1807; it was destined to become by far the largest with 105,000 volumes in 1875. Half of the atheneums had been founded by the early 1840s. Americans' interest in establishing this kind of library had almost disappeared by the time of the Civil War; only three had founding dates after 1860. However, once an atheneum was established, it had a relatively good chance of continuing to exist; at least twenty-four still existed in 1875.

SOCIAL LIBRARIES WITH BOOKS IN FOREIGN LANGUAGES

A small number of libraries were established before 1876 by members of foreign-speaking societies. Most of these were formed by associations that had other purposes—the German Turner (gymnastic) societies, for example—but a few collections were owned by societies formed with the main purpose of establishing and using libraries. The total number of these social libraries identified for this study was twenty; the number of libraries that were formed as adjuncts to other purposes was much greater; fifty-six of them are discussed in chapter 6, along with other libraries formed by various kinds of societies.

Almost all of the collections owned by library societies with members who spoke a language other than English were the German ones. Of the total of twenty, only three clearly were not German. A Scandinavian library association was formed in Neenah, Wisconsin, in 1869 (presumably with books in several languages), a Norwegian library association was established in Minneapolis in 1875, and a Swedish one in Burlington, Iowa, in the same year. An unusual kind, a German and French "circulating" library was established in Milwaukee in 1850; it may have been a commercial enterprise, but it had a librarian, which such businesses rarely had; the owner managed the collection.

Germans came to the American colonies and to the United States in increasing numbers beginning in the seventeenth century, particularly during times when they became unhappy because of religious, economic, or political conditions at home. By the 1850s German immigration was averaging about ninety-five thousand per year; fewer came during the war years but, during the ten-year span from 1866 through 1875, the number averaged about a hundred and six thousand per year.

The Germans liked to keep reminders of their European heritage; these were easily preserved in the form of books in libraries.[26] Founding dates are available for fifteen collections that clearly were established as German social libraries. As might be expected when numbers are so small, they may not accurately reflect the presence of Germans: there were four before the 1850s, seven during that decade, and four after that. The numbers in existence, counted at five-year intervals, were these: never more than two until 1855; then, the number varied between four and seven, and stood at seven in 1875. The pattern for libraries owned by other German societies is somewhat different; possible reasons for the differences in the two patterns will be discussed in the section of chapter 6 devoted to those societies.

No clear evidence has been found about foreign language social libraries intended primarily for persons other than Germans and Scandinavians. Ireland provided more new Americans than any other country during most years from 1820—the date when statistics about immigration became fairly reliable—to 1853. (Germany led during most years from 1854 through 1875.) It seems likely that many Irish immigrants spoke a form of Gaelic in the old country but there is no evidence indicating that any concerted effort was made to maintain the use of Gaelic in America. It has been impossible to identify any "strict" social library founded by Irish Americans before 1876; the reasons may be these: (1) The Irish settled mainly in cities and may have used social libraries that were already existing there. (2) The majority of the Irish came from a background that placed relatively little value on books and reading. (3) For many libraries, the type can be determined only from the name of the library. If the Irish were influential in establishing a library or were the main users of the library, there may be no way to learn about their participation. Occasionally, there are indications that libraries operated by Catholic churches were mainly used by Irish immigrants.

SOCIAL LIBRARIES AIDED BY GOVERNMENTS

From colonial times to the present, American state and local governments have aided voluntary organizations in several ways. The granting of charters (that is, incorporation, which regularly included some privileges) has been common. Also, towns have occasionally made financial contributions to social or other libraries without formal authorization by state governments. An unusual form of aid to what were basically social libraries occurred in the early nineteenth century in Indiana. The state government played such an important part in their establishment that they can be considered as quasi-social libraries.

The makers of Indiana's first constitution, that of 1816, provided that ten percent of the proceeds of the sale of lots at any county seat should be set aside for the use of a "library company" for the benefit of the citizens of the county.[27] As laws were passed establishing new counties, they almost always contained references to the establishment of these libraries.[28]

Apparently, these *county* libraries were established only when the local people showed enough interest to see that the money was collected, that a library board was elected, and that the money was given to the board. Little is known about the operation of the early Indiana county libraries, but the minutes of one at Bloomington in Monroe County, still exist and show that at one time the county library fund was lent to local citizens whose interest payments helped to support the library.[29] In that county, the library users also paid membership fees. However, this and the four other Indiana county libraries listed in the 1876 *Report* of the Bureau of Education were, by that time, considered to be free public libraries.

There can be little doubt that these Indiana county libraries were basically designed as social libraries that were to be aided by local units of government. Seventeen of the twenty-four libraries placed in this category were in Indiana. The earliest of the ten Indiana libraries with known founding dates was established in 1817. Eight of the ten had been started by 1826, the next one in 1844, and the last in 1852. A new constitution adopted in 1851 did not include a provision for the support of county libraries by the state or local governments.

The seven libraries in other states that have been classified as quasi-social were all ones in New England that had a degree of control by library associations and by local governments. Five of them were in Massachusetts and two in Maine. For six, the founding dates are known; they range from 1790 to 1857. For some libraries classified in this study as strict social libraries, so little is known that they may have been partly under the control of town governments. Furthermore, at any time, a single library could have ceased being an ordinary social library, particularly in the years after the Civil War when some social libraries faltered and were in the process of becoming libraries owned by towns or counties. These local governments may or may not have charged fees for their use.

REGIONAL DIFFERENCES

This chapter has considered each kind of social library separately. A different perspective can be obtained if each major region of the country is considered to see, for that region, which kinds of social libraries were more popular and which were less favored. A simple way to do this is to convert the number of social libraries of a particular kind in existence in each of the four regions (in Table 5.1) to a percentage of the total number for that kind in the whole United States, and then to compare these percentages with the corresponding percentages for all kinds of libraries (as shown in Table 1.1). For example, the number of strict social libraries in the Northeast, according to Table 5.1, was 1,531, which was 62.2 percent of the strict social libraries in the entire United States. According to Table 1.1 the Northeast had 42.5 percent of all the libraries in the study. For a simple comparison it is sufficient to note, for each kind of library, whether a particular region had a higher or lower percentage than it had of all the libraries in the study. On that basis, the Northeast definitely had a higher proportion of strict social libraries than it had of libraries in general.[30]

For nine of the fifteen kinds of social libraries shown in Table 5.1 (counting the small number of libraries on "other subjects" as a single group) the Northeast had a higher proportion of the United States total than it had of all kinds of libraries. Each of the six kinds of libraries where the Northeast appeared weak was one where another region was particularly strong. These six were the women's social libraries, the foreign language social libraries, the workingmen's libraries, the young men's social libraries, the mercantile libraries, and the social libraries aided by governments. As we have seen, women's social libraries were particularly numerous in Michigan; foreign language social libraries were most often found in the Midwest because German immigrants frequently settled there and almost all of the workingmen's libraries were located in Indiana, as were the social libraries aided by governments. For the other two kinds where the Northeast seemed to be weak, the reasons are not clear. The numbers are so small that the apparent strength of the young men's libraries in the Middle West and the apparent strength of the mercantile libraries in the South might disappear if only a few more libraries could be identified elsewhere.

The South, which had only 15.3 percent of the libraries in the study, had an even lower percentage of social libraries: 11.2 percent. Of the fifteen kinds of social libraries (counted, as above, for the Northeastern region) ten had percentages below 15.3. The five kinds for which the South had a higher proportion than might have been expected were the social law libraries, those for apprentices, those for mechanics, the mercantile libraries, and the atheneums. Numbers for all of these were small, so the South's apparent good showing may not be significant. Approximately half of the social libraries in the region were in the South Atlantic states.

The Midwest, like the South, had only five kinds of social libraries for which the region had more libraries than might have been expected. All five have been mentioned above in the section about the Northeastern libraries: the women's social libraries in the state of Michigan; the young men's libraries in the East North Central states; the foreign language social libraries throughout the Midwest; the workingmen's libraries in the state of Indiana; and the library societies that were aided by the Indiana state and local governments.

It is probably unwise to draw conclusions about the prevalence of various kinds of social libraries in the Far West because there were so few; the total for all social libraries was 4.6 percent of the libraries in the country, very close to the 4.7 percent for all of the kinds in the study. Of the social libraries in the Far West, about half were in California.

NOTES

1. Many studies mention social libraries. Histories of American reading habits or popular culture frequently report on them, and the literature about them is discussed on pp. 56–57 of *American Library History: A Comprehensive Guide to the Literature* by Donald G. Davis, Jr. and John Mark Tucker (Santa Barbara, Calif.: ABC-CLIO, 1989). Most of the 265 studies listed on pp. 60–71 of that volume are about social libraries.

2. The condition known as patriarchy has received a considerable amount of attention in recent years. Patriarchy in America is discussed in such books as Page Smith's *Daughters of the Promised Land: Women in American History* (Boston: Little, Brown, 1970) and Mary P. Ryan's *Womanhood in America from Colonial Times to the Present* 3d ed. (New York: Franklin Watts, 1983).

3. The literature about the attitudes of nineteenth century Americans toward "knowledge," "self-culture," and the reading of fiction is extensive. Among useful works are Richard D. Brown's *Knowledge is Power: The Diffusion of Information in Early America, 1700–1865* (New York: Oxford University Press, 1989) and Ronald John Zboray's *A Fictive People: Antebellum Economic Development and the American Reading Public* (New York: Oxford University Press, 1993).

4. In my article, "The Very Slow Decline of the American Social Library" in *Library Quarterly* 55 (April 1985): 207–25, I trace the history of the social libraries in more detail and speculate about reasons for their continuing popularity.

5. Jesse H. Shera, *Foundations of the Public Library: The Origins of the Public Library Movement in New England, 1629–1855* (Chicago: University of Chicago Press, 1949), 76–100.

6. Among recent works that deal with American women's associations and their activities before 1876 are *The Clubwoman as Feminist: True Womanhood Redefined, 1868–1914* (New York: Holmes and Meier, 1980) by Karen J. Blair; *Lady Bountiful Revisited: Women, Philanthropy, and Power* (New Brunswick, N.J.: Rutgers University Press, 1990), edited by Kathleen D. McCarthy; *Natural Allies: Women's Associations in American History* (Urbana, Ill.: University of Illinois Press, 1991) by Anne Firor Scott; and *Women and the Work of Benevolence: Morality, Politics, and Class in the Nineteenth-Century United States* (New Haven, Conn.: Yale University Press, 1990), by Lori D. Ginzberg.

7. Mrs. A. F. Bixby and Mrs. A. Howell, eds. *Historical Sketches of the Ladies' Library Associations of the State of Michigan* (Adrian, Mich.: Times and Expositor Steam Print, 1876). The life of one of these is examined in detail in "Outpost of New England Culture: The Ladies' Library Association of Kalamazoo, Michigan" by Daniel F. Ring, *Libraries and Culture* 32 (Winter 1977): 38–56.

8. John Langdon Sibley, in *A History of the Town of Union, Maine* (1851, Reprint, with a foreword by A. Carman Clark, Somersworth, N.H.: New England History Press, 1987), p. 317, writes that some young men tried to form a library and drew up a constitution, but that within two or three years several of the young men moved from the town and interest subsided.

9. I am not aware of any studies that shed much light on the lives of these libraries. They may have been similar to the libraries held by young men's societies that were formed mainly for non-library purposes, considered in chapter 6.

10. Haynes McMullen, "Social Libraries in Ante-Bellum Kentucky," *Register of the Kentucky State Historical Society* 58 (Apr. 1960): 106.

11. George Sheldon, *A History of Deerfield, Massachusetts* (a facsimile of the 1895–96 edition, vol. 2, Somersworth, N.H.: New Hampshire Publishing Company, 1972) p. 826.

12. Juvenile social libraries, along with other nineteenth century libraries for children, are discussed in Harriet G. Long's *Public Library Service to Children: Foundation and Development* (Metuchen, N.J.: Scarecrow Press, 1969.)

13. Bernard Elbaum, "Why Apprenticeship Persisted in Britain but not in the United States," *Journal of Economic History* 49 (June 1989): 345–46.

14. Stuart Bruchey, in *Roots of American Economic Growth, 1607–1861* (New York: Harper and Row, 1965), on p. 184, summarizes the effect of the spread of the factory system on apprenticeship.

15. Howard B. Rock, "A Delicate Balance: the Mechanics and the City in the Age of Jefferson," *New-York Historical Society Quarterly* 63 (Apr. 1979): 93–95.

16. In June, 1815, the "Mechanics' Social Library," in Exeter, New Hampshire was incorporated; the date when it opened its doors is not known, but an undated set of "Rules and Regulations" is owned by the Exeter Historical Society. Jesse H. Shera, in his book, *Foundations of the Public Library*, on p. 230, mentions a mechanics' library that was in operation in 1818 in Bristol, Connecticut.

17. The manuscript notes that Jesse H. Shera used in the preparation of his book, *Foundations of the Public Library*, mention one founded in Portsmouth, New Hampshire, in 1823 and one in Springfield, Massachusetts, founded in 1824.

18. John Frederick Lewis, *History of the Apprentices' Library of Philadelphia, 1820–1920: The Oldest Free Circulating Library in America* (Philadelphia: n.p., 1924), 23–25, 47–48.

19. The Maclure libraries established in Indiana are discussed in Jacob Piatt Dunn, *The Libraries of Indiana* (Indianapolis: Wm. B. Burford, 1893), 12–15; a much fuller treatment is contained in "Maclure Libraries in Indiana and Illinois," by Frances Helmerick McBride, 1967, a student paper in the Graduate Library School, Indiana University, 63p. (manuscript in my possession).

20. A significant exception was the Cincinnati Mercantile Library, which, during its first eleven years, subscribed to a number of periodicals and newspapers directly useful to businessmen; it also operated a merchants' exchange. "The Cincinnati Mercantile Library as a Business-Communications Center, 1835–1846," by Sallie H. Barringer and Bradford W. Scharlott, *Libraries and Culture* 26 (Spring 1991): 388–401.

21. William Douglas Boyd, Jr., "Books for Young Businessmen: Mercantile Libraries in the United States, 1820–1865" (Ph.D. diss., Indiana University, 1975), 181–85.

22. Libraries often lost money on lecture series, but profits at two prominent eastern mercantile libraries were occasionally large enough to be noticed in general periodicals. *National Magazine: Devoted to Literature, Art, and Religion* 2 (Apr. 1853), on p. 381, reported that the New York Mercantile Library made a profit in 1852 of $1,500. The same periodical, in vol. 3 (Aug. 1853) on p. 187, reported a profit for the Boston Mercantile Library of $1,584.60 for 1852 and, in vol. 4 (May 1854), p. 478, reported a profit there of $1,788.43 for 1853.

23. The index to *Libraries in American Periodicals before 1876*, compiled by Larry J. Barr, Haynes McMullen, and Steven G. Leach (Jefferson, N.C.: McFarland & Co., 1983) on p. 413, refers to 116 articles about American mercantile libraries.

24. Josiah Quincy, *The History of the Boston Athenaeum, with Biographical Notices of Its Deceased Founders* (Cambridge, Mass.: Metcalf & Co., 1851) pp. 6–9.

25. Charles Caldwell, *A Discourse on the Genius and Character of the Rev. Horace Holley, LL.D., Late President of Transylvania University* (Boston: Hilliard, Gray, Little and Wilkins, 1828), 152.

26.   Richard O'Connor's *The German-Americans, an Informal History* (Boston: Little, Brown, 1968) gives a clear account of the gradual assimilation of the German immigrants.

27.   The text of this part of the first Indiana constitution is quoted on pp. 114–15 of volume 1 of Charles Kettleborough's *Constitution Making in Indiana: A Source Book of Constitutional Documents with Historical Introduction and Critical Notes* (Indianapolis: Indiana Historical Commission, 1916).

28.   The Indiana county libraries are discussed on pp. 36–41 of "Legal and Government Aspects of Public Library Development in Indiana, 1816–1953" by La Vern A. Walther (Ed.D. diss., Indiana University, 1957).

29.   Manuscript minute book of the Monroe County Library, 1820–1855, now in the Monroe County Public Library, Bloomington, Indiana.

30.   In chapter 3, numbers were included to show what the situation would have been if the government of the state of Indiana had not, rather arbitrarily, distributed 939 township libraries. If this imaginary situation had obtained, all of the libraries in the Northeast would have been 47.0 percent of the total instead of 42.6 percent. The percentages for all kinds except public libraries would have been higher and percentages for public libraries would have been lower. In chapter 5 this hypothetical situation will be ignored; in later chapters it will be considered only rarely.

Chapter 6

Libraries Belonging to Organizations That Were Not Formed to Establish Libraries

The libraries discussed in chapter 5 have been considered as ones that most clearly indicate the desire of Americans to have and use books. However, many significant collections were owned by various organizations whose members, for whatever reasons, felt that the formation of a library should be only a part of the association's activity.

Sometimes the books clearly provided information about whatever subject was of most concern to the members of the group (as law books owned by a bar association); sometimes the collections were general or miscellaneous (as the contents of libraries owned by women's societies); and sometimes the collections were mixed (as in libraries owned by the Young Men's Christian Associations, which deliberately offered some secular books as enticements to attract readers with little or no interest in religion).

Earlier, it was mentioned that the order in which various kinds of libraries are discussed in this study may be unimportant. However, there may be some advantage, in following here as closely as possible, the same order as in the part on social libraries. Table 6.1 presents the same kind of information as Table 5.1. Some kinds of societies that considered the maintenance of libraries part of their purpose were quite similar to the library societies discussed in chapter 5. For example, the members of bar associations, covered in chapter 6, may have been as concerned about their libraries as were the members of law library societies, discussed in chapter 5.

Three kinds of libraries that were formed by voluntary organizations are not considered in this chapter but are examined in chapter 7: libraries owned by colleges or professional schools, hospital libraries, and libraries in asylums that existed for the care of persons with disabilities. These three kinds of institutions often belonged to voluntary organizations, but substantial numbers were operated by the federal, state, or local government. Changes in the role of private and public ownership over the years have seemed to provide a sufficient

Table 6.1
Libraries Belonging to Organizations That Were Not Formed to Establish Libraries

	Northeast	South	Middle West	Far West	All U.S.
Organizations concerned with particular subjects					
Religion					
Churches	219	92	25	34	370
Young Men's Christian Assns.	98	37	46	8	189
Other religious organizations	37	11	18	11	77
Agricultural societies	117	20	136	21	294
Scientific and technical societies	60	5	24	9	98
Historical societies	48	14	21	8	91
Literary societies, book clubs, and reading clubs	37	8	9	3	57
Medical societies	26	5	4	2	37
Bar associations	10	5	6	2	23
Boards of trade, merchants' exchanges, and chambers of commerce	9	7	3	4	23
Musical societies	10	4	5	0	19
Art societies	6	0	1	1	8
Organizations for persons of a particular age or gender					
Young men's associations	44	5	30	1	80
Women's associations	13	0	7	1	21
College students' societies	150	168	168	10	496
Other organizations					
Lyceums	58	31	27	7	123
Fraternal orders	30	28	21	44	123
Fire companies	8	24	2	5	39
Foreign language societies	16	9	26	5	56
Miscellaneous, general, and unclassified					
Miscellaneous	46	10	4	5	65
General	9	0	0	1	10
Unclassified	14	5	6	3	28
Total	1,065	488	589	185	2,327

reason for considering these libraries separately from others.

Another kind of library could have been included in chapter 6 but will be held for chapter 8—the one for libraries that belonged to governments: the garrison or military post library. At each post, the library was authorized by the federal government but was organized and managed by the officers stationed there.

ORGANIZATIONS CONCERNED WITH PARTICULAR SUBJECTS

Religion. Several conditions favored the establishment of libraries belonging to religious organizations in the American colonies and the United States before 1876. (1) Many Americans saw the world from a religious view. (2) The presence of religious freedom encouraged the development of voluntary organizations whose members held a variety of beliefs and purposes; one effect of the Second Great Awakening during the first part of the nineteenth century was to encourage the birth of new religious groups. (3) The members of these groups, like the members of older churches or sects, wished to provide reading matter that supported their organizations' views. Of all the libraries belonging to voluntary groups that were not primarily library societies, at least a fourth (27.3 percent) were clearly concerned with religion.

Churches. In America, the local churches were the main vehicles for the expression of religious feelings and the conduct of religious practices. This section includes libraries intended for the general use of members; Sunday school libraries, intended for the religious instruction of children, were usually operated by churches but were recognized as separate and are discussed in chapter 12.

The 370 church libraries that could be identified for this study were almost certainly not representative of the much larger number that existed, so any conclusions about their geographic or chronological patterns would be unreliable. There are four reasons why the available sources of information have furnished unrepresentative data: (1) Church libraries were often very small so they seldom appear in published lists of American libraries. (2) They were deliberately omitted from the list of more than three thousand American libraries appearing in the U.S. Bureau of Education's *Public Libraries*, Part 1, published in 1876. The compilers of that list reported that church libraries (and Sunday school libraries) were almost as numerous as the churches in the country. (3) The only information derived from church archives was from records kept in England concerning the gifts sent to churches in the American colonies by Thomas Bray and his associates. (4) The amount and nature of information about church libraries in the manuscript census returns for 1850 through 1870 varies considerably between states.

The Bray libraries, discussed in chapter 2, account for most of the church libraries that could be identified in the British colonies and the United States before 1786. Records concerning those collections have been made available because several scholars have published studies dealing with them. No detailed investigations concerning later church libraries have been discovered. The 145 libraries in the British colonies, in addition to the seven that clearly started in the Spanish colonies before 1786, make up a high percentage (41.1) of all the church libraries in the study; for no other kind of library were there more than 5 percent that were established in the years through 1785.

The available manuscript census returns for ten states from 1850 through 1870 were examined. For nine of the states (from widely separated parts of the country) only eight church libraries could be identified, but for the 1850 returns for a single state, Pennsylvania, forty of these libraries were found that appeared in no other information sources. Surely, the instructions for census takers in Pennsylvania must have been different from those in the other nine states.

The collections in the California missions deserve special mention. Sufficient information has been discovered for only nineteen, and founding dates were located for only three of those. Records have been preserved concerning library inventories that were taken at the time in the 1830s when some missions were being secularized. As a result, the largest number that could be identified at any of the five-year intervals was fourteen for the year 1835. Undoubtedly, several of these libraries had been in existence for some time before that date.[1]

For the United States as a whole, the paucity of information about many of the collections must make any generalizations very tentative in regard to the number existing at any one time. The records show no more than eleven at any of the five-year benchmarks through 1780, then never more than nineteen through 1830. The number rose somewhat erratically from 1835 to 1875, varying between eighteen and sixty, and averaging at about forty.

Young Men's Christian Associations. Among organizations with religious purposes, the YMCAs came late; however, they quickly spread across the country after the first was established in Boston in 1851. Before the decade of the 1850s many associations of young men had formed libraries and some of them had religious or moral purposes. Following the example of British associations, which had existed since 1844, the American YMCAs were at first established in cities to serve young men's religious needs. By 1875 they had spread to smaller towns, and some had begun to serve particular groups: railroad employees, German-speaking persons, or college students. By 1875, a total of 189 associations had established libraries.

The YMCA libraries were planned as important instruments to fulfill the purposes of the organizations. They regularly held secular as well as religious books, in order to attract young men who may have had little or no interest in religion. The December, 1859, issue of the Association's organ, *Young Men's Christian Journal*, emphasized the library's function in soul-winning, pointing out "where the Librarian is the only officer in daily attendance at the rooms, as in most American Associations, his responsibilities are certainly very great. He is the main representative of the institution. . . ." He should know books and authors, be friendly and helpful to the users, and above all, "have a deep personal interest in their spiritual well-being."[2] Even though the rooms were open to young men of any religious persuasion, the libraries, like their parent organizations, were always controlled by Protestant men.

In several cities, YMCAs established libraries very quickly, sometimes with new books and sometimes with hand-me-down collections acquired from other libraries, dead or dying.[3] By the year 1876, a YMCA in Cincinnati was claiming to have a library founded in 1848, three years before any YMCA existed in the United States. Apparently, that association was taking credit for a collection formed before it had come under control of the YMCA. One reliable source reported that its library was started in 1851 and that the association was first known as a YMCA around 1863.[4]

The portion of the collections that were not religious varied between libraries. Referring to libraries in both Canada and the United States, one report in 1858 estimated that a third of the books and half of the periodicals were not religious.[5] The secular books seem to have been more popular. The author of the section about YMCA libraries in the U.S. Bureau of Education's *Public Libraries of the United States of America* gives circulation figures for 1874 in a library that he considered typical. Books on religion made up only 9.5 percent, although his categories such as "biography" might have contained information of a religious nature; "fiction and tales" provided 29.5 percent of those that circulated.[6]

One event may have affected the rate of founding of YMCA libraries and another certainly did. The panic of 1857 caused unemployment in the cities and was responsible for an increase in the activities of the YMCAs. The pattern of founding for YMCA libraries at about that time may have been influenced by the economic dislocation and higher unemployment. Available records show eight new libraries in 1856, seven in 1857, fifteen in 1858, and then only four in 1859. The Civil War, of course, affected libraries serving young men. In some towns, the libraries ceased to exist when the war began, but the association was active in the Christian Commission that aided the soldiers in several ways, including the provision of libraries for the camps.[7] In at least fifteen of the towns where a YMCA library closed, a new one started after the war. As might be expected, the situation in the South was different from the situation in the North: The percentage of YMCA libraries in the South (19.6) was higher that its percentage for most other kinds of libraries, but about two-thirds of its YMCA libraries were founded before the war, and in the North, slightly more than half started after the war. Of the 116 libraries existing in 1875, sixteen were in the South.

Other Religious Organizations. It is difficult to be sure about the number of various kinds of libraries that belonged to religious organizations for two reasons: (1) Some groups (for example, Universalists) were sometimes considered associations whereas we might think of them as churches, and (2) it is not always possible to know whether a group was essentially interested in religion or in some general reform. Therefore the assignment of some libraries in this section can be open to question.

Among the seventy-seven libraries in this section, no kind was in the majority; however, two kinds had considerably more than any of the others: seventeen belonged to organizations concerned with the extension of Christianity (missionary societies or mission boards of national churches) and thirteen belonged to temperance organizations. The missionary libraries included five that were expressly for seamen,[8] and the temperance libraries included one for an organization that was only beginning to grow: the Women's

Christian Temperance Union. No libraries were discovered that belonged to societies that took part in one of the most important reform movements in the decades just before the Civil War: the anti-slavery movement. There were nine collections belonging to boards or commissions of Protestant churches excluding the missionary boards mentioned above and excluding eight church historical libraries in this study. The Catholic church owned one of the missionary libraries mentioned above, and Catholic societies owned at least seven others. Only four libraries belonged to Jewish organizations.

In most ways, the chronological and geographical pattern for the establishment of collections belonging to these various societies was similar to that of several other kinds of libraries: none before 1800, then a slow—and irregular—increase in the number being founded until the outbreak of the Civil War, followed by a faster rate after the war. By 1875, thirty-six existed, twenty-two of them in the Northeast.

The pattern of distribution was different from that of most kinds of libraries in one way: of the seventy-seven that had been founded at some time before 1876, twenty-two were to be found in one of three eastern cities: Boston, New York, or Philadelphia. Sixteen of the libraries in these three cities were at the national headquarters for various denominations or for other religious organizations.

Agricultural Societies. Considering that a high proportion of Americans were farmers during all the years before 1876 and considering the tendency of Americans to form associations, it is not surprising that there were many agricultural societies and that members of these societies should want to collect libraries. Most of these libraries were very small, and not enough information is available to indicate what proportion of the books were about agriculture, what proportion were about science or technology useful to farmers, and what proportion were of a general or miscellaneous nature.

The names given to these societies show us their members' initial intentions, though the nature of the book collection belonging to an individual association may have changed over the years. Of the 294 that could be identified, 109 were called agricultural societies; sixty-nine others were more modestly called farmers' clubs. A degree of specialization may have been indicated by the names for fifty of them: "agricultural and horticultural society" or just "horticultural society." About a dozen mentioned fruit growing or gardening in their titles, and just one mentioned any animals: the Penobscot Sheep Keepers' Association, formed in Bangor, Maine, in 1863. Twenty-five of the collections were also intended for mechanics, but farmers were always mentioned first in their names.

Founding dates were available for only fifty-six of the collections owned by agricultural societies. Half of them had been founded by the mid-1850s; more were being founded just after the Civil War than at any other time.[9] Geographically, the records are more helpful, providing a basis for several generalizations. When the numbers of libraries known to have existed at each five-year point are compared, it appears that almost all were in the Northeast before the 1850s. Frequently, from the end of the period the Northeast had more than half that are known to have existed during benchmark years. However, very little could be learned about the length of life of many of the collections, so they do not appear in the records that show the number in existence at particular times. Considering the total that existed at any time before 1876 in each state, New York, well known for improvements in farming methods, had thirty-seven, a few more than in any other state. But so many of the North Central states had respectable numbers of libraries that the total for the entire Midwest was 136, whereas the total for the entire Northeast was 117. There were few agricultural society libraries outside of those two major regions; the largest number in any state or territory in the other regions (seventeen) was in Utah, where the Latter-day Saints were much interested in making the desert bloom. No records of more than four could be found in any other state or territory outside of the Northeast or Middle West.

Scientific and Engineering Societies. During the colonial years and in the early nineteenth century, Americans had ample opportunities for participating in scientific activities and even the most deeply religious person could conduct scientific inquiry without any qualms of conscience. Religious leaders saw the universe as evidence of the power of God; the discovery and classification of native American plants and animals was seen as a process for uncovering aspects of this handiwork. At least into the 1860s, most Americans felt that neither the direction taken by science nor its power was reason to see it as a threat to religious faith.[10]

So it is not surprising that Americans, before 1875, formed numerous scientific societies and that some of them acquired collections of books as well as "cabinets" containing objects of scientific interest. The concept of science was broader than it is today, usually embracing technology, at least; and the interests of members could easily include what have come to be called the humanities, with the result that some libraries considered to be scientific may have been more inclusive than that term now implies. Ninety-eight society libraries seem to have been predominantly scientific in nature. Only seven of them were founded in the eighteenth century; the American Philosophical Society in Philadelphia, whose library was founded in 1743, is the best known of these early ones. The rate of founding remained quite slow until the 1850s; of the eighty-six with known founding dates, fifty-seven were started from 1851 through 1875. Thirty of the libraries did not appear until after the Civil War, and sixty-four still existed in 1875.

Approximately three-fourths of the libraries belonged to societies with broad purposes: the natural sciences or "natural history." However, by the 1850s, more specialized groups were acquiring collections: for example, entomological societies and societies that operated astronomical observatories. Six of the libraries were owned by societies that were clearly intended for engineers, and four of the six were for civil engineers, beginning with one in Boston in 1851 and one in New York City in 1852. Civil engineering developed, in the United States, before other branches of the field because of the obvious need for roads, canals, and bridges. In the factories, machinery was usually designed without the help of mechanical engineers.

Geographically, the libraries owned by scientific and engineering societies present a pattern that is somewhat different from that of the entire group of societies. The Northeast had 61.2 percent of the scientific ones and only 45.8 percent of all the libraries considered in the main part of this study as belonging to voluntary organizations that were not library societies. Part of the reason for the prevalence of scientific collections in the Northeast may be that the collections had a tendency to gather in larger cities: New York City and Philadelphia each had nine, and Boston had six. Chicago had eight, but no other city had more than three.

Historical Societies. Soon after the winning of the Revolutionary War, Americans began to think of their country as having entered the mainstream of history, and some of them began to be concerned about the preservation of the record of that entrance. Because the habit of the time was to form associations, it followed that historical associations began to appear with the collection of manuscripts, documents, newspapers, and books as one of their main purposes. Such associations had existed in Europe for at least two hundred years, but as Leslie Dunlap has pointed out in his careful and detailed survey, *American Historical Societies, 1790–1860,* there is little evidence of direct imitation of foreign societies.[11] College libraries already contained examples of the most popular historical writing, but no group of libraries was systematically collecting all the forms of materials needed to support serious study of the past.

This dominant interest in the materials of scholarship makes the libraries of the historical societies the first true research libraries in America. Sometimes the societies collected so avidly that there might not be complete agreement as to the significance of all the items in their collections, particularly some of the museum objects. Dunlap mentions a bullet, in the possession of the New York Historical Society, that was reported to have been swallowed twice by the same British soldier during the American Revolution.[12] But most of the materials collected by these associations were and are invaluable to anyone studying, firsthand, the records of the American past.

It is difficult to say how many historical society libraries were founded in the United States before 1876. One of the authors of the section about them in the Bureau of Education's *Public Libraries of the United States of America,* issued in 1876, claimed that more than 160 historical societies had been founded, "the greater number of which have perpetuated their organizations." The editors of the same volume presented a list of sixty-four libraries belonging to historical societies in existence then, but admitted that a few of them could be considered scientific societies because of their members' wide range of interests.[13] For the present study, ninety-one collections could be identified that had, before 1876, belonged to societies whose predominant interest seemed to be historical. This number includes eight that were owned by societies affiliated with particular denominations (the Lutheran Historical Society of Gettysburg, Pennsylvania, for example); these could have been included in the totals for religious societies, considered elsewhere in this chapter.

Chronologically, the libraries belonging to historical societies present a pattern similar to that of several other kinds of associations. At first, a few appeared in the Northeast, beginning with the library of the Massachusetts Historical Society in 1791. Then, by the 1830s they were beginning to spread into all parts of the country. Measured at five-year intervals, the number for the entire United States increased steadily from 1820 to 1875. At the end of the period, the Northeast had thirty-two of the fifty-six libraries in existence, and the other collections were scattered among nineteen states, with not more than three libraries in any single state.

The historical society collections were different in one way from collections formed by other kinds of societies. In the later years, the western libraries often appeared soon after settlement began. For example, in 1849 it was reported that the Iowa Historical and Geological Institute in Burlington had been organized in 1843, "but ten years after the departure of the 'red men'," and that constant additions were being made to its library.[14]

Literary Societies, Book Clubs, and Reading Societies. During the years before 1875, the term "literature" often had the meaning that we attach to the term "knowledge," so we cannot be sure that the members of literary societies confined their interests to poetry, drama, and fiction. In many cases, it is likely that the term *literary* in the name of a society just meant that its members had serious interests that transcended local concerns. Book clubs or reading societies were of two kinds: those which accumulated libraries for the use of their members, and those whose members exchanged books without forming a club library. Societies of only the former variety are included in this study.

Fifty-seven libraries belonging to literary, book, or reading societies, were identified which apparently were not intended for persons of a particular age or gender. Not counted in this group are twenty young men's literary societies that have been included with other young men's associations and six women's literary or book clubs that have been considered along with other women's societies.

Of the fifty-seven literary, book, and reading societies that do not seem to have been intended primarily for young men or for women, thirty-five had the word "literary" in their names and thirteen were called book clubs or reading societies. As with most other kinds of societies, these organizations were more likely to be found in the Northeast: New England had twenty-five and the Middle-Atlantic states, twelve. If the twenty-six literary societies for young men and for women had been included, the proportions would not have been very different: of the eighty-three total, there would have been forty in New England and sixteen in the Middle-Atlantic states.

The earliest literary or reading society of any kind that could be identified for this study was the Book Society formed in Hartford, Connecticut, in 1753. Only a few were organized in any of the decades before the 1850s, when thirteen were formed (twenty-four including the ones for young men and for women). The figure for 1866 through 1875 was only nine (fifteen including the ones for young men and for women). The number in existence stood at only nine in 1875 (fourteen including those for young men and for women). There had been more during the 1850s: in 1855 the total reached thirteen not including the ones for women and for young men, or eighteen including those. These numbers are all small and therefore of uncertain value. However, it is possible that they indicate a diminished amount of interest in these libraries after the war.

Medical Societies. By the time of the American Revolution, medicine had been recognized as a "scientific" profession, but during much of the nineteenth century its practitioners were only moderately successful in curing disease. Ordinary citizens sometimes began to practice medicine with little or no training, and splinter groups—homeopaths and others—began to offer their own varieties of cures.[15]

Physicians began to form medical societies before the Revolution, and these societies continued to appear during the years included in this study. Two of the purposes of these organizations were to improve the practice of medicine through discussions at meetings and through the publication of medical journals. A few of them also built libraries as a means of collecting and disseminating medical information.

Only thirty-seven libraries belonging to medical societies were identified for this study. The two earliest were both founded in 1789: one belonging to the College of Physicians in Philadelphia and the other belonging to the Medical Society of South Carolina in Charleston. The one in Charleston was the only medical society library existing outside of the Northeast before the Medical Society of the District of Columbia established one in 1819. After that, most continued to appear in the Northeast. By 1875, seventeen states had at least one such library. Massachusetts had eleven, New York State eight, and no other state had more than three. The number of medical society libraries in existence increased very slowly until about 1850. Then, counted at five-year intervals, the numbers rose somewhat more rapidly from ten in 1850 to twenty-four in 1875.

Bar Associations. In a country like the United States, with various new state and local governments occasionally springing up in an environment that encouraged individual enterprises, it was to be expected that men often felt the need to understand—and sometimes to circumvent—the laws. The number of lawyers grew rapidly and so did the amount of legal literature in the years before 1876.[16] In this chapter we have already noticed the tendency of lawyers to form library societies. Some of the other societies formed by lawyers—bar associations—also had libraries.

The number of bar association libraries identified for this study (twenty-three) is considerably smaller than the number of collections owned by lawyers' library associations (fifty-two). The difference is hard to explain. Actually, neither of these numbers may be significant because various governmental units provided large numbers of law libraries, to be discussed in chapter 8. It may be that a voluntary association collected books only when a court or legislative body in its community did not meet the need.

The organization known through much of its history as the Law Association of Philadelphia had a library as early as 1802; other bar associations occasionally formed collections. By 1875, nineteen existed; nine of these had been founded during the ten-year span from 1866 through 1875.

Boards of Trade, Merchants' Exchanges, and Chambers of Commerce. Organizations with any of these names can appropriately be considered together, because all of them facilitated commercial activity. However, the term "chamber of commerce" may have implied that the organization also served to represent business interests in the community. Little is known about some of the twenty-three libraries belonging to these associations of businessmen; a few clearly emphasized current information to be obtained in newspapers and periodicals.

The earliest identifiable library of this kind was one that appeared in 1784 in Charleston, South Carolina. There were only three more with founding dates before 1849. The general prosperity and improvements in transportation during the late 1840s and early 1850s encouraged the formation of these associations; at least six libraries appeared from 1849 through 1858. Six more were founded from 1869 through 1875. As might be expected, these libraries rarely appeared anywhere except in cities; sixteen of them were in seaports. A few may have been specialized because they belonged to exchanges that had special interests— maritime trading or trading in produce. The number in existence at different times is what one might expect: not more than four at any five-year measuring point before 1850 and then an increase to fourteen by 1875.

Musical Societies. Nineteen musical societies had libraries before 1876. For most of them it is not possible to know what proportion of the collection consisted of books about music and what proportion consisted of books or sheets containing the music itself. Twelve societies had German names: one in New York, two in Pennsylvania, four in Illinois, one in Missouri, and four in Texas.[17] The seven societies with names in English were located in the East: five in Massachusetts and two in New York.

What may have been the earliest library belonging to any of these musical societies was the one organized by the New York Philharmonic Society in 1843. Eleven out of the nineteen were founded or first mentioned during the 1850s, and nine still existed in 1875.

Art Societies. Only eight libraries that belonged to art societies could be identified; at least six of these societies seem to have operated art schools or museums. Five of the organizations were located in cities: three in New York City and two in Philadelphia. Two more were in places that may have been considered cities by 1875: Chicago and San Francisco. The only small town to have one was Manchester, New Hampshire. Although the earliest, in the American Academy of the Fine Arts in Philadelphia, got started in 1802, five of the eight did not open until after the Civil War. At least six existed in 1875.

ORGANIZATIONS FOR PERSONS OF A PARTICULAR AGE OR GENDER

In the chapter concerned with social libraries (chapter 5), the ones that were intended for persons of a particular age or gender were grouped together. Three other kinds of libraries intended for persons of a particular age or gender were the ones established by young men's societies, women's societies, and societies formed by college students. Most of the student societies were for young men; only a few libraries were owned by societies that existed for women students.

No societies for children, corresponding to the juvenile library societies, could be identified among the societies that did not have the establishment of libraries as their main purpose. Perhaps the very numerous Sunday schools or other schools met at least a part of the need for children's reading.

Young Men's Associations. The libraries belonging to young men's societies that did not have the formation of libraries as their main purpose may have been quite similar to those owned by the young men's library societies; most seem to have been general in subject matter although some of the parent societies had religious or moral purposes. There seem to have been more collections that were owned by the (non-library) societies; eighty of them have been identified for this study, and only fifty-one were owned by library societies.[18]

About half (thirty-eight) of the societies that had the ownership of libraries as only one of their features were called young men's associations or young men's societies. A few called themselves "institutes" or "unions"; the word "literary" appears in the names of twenty of them, perhaps just to indicate a serious interest in various subjects. Just a few clearly had religious or moral purposes; for most, no particular purpose is evident.

The geographical distribution of these societies was not much different from that of most libraries: more in the Northeast than in any other region, some in the Middle West, and only a few elsewhere. But chronologically, their distribution was unlike that of most kinds of libraries. Almost none appeared before the 1830s, a decade in which there was a systematic attempt to found young men's societies. New libraries were established frequently in the years before the Civil War, especially during the 1850s. Fewer appeared during the 1860s; apparently, none were started from 1870 through 1875. The number that existed at any one time did not increase notably between the 1840s and 1875 except that for some reason there were considerably more in 1855 than at any other five-year measuring point. The Young Men's Christian Associations, considered separately in this study, appeared in large numbers beginning in the 1850s and aggressively sought members, so their libraries may have been more attractive to many young men.

Womens' Associations. As mentioned earlier in this chapter, women were often active in the management and operation of the hospitals and asylums that were intended for men, women, and children. But there were at least twenty societies that were organized by and for women and that had libraries to support their main (non-library) purposes. Six of these were literary societies or reading clubs, four were called sewing circles or clubs (and may have been charitable in purpose, making clothes for the poor), and several were just called ladies' associations or ladies' circles.

It is not surprising that eight out of the fifteen with known founding dates were started after the Civil War. As with the much more numerous women's library associations mentioned in chapter 5, American society in the first half of the nineteenth century seems not to have been as conducive to the growth of these organizations as it was just after the war. Apparently, not more than two of these (non-library) societies existed at any time before the Civil War; by 1875, ten were in operation.

College Student Societies. College students in the years before 1876, were, like other Americans, quick to form societies. A safe generalization is that every liberal arts college for men had at least two student societies, each of which established a library early in its career. There were a few societies for women, both in the small number of women's colleges and in the even smaller number of coeducational schools; at least six of these societies had libraries.[19]

Although these organizations have often been called literary societies, it must be remembered that the term "literature" was closer to what we think of as "knowledge" than to "belles lettres." The topics of debates conducted by most societies seem to have been quite varied. Although information is lacking about the contents of many of the 496 libraries that could be identified, a few were clearly specialized; at least twenty-seven emphasized religion, and a few seem to have been concerned with science.

As might be expected, the geographic distribution of the libraries belonging to the student societies was quite similar to the distribution of libraries belonging to all colleges and professional schools, considered in the next chapter. The relatively small number of college libraries in the Northeast and the high number in the South—when compared with the number for all libraries in the study—are discussed in that chapter.

The general history of these student societies and their libraries has been told by Thomas Harding and others.[20] However, for the present study, determining exactly what society libraries were formed at what times and in what places has been difficult because early lists of college libraries often did not mention society libraries or just reported that the students' libraries on the campus had a total of a certain number of volumes. One result of the lack of information about this kind of library is that the proportion of collections with known founding dates is low: The number with dates is only 61.9 percent of the total that are known to have existed before 1876. If the ones with known founding dates are representative, there was no noticeable increase in the rate of founding from the 1830s through 1875. The rate increased and decreased several times; fifty-three were started in the 1830s and only fifty-eight in the ten years from 1866 through 1875. The rate for college libraries (to be discussed in chapter 7) increased steadily during those years: from sixty-seven in the 1830s to 209 between 1866 and 1875.

The failure of the rate of founding for student society libraries to increase may have been related to the students' attitudes toward those organizations. Historians have observed a decline in the popularity of the societies that began around the time of the Civil War, as students became more interested in athletics and in other kinds of organizations. No libraries belonging to one kind, the Greek-letter fraternities, could be identified for this study.

If students lacked much interest in their traditional societies in the years just after the Civil War, at least they did not get rid of those they had. In 1875 at least 306 existed; the number had increased at each of the five-year measuring dates since 1785. Of the nine sub-regions, all except New England and the Mountain area had more in 1875 than at any earlier date; New England had somewhat fewer than in the years just before the war, and the Mountain states had none at any date.

OTHER ORGANIZATIONS

In addition to groups of people who had particular subject interests and groups of particular ages or genders, there were other associations whose members included the maintenance of a library as one of their purposes. Four groups who seem to have often been especially interested in forming libraries were members of lyceums, fraternal orders, fire companies, and societies made up of persons who spoke a language other than English.

Lyceums. Josiah Holbrook used the Greek word *lyceum* to identify a kind of association (not, at first, called a lyceum), which he founded in Millbury, Massachusetts, in 1826. This and other early lyceums had three main purposes: the improvement of instruction in public schools, the provision for adult education through discussion and lectures, and the establishment and encouragement of libraries and museums.[21] Several manifestos were published during the first few years of the movement. The first, in the October, 1826, issue of the *American Journal of Education*, proposed that these mutual education societies should have libraries, but said nothing against the existing social libraries. Later articles reported that many social libraries had fallen into disuse, and the *American Annals of Education* (the successor to the *American Journal of Education*) for November, 1831, carried an article that claimed that when a lyceum was started in a town, its members either began to use the old library or formed a new one.[22]

The members of the lyceums were mostly professional men and businessmen, but women were welcomed as members in some associations. Although women were not numerous within the membership of most lyceums, they played one important role in the life of many lyceums that has been overlooked by most modern historians. Attending a lecture was a form of social life in which young men could properly invite young women to accompany them, so they did.[23]

The number of lyceums increased rapidly. Eight years after the establishment of the first one, there are said to have been nearly three thousand of them, many sending representatives to county, state, and national meetings. They were particularly strong in New England but existed in good numbers in the Middle Atlantic states and the Middle West. In the 1830s they flourished in the South, but the southern way of life in the two decades before the Civil War did not encourage the growth of a northern institution, which appealed to middle-class people who wished to freely debate and, sometimes, to support a variety of reforms.

In the north, the debating part of the lyceums' programs declined as railroads spread in the 1840s and 1850s, permitting popular lecturers to inspire, educate, and, after the Civil War, astonish or amuse lyceum audiences in remote parts of the country. Emerson was one of the first prominent easterners to carry culture into the west; he was followed soon by other writers and reformers and later by retired generals, humorists, and magicians. Emerson's career as a lecturer illustrates the close connection between the lyceums and library associations. He often spoke under the auspices of library associations whose members, like the members of lyceums, hoped that by charging their audiences more than Mr. Emerson charged the associations, they could acquire money to spend on books.[24]

Sometimes a lyceum's library became the center of its activity during the years when its other functions were atrophying. In fact, if not in name, it thus became a social library. Sometimes, if interest in the organization died completely, the book collection was given to a new or existing social library or, after 1850, perhaps to a public library.

If there really were nearly three thousand lyceums in the United States at one time, most of them either failed to establish libraries or had libraries that were not prominent enough to find their way into the lists used as the basis for the present study; only 123 have been identified. The geographical distribution of libraries connected with lyceums was about the same as the distribution of all libraries, except that the South had more than might be expected and the Middle West had fewer. The South had about a fourth of all lyceum libraries; it had only about a sixth of all libraries (excluding school and Sunday school libraries). The Middle West had 21 percent of the lyceum libraries and 37 percent of all libraries. This pattern may be surprising because the lyceum movement was strong in the Midwest, and southerners are thought to have been cool toward this kind of association. It is barely possible that this pattern of distribution was due to chance.

There were no noteworthy differences among the various regions as to the fifty-nine dates of founding that could be discovered. Almost everywhere, most lyceum libraries were established in the 1830s, 1840s, or 1850s, although a few were started after the Civil War. In 1860, at least sixteen existed; by 1875 the total number that could be identified was twenty-two.

Fraternal Orders. Freemasonry came to the British colonies from the mother country during the second quarter of the eighteenth century, a period when the movement was spreading to many countries. In America, Masonry was popular during the Revolutionary period and was joined by other fraternal organizations in the early nineteenth century. The Independent Order of Odd Fellows, which first appeared in 1819, was the most prominent of these.

The fraternal orders offered their members a sense of belonging, just as other societies did, but perhaps in greater measure than most organizations because the member became a brother who shared secret knowledge of some kind, shared ideals and shared benefits not available elsewhere; the lodges often provided support for aged members, for widows of deceased members, and for orphans.

Libraries belonging to fraternal organizations were more numerous than were libraries belonging to most other kinds of societies before 1876; records concerning a total of 123 have been identified for this study. However, little information has been discovered about their content; presumably their collections were similar to those in social libraries. Generally, they were intended for use by members, but records indicate that sometimes they were available to the public. The sources used for the present study contain no references to any separate libraries owned by the women's auxiliaries that were attached to some lodges.

Founding dates are available for ninety-nine of the fraternal libraries, 80 percent of the total. The earliest that could be identified was a Masonic library in Richmond, Virginia, that still exists and claims a founding date of 1777. Only a few were established before the 1840s when eleven were started; the 1850s saw seventeen new ones; and eleven more were formed during the Civil War years, 1861 through 1865. After the war they were being founded more rapidly: forty-five from 1866 through 1875. The number in existence at any one of the five-year measuring points increased very slowly until the 1840s, then more rapidly until 1875 when there were eighty-four in existence.

A variety of fraternal orders had formed libraries by 1875; they were to be found in thirty-one states. However, 105 out of the total 123 clearly belonged to lodges affiliated with either the Masons or the Independent Order of Odd Fellows (IOOF). The latter had sixty-five of the collections and the former, forty. The IOOF had more mainly because of the large number in a single state, California, which had twenty-four.[25]

Fire Companies. In America, the materials and methods used in building during the colonial period and much of the nineteenth century made destructive fires inevitable. During the eighteenth century, property owners sometimes formed associations to fight these fires; Benjamin Franklin organized one in Philadelphia, and George Washington joined another in Alexandria, Virginia. During the first half of the nineteenth century, fire companies often had two classes of members: active ones who raced to the fire and attempted to put it out, and honorary ones who were not expected to help. Members of both of those classes participated in social events of various kinds; sometimes the companies became virtual fraternities.

It was only natural for these associations, like others in which social intercourse was important, to form libraries for the members' use. Apparently, their collections were general in subject matter, similar to collections in several kinds of social libraries; sometimes they were called library associations. The thirty-nine that could be identified for this study were, without a doubt, only a small fraction of those in existence. John C. Colson, in a detailed study of fire company libraries in Baltimore, identified fifteen library associations organized by fire companies, only two of which appear in any general sources.[26]

The earliest fire company library with a known founding date was established in Leicester, Massachusetts, in 1812; no others were founded before the latter half of the 1830s. More than half of the libraries with known founding dates were organized during the 1840s and 1850s; only six have dates after the Civil War. The number in existence did not increase between 1845 and 1875; available records never show more than six at any five-year point during those thirty years. The number of libraries that could be discovered was so small that no specific statement about the geographic distribution of fire company libraries is justified; however, there was at least one library in each of seven of the nine sub-regions of the country.

The failure of these libraries to exhibit the usual pattern of increased numbers toward the end of the period is consistent with what is known about the fire companies. Two conditions caused them to weaken by the late 1850s: (1) the cost of new, improved fire fighting equipment was too high for many small voluntary associations to afford, and (2) law-abiding citizens became dismayed at the hooliganism of some "active" members at fires when they tried to prevent rival companies from succeeding in their efforts. City governments often had to take over the work of fire prevention, hiring firemen whom they could control. Perhaps this process can be considered as part of the general tendency, in this country, for governments occasionally to assume, the provision of various services that had been supplied by voluntary organizations—police protection, libraries for the public, care of the mentally ill, and others.[27]

Foreign Language Societies. Chapter 5 discussed societies whose main object was the formation of libraries in foreign languages, and it was mentioned that most of the foreign language libraries were held by societies organized for some non-library purpose. This latter group, like the former one, contained mainly books in German; only three out of a total fifty-six were in any other language. Twelve German singing societies had libraries that are not included in this total but are counted with collections held by other musical societies.

Collections held by German societies, which were not formed with the maintenance of a library as their main purpose, exhibit a chronological pattern that is somewhat like that of the German social libraries: of the forty-seven with known founding dates, eighteen were started during the 1850s, and, even though German immigration was as great from 1866 through 1875, only eleven were formed during that ten-year period. In another way, the distribution of the collections owned by the various non-library societies was different: the number in existence at each of the five-year measuring points increased from the 1850s into the 1870s. Of the total of fifty-three libraries, a total of thirty-nine still existed in 1875, whereas, for the German social libraries, there were only seven out of fifteen. If this difference was not due to chance, it may have been caused by the tendency of libraries connected with some other organization to have had longer lives than libraries that existed as separate entities.

Libraries for immigrants, as might be expected, usually appeared in the parts of the country where groups preferred to settle. No society libraries with collections in German have been recorded for any state except Pennsylvania before the 1840s. By 1876, more libraries for Germans had appeared in the Middle West than in any other major region. Eight Midwestern states had them, but they had been established also in eight other states. At least one collection was in the possession of a society intended for Irish Americans. The Mathew Institute, in Boston, existed around the year 1850. The organization was concerned with temperance; it provided lectures and encouraged debates.

Miscellaneous Societies. There were sixty-five collections belonging to organizations whose purposes were shared by so few others that it did not seem worthwhile to establish separate categories for them. Examples were the Chess and Literary Association of Shasta, California, the American Oriental Society of Boston, and the Universal Peace Union of Philadelphia. Included here are a few collections belonging to "philomathic" or "philomathean" societies. If these libraries supported the love of learning indicated by the titles of their parent organizations, they contained books of a serious nature on a variety of subjects. However, a majority of the societies considered as miscellaneous seem to have had specialized interests, so it is not surprising that most of their libraries were located where the density of population was greater: the Northeast had forty-six of them, and the three major cities there—Boston, New York, and Philadelphia together—had twenty-one.

General Societies. This term has been used for a group of only ten libraries that belonged to organizations that were general in the sense that, apparently, they were formed just because a group of people wanted to have a society;

perhaps the members simply enjoyed each other's company. These libraries appeared late in the period: seven were founded or first mentioned in 1863 or later and six of the total were founded in New York City from 1851 through 1872. Examples are the Lotus Club in that city and the Bohemian Club in San Francisco. The total is so small and I have so little information about the parent societies that it is unsafe to draw conclusions about them.

Unclassified Societies. This term is used for a group of twenty-eight libraries belonging to organizations that were clearly societies but whose purposes were not at all clear from the available information. Correspondence with librarians or local historians might have made it possible to move some of them into other groups. Examples are the Webster Club Library of Woodstown, New Jersey and the collection belonging to the Mount Pisgah Alumni Association of Ayletts, Virginia. Fourteen from this group were in the Northeast, and the rest were distributed across the country in nine states. Their chronological pattern was unremarkable: they first appeared in the late eighteenth century and were discovered a little more frequently in the decades starting about 1840. Seven still existed in 1875.

REGIONAL DIFFERENCES

One way in which to consider the prevalence of libraries owned by organizations formed for non-library purposes is to look at differences among the four major regions in the same way that was done in the "Regional Differences" section in chapter 5.

The situation in the Northeast was one of the few where the figures for all libraries in this section, in Table 6.1, when converted to a percentage of the total for the United States, comes fairly close to the percentage for its area in the main part of this study as shown in Table 1.1; the Northeast is slightly above average (3.2 percentage points above).

Even though the Northeast had about the same proportion of collections owned by these non-library organizations as it had for all libraries in the study, it made a very good showing when individual kinds of libraries are considered. Of twenty-two kinds (counting *unclassified* as a kind), the Northeast's percentage was below its percentage of all libraries for only six kinds: libraries owned by agricultural societies, boards of trade, college students' societies, fraternal organizations, fire companies, and societies with members who spoke foreign languages. The number of libraries of each of these kinds was so small that chance may have played a part in sending them below the Northeast's percentage for all kinds of libraries in the study. However, if chance did not play a part, we can speculate about reasons why the Northeast did not show up well in a few cases.

The Northeast had more than its share of agricultural social libraries but less than its share of libraries owned by agricultural societies, possibly because of the affinity in New England for the social library as a form of organization. The poor showing for the Northeast in regard to collections belonging to college students' societies is to be expected because that region had relatively few colleges and college libraries. Fraternal libraries in California have been the object of a special study by Ray Held; he may have located a very high proportion of the ones in that state, and collections in other parts of the country are almost certainly not as well represented in this study. With the fire company libraries, the intensive study by John Colson of libraries in Baltimore has clearly caused the South to come ahead of the other regions. The situation with libraries belonging to various foreign language societies is the same as with foreign language social libraries: the large number of Germans in the Midwest caused that region to have a disproportionately large number of libraries.

In the South, the proportion of organizations that had libraries was noticeably higher than the South's proportion of all libraries in the main part of this study (21.0 percent instead of 15.2 percent). This situation was not the result of strength in any particular kind of libraries; for thirteen of the twenty-two kinds the South had more than its share and for nine it had less.

Generally, the Middle West had a smaller proportion of the libraries belonging to non-library organizations than it had of all libraries in the study, 25.3 percent as opposed to 37.4 percent. The only three kinds for which it had more than its share were ones belonging to agricultural societies, to young men's societies, and to foreign-language groups. It is not surprising that the region had more than its share of collections belonging to farmers' groups. The good showing for young men's societies is consistent with its good showing for young men's social libraries; however, there is no obvious reason for this superiority. The prevalence of foreign language collections is probably there for the same reason as the prevalence of foreign language library societies—the tendency of Germans to settle there.

The Far West had a somewhat greater proportion of collections belonging to these non-library organizations than it had of all of the libraries in the main part of the study (8.0 percent instead of 4.7 percent). The good showing for that region was, as might be expected, the result of the situation in California. Non-library societies in that state had more collections than the records shown for all the other far western states combined: a total of 123 out of 185. For eighteen out of twenty-two kinds of libraries belonging to non-library organizations, the Far West had a higher proportion than it had of all libraries of any kind in the country. However, as with library societies, the numbers were so small that chance could easily have played an important part in determining which libraries were present in available records.

To summarize, for these societies that had been organized for some purpose other than to have a library, the only major region that had fewer collections than might have been expected was the Middle West. However, the pattern of distribution among the four regions was somewhat closer to the pattern for all libraries in the study than was the pattern for social libraries.

A rough measure of the difference between the two groups of libraries in respect to their variation from the pattern for all libraries can be obtained in this way: If the pattern of percentages for the number of all libraries in the study (42.6 in the Northeast; 15.2 in the South; 37.4 in the Middle West; and 4.7 in the Far West) is considered normal and if the variations above or below those figures for the four regions are added together, the total variation for social libraries is 29.6 points, and the variation for the non-library societies is 24.4.

NOTES

1. Two articles provide information about libraries in California missions: "Libraries in Provincial California" by J. N. Bowman, *Historical Society of Southern California Quarterly* 43 (Dec. 1961): 426–39 and "The Story of California's First Libraries" by M. J. Geiger, *Southern California Quarterly* 46 (Mar. 1964): 109–24.

2. "Officers and their Duties. The Librarian" (signed "McC") *Young Men's Christian Journal*, 5 (Dec. 1859): 160–61.

3. The city of Louisville, Kentucky, may have held the speed record for moving collections from one library to another. In 1871, a local historian and bookman, Reuben T. Durrett, came across a volume that was owned by the Louisville YMCA after having belonged to six other libraries since the year 1816. M. Joblin & Co., *Louisville Past and Present: Its Industrial History as Exhibited in the Life-Labors of Its Leading Men* (Louisville: John P. Morton and Company, 1875), 254–68.

4. The date of 1848 is given on p. 1107 of the U.S. Bureau of Education's *Public Libraries in the United States of America: Special Report*. Part 1. (Washington, D.C.: Government Printing Office, 1876); a short history of the organization is given on p. 720 of Charles Theodore Greve's *Centennial History of Cincinnati and Representative Citizens* (Chicago: Biographical Publishing Co., 1904) vol. 1.

5. "Extract from Central Committee's Report to the Charleston Convention," *Quarterly Reporter of the Young Men's Christian Associations in North America* 3 (July 1858): 89.

6. "The Libraries of Young Men's Christian Associations" by Cephas Brainerd in U.S. Bureau of Education, *Public Libraries in the United States of America: Special Report*. Part 1, pp. 386–88.

7. David Kaser, *Books and Libraries in Camp and Battle: The Civil War Experience* (Westport, Conn.: Greenwood Press, 1984), 100.

8. Libraries aboard ships at sea are not included in this study. They are discussed in Harry R. Skallerup's *Books Afloat and Ashore: A History of Books, Libraries, and Reading Among Seamen During the Age of Sail* (Hamden, Conn.: Archon Books, 1974).

9. My records are not of much help in determining when various agricultural society libraries were founded because most of my information has been obtained from two contemporary surveys that seldom told when each library was founded: "Societies for Promoting Agriculture, State Boards, Etc." pp. 90–213 in U.S. Patent Office, *Report of the Commissioner of Patents for the Year 1858. Agriculture*, 35th Cong., 2d sess., 1859, S. Exec. Doc. 47 and "Agricultural and Horticultural Societies and Clubs" pp. 364–403 in U.S. Commissioner of Agriculture, *Report of the Commissioner of Agriculture for the Year 1867*, 40th Cong., 2d sess., 1868. H. Exec. Doc. 40.

10. Theodore Dwight Bozeman, in *Protestants in an Age of Science: The Baconian Ideal and Antebellum American Religious Thought* (Chapel Hill, N.C.: University of North Carolina Press, 1977), examines the attitudes of Protestant theologians.

11. Leslie W. Dunlap, *American Historical Societies, 1790–1860* (Madison, Wis.: Cantwell, 1944).

12. Dunlap, *American Historical Societies*, 74–75.

13. "Historical Societies in the United States: I. History and Condition" by Henry A. Homes, pp. 312–32 and "Table of Historical Societies in the United States," pp. 375–77 in U.S. Bureau of Education, *Public Libraries*.

14. Letter from David Rorer, Corresponding Secretary of the Iowa Historical and Geological Institute of Burlington, Iowa, quoted on p. 185 of Charles C. Jewett's

Appendix to the Report of the Board of Regents of the Smithsonian Institution, Containing a Report on the Public Libraries of the United States of America, January 1, 1850, 31st Cong., 1st sess., 1850, Sen. Misc. Doc. 120.

15. John Duffy, *From Humors to Medical Science: a History of American Medicine.* 2d ed. (Urbana: University of Illinois Press, 1993), especially pp. 143–50.

16. Lawrence M. Friedman's *A History of American Law*, 2d ed. (New York: Simon & Schuster, 1985) includes a comprehensive treatment of the role of law and lawyers in American society before 1876.

17. The ones in Texas are discussed in Theodore Albrecht's "The Music Libraries of the German Singing Societies in Texas, 1850–1855," *Music Library Association Notes* 31 (Mar. 1975): 517–29.

18. I have been unable to find much information about the young men's societies. C. Seymour Thompson on pp. 111–16 of his *Evolution of the American Public Library, 1653–1876* (Washington, D.C.: Scarecrow, 1952), mentions them briefly, as does Carl Bode, on pp. 244–45 of *The American Lyceum: Town Meeting of the Mind* (Carbondale and Edwardsville, Ill.: Southern Illinois University Press, 1968).

19. I found references to more than twenty societies for women students and three that admitted both genders by scanning Thomas S. Harding's *College Literary Societies: Their Contribution to Higher Education in the United States, 1815–1876* (New York: Pageant Press International, 1971) and the dissertation on which that book was based. I have located information about libraries in six of these.

20. Harding, *College Literary Societies.* The most detailed analysis of differences between student society libraries and the libraries provided by colleges is to be found in "A Comparative Analysis of Nineteenth-Century Academic and Literary Society Library Collections in the Midwest" by Michael J. Waldo (Ph.D. diss., Indiana University, 1985).

21. The most useful history of the lyceum movement is Carl Bode's *The American Lyceum: Town Meeting of the Mind.* However, this author, like some others, considers almost any library association that sponsored lectures to be part of the lyceum movement.

22. "Associations of Adults for Mutual Education," *American Journal of Education* 1 (Oct. 1826): 594–97; "Results of Lyceums," *American Annals of Education*, 3d ser., 1 (Nov. 1831): 528.

23. Mary Whiteford Graham, in "The Lyceum in Ohio from 1840–1860" (Ph.D. diss., Ohio State University, 1950), on p. 152, reports that Ohio lyceums provided opportunities for young men and women to get to know one another; surely, the situation in that state was not unique.

24. Haynes McMullen, "Ralph Waldo Emerson and Libraries," *Library Quarterly* 25 (Apr. 1955): 155.

25. Ray E. Held's book, *Public Libraries in California, 1849–1878* (Berkeley, Calif.: University of California Press, 1963) and his article, "The Odd Fellows' Library Associations in California," *Library Quarterly* 32 (Apr. 1962): 148–63. For fourteen of the thirty-three libraries belonging to fraternal orders in California, Held's work has been my only source of information. However, even without the ones that only Held mentions, that state had more than any other.

26. John Calvin Colson, "The Fire Company Library Associations of Baltimore, 1838–1858," *Journal of Library History* 21 (Winter 1986): 158–76.

27. Voluntary fire companies did not completely disappear. I have lived in two small towns where they still exist and in another where volunteers assist professional firemen.

Chapter 7

Libraries Belonging to Institutions, Some of Which Were Operated by Private Organizations and Some of Which Were Operated by Governmental Units

The kinds of libraries considered in chapters 5 and 6 all belonged to voluntary societies. The kinds of libraries gathered in the present chapter could have belonged either to societies or units within some government. Of course governments occasionally contributed in some way to the support of libraries established and operated by voluntary organizations, and in later years, some associations (particularly women's clubs) assisted local governments in the establishment of free public libraries. However, there were three kinds of libraries in the years before 1876 that were of concern both to members of associations and members of governmental bodies: those belonging to institutions of higher education, to hospitals, and to institutions established to care for persons with disabilities, institutions which have been called asylums in this study.

Table 7.1 shows that the general pattern of the distribution of these libraries in the different regions of the United States is somewhat like the distribution of all libraries in this study: more in the Northeast, fewer in the Middle West, fewer still in the South, and fewest in the Far West. However, this table also shows that any conclusion based on the general pattern for the three main kinds of libraries, considered together, has little meaning because the pattern for libraries in colleges and professional schools is quite different from the patterns for the other two kinds.

When the founding dates for the three kinds are considered together, a steady progression can be seen: from fourteen in the 1790s to 247 in the 1850s. There were only eighty-six in the years from 1861 to 1865, then a total of 310 for the ten-year span from 1866 to 1875. There were two noticeable differences between the patterns for the college and professional school libraries on the one hand and the hospital and asylum libraries on the other hand: (1) The collections in the academic libraries appeared earlier: twenty-one before 1791 whereas only two of the others were founded before that year. (2) In later years, the number of

Table 7.1
Libraries Belonging to Institutions, Some of Which Were Operated by Private Organizations and Some of Which Were Operated by Governmental Units

	Northeast	South	Middle West	Far West	All U.S.
Libraries in colleges and professional schools					
Liberal arts colleges for men	91	156	188	31	466
Liberal arts colleges for women	8	18	13	0	39
Theological seminaries	58	30	43	2	133
Medical schools	30	19	30	2	81
Law schools	11	8	12	0	31
Engineering and scientific schools	17	2	3	2	24
Agricultural colleges	5	5	5	0	15
Other schools	8	4	2	0	14
Total	228	242	296	37	803
Libraries in hospitals					
Medical	20	2	2	0	24
For patients	6	2	0	2	10
Medical and for patients	0	0	1	0	1
Uncertain	10	2	5	0	17
Total	36	6	8	2	52
Libraries in asylums					
Orphanages	59	14	16	2	91
For the mentally ill	27	11	15	1	54
For the physically disabled	7	3	10	1	21
For soldiers and sailors	12	4	3	0	19
For women	7	0	1	0	8
Others	25	2	5	1	33
Total	137	34	50	5	226
Total in all institutions	401	282	354	44	1,081

libraries being established in hospitals and asylums increased much more rapidly than did the number of new college or professional school libraries. New collections in hospitals and asylums increased from forty-nine in the 1850s to 103 in the ten years from 1866 through 1875 whereas the increase in new academic libraries went from 197 to only 207 in the same length of time.

Because all of these libraries were attached to other organizations, it is possible that the times when more academic libraries were being founded were the times when more colleges and professional schools were being established. In the case of academic libraries, this is probably true because, typically, a college or professional school formed a library very close to the time when students first attended, and it seems likely that the sources used for this study came fairly close to listing all of the colleges that existed.[1]

For hospitals and asylums, on the other hand, it is clear that the libraries that have found their way into the available records were owned by only a fraction of the existing institutions. And the fraction varied among the different kinds of institutions. For example, as we shall see, it seems to have been much higher among mental asylums than among almshouses.

The three major kinds of libraries in this chapter (those in colleges or professional schools, those in hospitals, and those in asylums) shared one characteristic, although they shared it with some other libraries as well: they all belonged to agencies that were intended to help persons who were not agency members. Benevolence was a motive in establishing and maintaining the organizations that owned these collections.

In this chapter, the entire group of 1,081 libraries will be examined first, and then each of the three major kinds will be considered separately. The entire group was large enough to indicate that many Americans who were in some way concerned with the welfare of other persons believed that libraries were appropriate tools for benevolent agencies to use in their work. However, Table 4.1 shows that the total number of libraries established by societies for their own members' use (considered earlier in chapters 5 and 6) was far greater. Most of the libraries in the first two groups in Table 4.1 (that is, most of those in the total of 5,623 libraries) were intended to provide reading matter for members. And most of the libraries in the fourth group in Table 4.1, the ones that were established only by governmental units, were supported by taxpayers both for their own use and for any citizens who did not pay taxes. This was clearly true for the 1,407 locally supported free public libraries within that group.

Some Americans living before 1876 may not have cared whether institutions designed to help others were operated by governments or by voluntary organizations, but many of them did care. There was a definite feeling that higher education should be under the control of religious groups; in some states, government-supported colleges were neglected.[2] On the other hand, there is little evidence of opposition to government control of hospitals and asylums. Sometimes city governments and benevolent societies cooperated in humanitarian enterprises.[3]

Whatever the attitudes of Americans about the control of the kinds of institutions considered in this section, governments seem to have been in charge of relatively few. Of the total of 1,081 libraries, governmental units controlled 155; voluntary organizations controlled 843, and for eighty-three, all of them in hospitals and asylums, it was impossible to be certain, from the available information, what kind of organization was in control. The number of the libraries of uncertain ownership was great enough to prevent any more than very general statements about the role of governments as opposed to voluntary organizations.

There are other reasons for caution in using the information gathered about the libraries in this section. A few belonged to institutions that changed from private to governmental control or vice versa before 1876. As far as possible, the status of the institution at the time of the founding of its library has been considered in this study. A few of the colonial colleges had a measure of control by both governmental and private bodies. Because religious bodies seem to have had a larger measure of this control, the collections belonging to these "semi-state" colleges have been considered as having been under private control in the present study. Almost all of the college libraries belonging to governmental units were operated by states: sixty-one out of the total sixty-six.

Governments played only a small part in the establishment of libraries in academic, hospital, or asylum libraries before the 1820s. Governments were responsible for the founding of only eight libraries before that decade; seven of those were in colleges or professional schools. During the 1820s, 1830s, and 1850s, the percentage of new libraries in institutions of higher education, in hospitals, and in asylums that were established by governments remained between 9 and 12 percent. In the 1840s it was higher: 15.5 percent, mainly because mental hospitals were being established in several states. In the ten years from 1866 through 1875, the percentage of new government libraries rose to 16.8 percent, partly because of the formation of libraries in the new state colleges and professional schools.

LIBRARIES IN COLLEGES AND PROFESSIONAL SCHOOLS

We have already seen that many libraries had to be located in small towns if they were to be of value to Americans. There were at least four reasons why libraries in colleges and professional schools needed to be in or near small towns: (1) During much of the period, the difficulty of travel and the expense involved made it desirable for a young person to be able to obtain higher education close to his or her home. (2) Because of the belief in the benefits of a general education, most persons did not need advanced or specialized courses obtainable in only a few of the "better" colleges. (3) Although control of a college was most frequently in the hands of a particular religious denomination, establishing the college in a town was often a matter of local pride, and private citizens with other religious affiliations contributed to its support.[4] (4) A library was considered essential in an institution, even though, by standards of a later day, the collection might not be well supported or heavily used.

In this study, first, all academic libraries will be considered as a group. Then, libraries in the following kinds of institutions will be considered separately: (a) liberal arts colleges for men, (b) liberal arts colleges for women, (c) professional schools in theology, medicine, law, science and engineering, and agriculture, and (d) a few schools that prepared students for other vocations.

The distribution of libraries in colleges and professional schools before 1876 was quite different from the distribution of all libraries in the study. New England had a much smaller proportion of academic libraries. It had only 8.7 percent of the collections in colleges and professional schools and 26.3 percent of those in all of the libraries in the study. Among the reasons for this difference in proportions were the tremendous enthusiasm in that region for social libraries, and a tendency to discourage the foundation of new colleges.[5] All three sections of the South were quite hospitable to colleges; that region as a whole had 30.1 percent of the college libraries and only 15.3 percent of the libraries in the study. Perhaps southern colleges were not as closely tied to their local areas as were the institutions responsible for the presence of other kinds of libraries. The feeling of southerners in the later years that young men should be educated in southern institutions could have affected this.

Two parts of the country where the proportion of college and professional school libraries were about the same as the proportion of all libraries were the Middle West and the Far West. The Middle West had 37.4 percent of all libraries and 36.8 percent of the ones belonging to institutions of higher education; the Far West had 4.7 percent of all libraries and 4.6 percent of those in colleges and professional schools.

When the dates of founding of libraries belonging to higher education institutions are considered, the information is unusually full—for about nineteen out of every twenty libraries. However, the information is not always reliable: sources often disagree about the date for a library. An institution may have started as a secondary school, only gradually becoming a college as it began to offer more advanced courses; the library could have been older than the college. For the purposes of this study, in such a case, the date for the library has been considered to be the date when the institution began to offer college-level courses—if that date can be discovered with a reasonable amount of searching.

The earliest college library seems to have been Harvard's, established in 1638; no evidence has been discovered of any library in the Spanish West before the nineteenth century. On the east coast, a few more were founded during colonial and revolutionary days, but the rate of founding did not begin to increase significantly until the 1820s. After that, there was a fairly rapid increase through the 1850s; from 1851 through 1860, 197 libraries were founded. This increase occurred, at least partly, because of the Second Great Awakening when new religious groups wanted their own colleges.[6] Of course the population of the country increased during these years, but that increase does not seem to have been the main cause of the increase in the rate of founding; the number of collections in colleges and professional schools was growing faster than the population was increasing from the 1820s through the 1850s.[7] After a decrease during the Civil War, new libraries began to appear at about the same rate as before the war: from 1866 through 1875, 209 were established.

The role of the federal and state governments had little effect on the increase in the number of libraries in colleges and professional schools before the Civil War. Only sixty-six out of the 803 libraries serving higher education in this country before 1876 were controlled by governments. However, that number is open to question because a few institutions passed from private to public control before that date, and as mentioned above, a very few quasi-governmental colleges existed, which had representatives of both government and private interests on their boards of control.

Most of the institutions under government control appeared late in the period: only fourteen had been established before the 1840s, and twenty-nine did not appear until after the Civil War. In the South, no academic libraries of any kind were started from 1861 through 1871, but seven were founded from 1872 through 1875, all seven under state control.

The effect of the Civil War on the rate of founding of libraries in all kinds of colleges and professional schools was noticeable, but the difference between the percentage being founded after 1860 in the South and the North was not as great as might be expected. In the South, 28.4 percent of the libraries were established after 1860 and in the North, 36.7 percent. Within both the South and the North, the pattern for the regions and sub-regions was what one might expect. Always, the areas that were settled later had a higher percentage of libraries founded after 1860: in the South the lowest figure was 21.4 for the South Atlantic sub-region and the highest was 48.6 for the West South Central. In the Northeast, 30.2 percent of the libraries were established between 1861 and 1875 and, in the Far West, the percentage was 67.6.

We have already noticed that libraries belonging to institutions of higher education tended to have long lives. Almost exactly three-fourths (600 out of 803) were still listed in the available records as existing in 1875, and some of the others may have lasted that long. The distribution of these libraries in various parts of the country in 1875 was much the same as the distribution of all the collections belonging to colleges and professional schools that had been established before 1876. The only regions where there was a noticeable difference were the Northeast and the South. In the Northeast, 81.1 percent of all libraries were clearly still alive at the end of the period and in the South, 66.9 percent. For the Middle West, the percentage was 76, and for the Far West, 75.7, both figures close to the average for the entire United States of 74.7 percent.

It might be expected that the collections that disappeared from the available records before 1876 were the ones that were started in the eighteenth and the earliest part of the nineteenth century. Such was not the case. Of the eighteen founded through 1785, all lasted until 1875 except one at the Litchfield Law School at Litchfield, Connecticut, which existed only from 1784 until about 1820. Expressed in percentages of libraries that disappeared from the records before 1875, the years through 1785 lost only 5.8 percent. The percentages from the years 1786 through 1835 was higher (21.9), and the libraries first mentioned from 1846 through 1860 were much more likely to disappear (38.2 percent). As might be expected, only a few of the collections appearing in 1861 or later were missing in the records for 1875 (8.3 percent).

The reasons for the differences in the percentages of libraries that disappeared before 1875 are not clear. Perhaps, if the founding of some colleges and their libraries was related to sectarian religious feelings aroused by the Second Great Awakening during the 1840s and 1850s, the demise of a higher percentage of those libraries can be attributed to the diminution of such feelings by 1875.

Liberal Arts Colleges for Men. The title of this section may need a little qualification. It might have read "...for Men, Boys, and a Few Women" because some colleges admitted younger students than is customary today, and because, even though almost all of the colleges in this group were originally intended for males, women had been admitted, often rather grudgingly, to approximately a hundred American men's colleges by the end of the period.[8]

The chronological pattern for the founding of libraries in men's colleges was generally similar to that described above for all academic libraries, but there were a few differences. The collections in men's colleges constituted from 50 to 70 percent of the total for all colleges and professional schools except for a few times in the early years of the nineteenth century when an increase in the founding of other kinds—especially those in theological seminaries—brought the contribution of the men's colleges down below 50 percent. By the 1870s, several new kinds of institutions of higher education were growing in number, but the enthusiasm for establishing libraries in men's colleges did not diminish as these kinds of institutions appeared.

The figures for the geographical distribution of libraries in men's colleges, shown in Table 7.1, indicate that the Northeast had an even lower percentage of libraries in men's schools than it had for libraries in all colleges and professional schools, 19.5 percent for men's colleges and 28.4 percent for all kinds. Figures for New England, not shown in that table, list libraries in men's colleges as 3.6 percent of the total for the United States; that sub-region had 8.7 percent of the libraries in all academic institutions. As with all collections in colleges and professional schools, the South had more than its share, if we consider its share of all libraries to indicate what might be expected.

Liberal Arts Colleges for Women. Throughout much of the nineteenth century, reformers were advocating better education for women. One result of this was the admission of women to men's colleges, mentioned above; another result was the establishment of separate colleges for women.[9]

There can be some doubt about the figures for women's colleges shown in Table 7.1. Our ideas today as to what constitutes college-level work may be different from those of the persons who operated some of the schools; it is possible that a few of those libraries should be eliminated. Only two of the post-war libraries belonged to the stronger women's colleges that began to appear after the war: Vassar's in 1865 and Wellesley's in 1875. Smith College was founded in 1875, but its library has not been included in this study; it consisted of one book and two newspaper subscriptions during that year.[10]

The chronological pattern of founding for women's college libraries was quite different from the pattern for most kinds of libraries included in this study: fewer in the early years, more in the middle years, and fewer in the later years. Of thirty-six libraries with founding dates that could be discovered, twenty-two appeared during the 1850s. Only seven were established from 1866 through 1875. During those years, some feminists opposed separate education for women, but a connection between their views and these statistics cannot be proved. Because the total number of libraries in women's colleges was small, no particular importance should be attached to the geographic distribution shown in Table 7.1.

At least four collections in colleges or professional schools intended for women have not been counted here but have (perhaps arbitrarily) been included later in this chapter: one in a medical college for women in Boston, another for a medical college in Philadelphia (a library which belonged to the Philadelphia School of Design), and one belonging to the Vassar College Observatory.

Theological Seminaries. We have already noticed several ways in which Americans' pervasive concern for religious matters resulted in the establishment of libraries. An additional way was in the establishment of seminaries for training clergy. Even though many colleges provided instruction in religion, several Protestant denominations began to establish theological seminaries after the Revolution, some of which were affiliated with the colleges.[11]

The first library in a seminary appeared in 1784, the date when the first seminary was founded, that of the Reformed Church in America, located in New Brunswick, New Jersey. The chronological pattern for the founding of seminary libraries was somewhat different from that of the other kinds of libraries in colleges and professional schools. As with the others, there were few established before an increase began in the latter part of the decade from 1811 through 1820. But after the 1820s, the rate of founding for seminary libraries generally did not share in the rapid increase for academic libraries. In the 1820s, about a third of all academic libraries being established (34.0 percent) were in theological seminaries; in the 1830s about one in five (20.9 percent) of the new libraries were in those institutions, and by the ten-year span after the Civil War (1866 though 1875), seminary libraries constituted only 11.6 percent of those being founded. This pattern seems to indicate the effect of the religious movement called the Second Great Awakening more clearly than does the pattern for all academic libraries, mentioned earlier. This movement was at its height around the 1820s and 1830s, when seminary libraries constituted a relatively high percentage of those being founded in colleges and professional schools.

There were only a few libraries in Catholic seminaries before the 1840s, and the total number that appeared after that date was small. Only about twenty of the 133 seminaries in Table 7.1 belonged to Catholic institutions. Collections in Jewish seminaries were just beginning to appear by 1875.

The distribution of libraries belonging to theological seminaries in various parts of the country was somewhat different from the distribution of other kinds of academic libraries listed in Table 7.1. The Northeast had 43.6 percent of the seminary libraries and only 28.4 of all libraries in colleges and professional schools. Pennsylvania provided considerably more than did any other Northeastern state: twenty-one out of the total fifty-eight. Pennsylvania had a relatively high proportion of the three other kinds of religious libraries included in this study, as well. For collections belonging to each of these: churches, religious social libraries, and other religious societies, Pennsylvania had more than any other in the Northeast. And for these three, combined, Pennsylvania had 31.8 percent of the libraries in the Northeast, whereas, for all kinds of libraries, it had only 16.5 percent. Could it be that the long tradition of religious tolerance in that state had the effect of encouraging the establishment of a significant variety of organizations that had libraries?

Medical Schools. In considering libraries belonging to medical societies, in chapter 6, we noticed that physicians were only moderately successful in curing diseases before 1876 and that members of the profession often disagreed about procedures.[12] Perhaps the resulting lack of confidence of the public had something to do with the slow increase in the number of collections being established in medical schools. It is also possible that because schools were often operated by one or a few doctors, students used books from the physicians' personal collections, which were not considered school libraries.

Libraries in medical schools seem to have appeared earlier than those in theological seminaries. The Medical Department at the University of Pennsylvania in Philadelphia claimed that its library was founded in 1765, and Harvard's medical school at Boston was credited with a collection established in 1782. But the number of libraries in medical schools grew more slowly than the number in theological seminaries; founding dates before 1840 have been discovered for only twenty. They were established somewhat more rapidly after that date, but in 1875, only sixty-six seem to have existed at a time when eighty-eight of the theological libraries were still alive.

The figures in Table 7.1 show that, considering all libraries that existed before 1876, the eighty-eight collections serving medical schools were not as likely to be located in the Northeast as were the ones serving theological seminaries; that region had 43.6 percent of the ones in seminaries, but only 37.0 percent of those in medical schools.

Law Schools. In the section of chapter 6 about bar association libraries it was mentioned that the number of lawyers and the amount of legal literature increased rapidly before 1876. However, the number of libraries in law schools increased more slowly than the number in medical schools or theological seminaries. There may have been several reasons for this. Law students may have had access to any of the other sources of legal information that existed: the collections built by legal societies (already noted in chapter 6); the private libraries belonging to faculty members, who were often practicing lawyers; or collections that were owned by courts or other governmental bodies, which are considered later in chapter 8.

The earliest law school library on record was the one established at the Litchfield Law School in Litchfield, Connecticut, in 1784.[13] But Table 7.1 shows only thirty more that were founded before 1876; approximately half of these date from the years after the Civil War. The number is too small to justify definite statements about the geographic distribution. However, there is no indication that it was much different from that for medical schools. By 1875, recent activity in the Middle West had brought its total in the available records to eleven; the Northeast had eight and the South, five.

Engineering and Scientific Schools. In the section of chapter 6 concerning scientific and engineering societies we noted the widespread interest in science among Americans in the colonial period and the early years of the nineteenth century; many scientific societies had been founded by 1876, but only a few organizations seem to have had a particular interest in engineering.

The situation was somewhat different in regard to collections serving colleges or departments within schools that taught science or engineering. Science only slowly found its way into the college curriculum, and engineering courses had only a few students even after the need for roads, canals, and bridges created a demand for professional engineers. As in other professions, beginners often preferred to learn through practice under the guidance of a person established in the field.[14]

The total of twenty-four scientific or engineering collections shown in Table 7.1 consisted of eleven in schools that primarily taught civil engineering, three in schools of mining engineering, two in scientific colleges, four in observatories operated by colleges, and four in museums or botanical gardens operated by colleges. Actually, other libraries in institutions of higher education contained books that supported the teaching of engineering. Around the middle of the century a few liberal arts colleges included courses in engineering in their curricula, and after the Morrill Act of 1862 encouraged the teaching of agriculture and engineering in the same institution, several collections, mentioned in the next section of this chapter, probably had a substantial number of books related to engineering.

The libraries that supported the teaching of science or engineering before 1876 were concentrated in the Northeast. The seventeen collections shown in Table 7.1 for that region were about evenly divided between the New England states (with nine) and the others (with eight). Five of the nine New England libraries were connected with one institution: Harvard College.

The earliest scientific or engineering school represented in Table 7.1 was the Rensselaer Polytechnic Institute, which had a library from the date of its founding, 1824, but the U.S. Military Academy at West Point, New York, established in 1802, taught military engineering; some of its graduates became engineers as civilians. After Rensselaer, no other scientific or engineering library appears in the available records until the 1840s, and only a few were founded before the Civil War. Twelve appeared from 1864 through 1875, four of them serving scientific departments and eight of them in engineering schools. The passage of the Morrill Act may have been responsible for the increased number during these years.

Agricultural Colleges. Americans were even slower to accept the idea of post-secondary education related to agriculture than the idea of similar education for science and engineering. The first full-fledged agricultural college is usually considered to be the State Agricultural College that was established in Lansing, Michigan, in 1857. Its library was started during its year of founding, and only two others, at Pennsylvania State College and at Kansas State Agricultural College in Manhattan, were available before the Morrill Act of 1862 provided for federal aid to agricultural education as well as education for the "mechanic arts."[15] Of the total of fifteen institutions holding the libraries in the available records, seven were called *agricultural colleges* and another, the Bussey Institution, belonging to Harvard College, was actually an agricultural school. The other seven were called *agricultural and mechanical colleges*; The records do not indicate what portion of their collections was related to agriculture. These libraries were rather evenly scattered across the country as far west as Texas and Kansas. Each of fourteen states had at least one.

Schools Training for Other Occupations. The fourteen libraries classed as belonging to "other schools" in Table 7.1 consisted of seven in military schools, four in business colleges, two in teachers' colleges, and one in an art school. The U.S. Military Academy at West Point, mentioned above in connection with engineering education, had the earliest, established in 1802; all of the rest were founded in the 1840s or later. Ten of them were to be found in the East: eight in the Middle Atlantic states and two in the South Atlantic area.

The seven libraries in the military schools probably resembled those in engineering schools. All of the business colleges were proprietary schools, and two of them, one in Brooklyn and one in Trenton, New Jersey, were members of a well-known group, the Bryant and Stratton chain. The two teachers' colleges, one in Shippensburg, Pennsylvania, and one in Edinboro, Pennsylvania, were both offering post-secondary work before 1876, but they, like many other teachers' colleges, were classed as secondary schools in the 1876 *Report* of the U.S. Bureau of Education. The Philadelphia School of Design for Women already had a library when it began offering college-level courses in 1846. It is possible that none of the seven schools in the fields of business, teacher education, or art would be considered a college today, and it is likely that others of their kinds had collections that could be considered college libraries.

LIBRARIES IN HOSPITALS

During most of the years before 1876, Americans who became physically ill were cared for at home when possible. Hospitals mainly provided care for persons who could not be taken care of at home—including those without a home, such as strangers in town, sailors, or the indigent. Physicians and hospital employees provided much the same kind of care as other people could because medicine had not yet become an esoteric, advanced art. Most hospitals were maintained by groups of charitably inclined persons, the same kind of people who were responsible for the institutions considered in this study under the heading of asylums.[16]

The distinction between hospitals intended for the physically ill (considered in this section) and the institutions for the mentally ill (sometimes called hospitals) could not always be maintained, although the managers often preferred to keep the mentally ill in a separate facility.

Two kinds of libraries in hospitals for the physically ill were recognized: the ones intended for patients and the ones for the medical staff. Of the fifty-four libraries that could be identified, twenty-five were clearly medical, for the staff, and nine were for patients. However, the intended use for twenty others was unclear so nothing precise can be said about the relative prevalence of the two types. At one hospital, the library was meant to serve both the medical staff and the patients.

Hospital libraries were rare before the nineteenth century. The earliest was at the Pennsylvania Hospital in Philadelphia, established in 1762 according to most authorities, but of the forty-seven with known founding dates, only nine had appeared before the 1840s; from then on, the rate of founding was more rapid; it did not change much before 1865; it increased somewhat after the war.

Various governments established hospitals that had libraries; the federal government operated at least eight, state governments operated six, and local governments, four. However, there were nine other hospitals that may have been under government control. The earliest library in a government hospital with a known founding date was the U.S. Marine Hospital in Chelsea, Massachusetts, which was opened in 1821. There was no tendency for governments to replace voluntary organizations in the establishment of hospital libraries; in each of the five-year measuring periods from 1851 through 1875, more were being founded by non-governmental bodies than by governments; Americans were still viewing the establishment of these libraries as primarily the duty of benevolent groups.

Before 1876, the great majority of the hospital libraries were to be found in the Northeast: thirty-eight out of fifty-four. Almost all the rest were in the South or Middle West. The available records show only two libraries west of the Mississippi River; both of them were tiny collections for patients at military forts in Wyoming. Northeastern libraries had long lives; all of the New England libraries still existed in 1875 as did all but one of those in the Middle-Atlantic states.

LIBRARIES IN ASYLUMS

Already, in this chapter, a distinction has been made between libraries intended for the use of persons who established and maintained the collections, and libraries intended for the use of other persons. An important group of the latter were to be found in institutions provided for the care of people who were unable to care for themselves. Libraries for patients in hospitals, of course, belong to this group. For the purposes of this study, all other collections in residential establishments have been considered together under the term *asylums*, a term that was often used before 1876.

Historians have written, in recent years, about the concern that Americans expressed for the welfare of the less fortunate before 1876. The scholars have critically examined the motives of those who tried to help others.[17] The present study cannot consider motivation in detail, and is limited to noticing when and where Americans decided that collections of books were appropriate adjuncts for institutions that were established for charitable purposes.

Of the 226 asylum libraries that could be identified, 137 were in the Northeast; within that region, New York, with sixty-two, had more than any other state, and Pennsylvania was next with thirty-eight. It is not surprising that so many were to be found in the Northeast because the need for asylums was most obvious in cities. However, New England had only thirty-four, whereas the Middle-Atlantic states had 103.

The rate of founding for libraries in asylums was generally like that for most other kinds of libraries but was very different in one particular way. Few were founded before the 1830s. The number increased from the 1830s into the early 1850s. The number appearing in the late 1850s decreased somewhat, perhaps due to chance, but there was a marked increase during the Civil War, a time when Americans were establishing fewer libraries of other kinds. The number for 1861 through 1865 was twenty-six, more than the number established during any of the earlier five-year measuring periods. After the war, the number was higher yet: fifty-one from 1866 through 1870 and 38 for 1871 through 1875. The increase after 1861 was not caused by any single kind of library, but collections in orphanages were founded more frequently than others. Libraries for Army veterans also increased, but the total number of these at any time was small: only nine could be identified for all the years before 1876.

The disruption caused by the Civil War could have had either of two effects on the founding of libraries in establishments that depended on charity. The need for asylums might have become greater, but the ability to finance them could have decreased. In the South, where economic conditions were bad after the war, new collections appeared in asylums, but at a slower rate than in the North. Of the ones for which founding dates could be discovered, seventeen southern libraries appeared before 1861 and only twelve from 1861 through 1875, whereas, in the North, the number increased from seventy-two before 1861 to 103 in the years beginning with 1861.

At the end of the period included in this study, at least 204 asylum libraries still existed, approximately nine out of every ten with known founding dates (89.4 percent). Perhaps this good showing was partly caused by the fact that so many had been established just before 1875: the total of 115 for the years beginning with 1861 was 56.4 percent of all those with known founding dates.

Governmental units were responsible for a substantial portion of the asylums that had libraries, although as with hospitals, it is impossible to give an exact number because the ownership of so many asylums could not be determined for this study. Governments controlled sixty-seven of the institutions, and voluntary associations controlled eighty-two, but for seventy-seven, ownership could not be determined.

Of the libraries belonging to units of governments, fifty-one were maintained by states, ten by the federal government, and six by local governments. As with hospitals, there was no tendency of governments to replace non-governmental organizations as founders of asylum libraries over the years; collections belonging to both groups increased at approximately the same rate. Of the libraries established from 1861 through 1875, governments were responsible for 22.6 percent.

Orphanages. During the middle decades of the nineteenth century the welfare of children was perhaps of greater concern to Americans than was the welfare of any other part of the population. So it is not surprising that of the 226 libraries belonging to asylums of all types, more were to be found in orphanages than in any other kind: a total of ninety.

Libraries existed in various kinds of institutions for the care of children. Some homes were intended for girls, some for boys, some for children of soldiers or sailors, some for children of different ethnic backgrounds, and some for delinquent children. Some were primarily schools; their libraries may have been similar to those in other schools. As with several other kinds of charitable establishments, more were found in the Middle Atlantic states than in any other geographic subdivision. New York had twenty-six, Pennsylvania nineteen, and no other state had more than eight.

Orphanages were rare in America in the eighteenth century and the early decades of the nineteenth century, so it is not surprising that no records of libraries existing before the 1820s were discovered for this study. They appeared occasionally into the 1850s and then more rapidly: fifteen were established during the war years, 1861 through 1865, more than in any previous five-year period. The rate of founding was even greater after 1865: forty-eight were established from 1866 through 1875. Interest in child welfare was increasing in the years just before war broke out, and one of the results of the war was a more rapid growth of concern during and just after the war.[18] The increased provision of libraries in orphanages could have been the direct result of this general increase in concern for the welfare of children. In the South only six orphanage libraries appeared before the war; no new ones were started until 1865, but eight were established from that year through 1875. By 1875 all except one of the orphanages still had libraries. However, this situation did not imply unusual longevity for this kind of library because half of them were established in the final ten years of the period.

Asylums for the Mentally Ill. Libraries were considered to be valuable assets in the treatment of insanity during the years from about 1830 to 1855, a period when "moral and humane" treatment of mental patients was being advocated by superintendents of asylums and "retreats." For many other kinds of libraries, we can assume approval simply because Americans founded so many of them. But for collections in mental institutions we have a body of printed material written by "experts" who advocated the provision of libraries to aid in treatment by helping the patients to focus on something other than their troublesome environment.[19]

Of the fifty-four libraries in asylums or hospitals for persons who were mentally ill, twenty-seven were in the Northeast. The others were distributed approximately as were other asylums; only one was to be found in the Far West. The dates of founding for collections in asylums for the mentally ill could be determined for only forty: two in the 1820s, four in the 1830s, then an average of about one per year until the Civil War. Only three were established from 1861 through 1865; then there were eleven from 1866 through 1875. Apparently, no new ones appeared in the South after 1864. At the end of the period, records show forty-three that still existed; they were distributed in approximately the same way as the total number that had been founded at any time: twenty-two in the Northeast, seven in the South, thirteen in the Middle West, and only one in the Far West.

Homes for Soldiers and Sailors. If the title for this section were to consider chronology it would read "...Sailors and Soldiers" because all of the ten libraries for seamen had been founded before sources mention eight of the nine collections in homes for soldiers.

The earliest libraries for sailors were two, established in 1699 in small seaport towns in South Carolina. There are no records concerning others until the 1830s; by that time, small libraries were often provided for ships that were to go on extended sea voyages (not included in the present study).[20] Four of the ones on land were founded during the 1830s; the remaining five appeared from 1843 through 1863. At least two of this total of ten were intended for navy men.

The first of the nine collections in soldiers' homes was established in 1850; all the rest were founded after the Civil War or were first mentioned during the post-war years. Most were operated by the federal government. The contents of these libraries may have been similar to the contents of the much larger number of garrison libraries, which were mostly established by the men themselves with the financial aid of the government and with, in many cases, gifts from charitable organizations. The post libraries are considered in chapter 8 at the end of the section on libraries belonging to the federal government. Six of the collections in homes for soldiers were located in states along the eastern seaboard, two were in Ohio, and one in Wisconsin.

Homes for the Physically Disabled. Twenty-one libraries served institutions that were formed to aid persons with particular physical disabilities; some of these agencies may have been primarily schools. Of the twenty-one, there were twelve in institutions for the deaf, two in institutions that served both the deaf and the blind, and four in institutions that were only for the blind. Presumably the libraries for the blind contained books with raised symbols of one or more of the systems that existed before 1876. One other agency was for "the ruptured and crippled," one was a "consumptives' home," and one was an "inebriates' asylum." Perhaps the last two named above could have been included with the hospitals that were considered earlier in this chapter.

The library in the institution for alcoholics is noteworthy because it is the only one identified for this study even though American reformers saw the use of alcohol as one of the main reasons for crime and general misery during much of the nineteenth century.[21] Surely, various other asylums must have joined, in some way, in the fight against the demon rum.

The libraries serving establishments designed for the benefit of the disabled were distributed in a pattern that was not very different from the pattern for all the kinds of libraries in this study: six in the Northeast, three in the South, and nine in the Middle West; the only one farther west than the state of Missouri was in Berkeley, California. Few libraries in establishments for physically disabled persons appear in the records before the 1850s. One for the deaf was founded in 1817, and one for the blind in 1831. The rest appeared sporadically from 1849 through 1865. It is difficult to say anything definite about the role of government because the ownership of nine libraries could not be determined. Agencies of state governments established eight, and only two were clearly owned by voluntary organizations. Sources listed only ten as existing in 1875.

Homes for Women. Before 1876 it was difficult for single women to make a living. For many, domestic servitude or sewing were the only possibilities; during part of the period, some would find employment in factories, but wages were very low. The libraries for women that have already been mentioned in this study seem to have been established mainly by married women of the middle class. There was some concern for the welfare of women who had little or no income, but the total number of libraries in homes for these women was small: only eight could be discovered, all of them provided by voluntary associations.

Seven of the eight collections in homes for women were in the Northeast. As with several other kinds of charitable establishments, New York State had the most: four. The eight libraries included some intended for particular groups of women: for working women, women prisoners, or older women. One of the few institutions of any kind for Jews was a home for Jewish widows and orphans established in New Orleans in 1875. In this study its library has been counted with those in orphanages and has not been included in the total for women. The earliest library in an institution for the care of women was in a "female asylum," established in 1809. Only four appeared before 1860; the other four had founding dates from 1860 through 1870. Seven of the eight still existed in 1875.

Other Asylums. Apparently, very few libraries existed to serve two kinds of asylums or homes: almshouses and homes for men. Many almshouses for the indigent were in operation, but only three libraries for them could be identified for this study, and one of those, in Philadelphia, was a medical library. Only one home for men (other than soldiers or sailors) was identified. There was a definite feeling against benevolence that might encourage indolence among men; however, in the later years some homes for elderly men appeared.[22] Of course, men who could earn a living had access to many kinds of libraries already considered in this study.

Unfortunately, the intended beneficiaries of twenty-nine asylums or homes could not be determined. However, it seems likely that a good share of them were orphan asylums. Eight were called *houses of refuge,* a term that was ordinarily used for homes for juvenile delinquents. These may have been very much like the reform schools that are included in the next chapter. All but seven of the asylums for which the purpose could not be determined were in the Northeast. New York State had fourteen, eight of them in New York City. No other state had more than five. Twelve had been founded before the Civil War; the rest were formed from 1864 through 1873. All still existed in 1875.

REGIONAL DIFFERENCES

The institutions whose libraries have been considered in chapter 7 can be divided into two distinct groups as far as regional differences are concerned: colleges and professional schools on the one hand and hospitals and asylums on the other. Perhaps the geographical distribution of libraries in colleges and professional schools has been described sufficiently in the first part of this chapter. And because the purposes of hospitals and asylums were so much alike, it may be well to consider them together.

The hospital and asylum libraries were much more likely to be found in the Northeast than were most other libraries. For all of the libraries in the study, 42.6 percent were in the Northeast; for hospital and asylum libraries, that region had 62.2 percent. And within the Northeast, the Middle Atlantic states had an unusually high proportion, 45.0 percent of the country's total. For all libraries, that sub-region had only 16.3 percent. Within the Northeast, the cities of New York and Philadelphia had a high proportion of these libraries: of the total of 173 collections, thirty-nine were in New York and twenty-eight in Philadelphia. Boston had thirteen of the forty-eight in New England. This concentration in coastal cities is not surprising because they had, at least beginning in the 1830s, unusually large numbers of persons of the "lower classes" who were in need of care. Smaller towns in the East and elsewhere were more likely to have only small almshouses, which apparently seldom had libraries.

In the South, libraries in hospitals and asylums constituted almost as high a proportion as the South had of all libraries: 14.4 percent of the ones belonging to hospitals and asylums, and 15.2 percent of all kinds of libraries. Again, a relatively high proportion appeared in coastal cities: of the forty in the entire South, twenty-nine were in the South Atlantic sub-region, and fifteen of those were in Baltimore, Washington, D.C., or Columbia, South Carolina.

The situation in the Middle West and the Far West is probably shown with sufficient detail in Table 7.1. Numbers for some categories there are so small that they have little significance. For most kinds of asylums, the Middle West had fewer than the Northeast and more than the South. Figures not shown in that table reveal a pattern for the nine sub-regions similar to the pattern for all kinds of libraries; not so many in the areas of later settlement, where there were fewer towns of any size.

NOTES

1. Several years ago, when my records included a total of 799 libraries instead of the 803 on which the present study is based, I discussed the tendency of colleges to establish libraries close to the dates of founding of the colleges, and I compared the number of libraries in my records with the numbers on several lists of early schools. "The Founding of Libraries in American Colleges and Professional Schools before 1876" in the book *For the Good of the Order: Essays in Honor of Edward G. Holley*, ed. Delmus E. Williams and others (Greenwich, Conn.: JAI Press, 1994), 37–54.

2. Donald G. Tewksbury, *The Founding of American Colleges and Universities before the Civil War* (Hamden, Conn.: Archon Books, 1965), 135.

3. This was true in New York City before 1830. "From City Fathers to Social Critics: Humanitarianism and Government in New York, 1790–1860," by M. J. Heale, *Journal of American History* 63 (June 1976): 21–41.

4. Historians have disagreed about the relative importance of "localism" versus "denominationalism" in the spread of colleges across America. For example, James Findlay's "Agency, Denominations, and the Western College, 1830–1860: Some Connections between Evangelicalism and American Higher Education," *Church History* 50 (Mar. 1981): 64–80 emphasizes the role of the churches. Anne L. Wilhite discusses local "boosterism" in her "Cities and Colleges in the Promised Land: Territorial Nebraska, 1854–1867," *Nebraska History* 67 (Winter 1986): 327–71.

5. Colin B. Burke in *American Collegiate Populations: A Test of the Traditional View* (New York: New York University Press, 1982) on p. 33 mentions New England restrictions on the founding of colleges.

6. The ideas and events associated with the Second Great Awakening are described in detail in William McLaughlin's book, *Revivals, Awakenings, and Reform: An Essay on Religion and Social Change in America, 1607–1977* (Chicago: University of Chicago Press, 1978), 98–140.

7. I have compared the rate of founding of college and professional school libraries with the growth of population on pp. 39–42 of "The Founding of Libraries in American Colleges and Professional Schools Before 1876" cited above. Edward G. Holley's "Academic Libraries in 1876," *College and Research Libraries* 37 (Jan. 1976): 15–47 reviews the status of libraries in American colleges and professional schools at the end of this period.

8. Rosalind Rosenberg, "The Limits of Access: The History of Coeducation in America," on p. 109 in *Women and Higher Education in American History: Essays from the Mount Holyoke College Sesquicentennial Symposia*, ed. John Mack Faragher and Florence Howe (New York: W. W. Norton, 1988) reports that those in charge of ninety-seven men's colleges had decided to admit women by 1872.

9. Nineteenth century trends are well covered by Barbara Miller Solomon's *In the Company of Educated Women: a History of Women and Higher Education in America* (New Haven, Conn.: Yale University Press, 1985).

10.   Letter from Maida Goodwin of the Smith College Archives to me, 6 August 1992.

11.   *Encyclopedia of Library and Information Science*, s.v. "Seminary Libraries" traces the history of some major American seminary libraries. The conditions associated with the founding of seminary libraries during the first part of the nineteenth century are summarized in "The Theological Seminary in the Configuration of American Higher Education: the Ante-Bellum Years," by Natalie A. Naylor *History of Education Quarterly* 17 (Spring 1977): 17–30.

12.   Paul Starr discusses the various nineteenth century attitudes of Americans toward the medical profession in *The Social Transformation of American Medicine* (New York: Basic Books, 1982).

13.   Its library is described in some detail in Marian C. McKenna, *Tapping Reeve and the Litchfield Law School* (New York: Oceana Publications, 1986), 111–17.

14.   Thomas N. Bonner, "The Beginnings of Engineering Education in the United States: The Curious Role of Eliphalet Knott," *New York History* 69 (Jan. 1988): 35–54, describes the work of various schools.

15.   The history of the libraries in these schools has been discussed by Evangeline Thurber, "American Agricultural College Libraries, 1862–1900," *College and Research Libraries* 6 (Sept. 1945): 346–52; and Edward G. Holley traces the effect of the Morrill Act in *The Land-Grant Movement and the Development of Academic Libraries: Some Tentative Explorations* (College Station, Tex.: Texas A&M University Libraries, 1977).

16.   Charles E. Rosenberg's book, *The Care of Strangers: The Rise of America's Hospital System* (New York: Basic Books, 1987) contains much information about the years before 1876.

17.   *American Philanthropy* by Robert H. Bremner, 2d ed. (Chicago: University of Chicago Press, 1988) provides an excellent overview of the history of American benevolence. *In the Shadow of the Poorhouse: A Social History of Welfare in America* by Michael B. Katz (New York: Basic Books, 1986) pays particular attention to the role of governments and voluntary organizations in relief work.

18.   Robert H. Bremner, *The Public Good: Philanthropy and Welfare in the Civil War Era.* (New York: Knopf, 1980), 85.

19.   Lisa M. Dunkel, "Moral and Humane: Patients' Libraries in Early Nineteenth-Century American Mental Hospitals," *Bulletin of the Medical Library Association* 71 (July 1983): 274–81, and Priscilla Older, "Patient Libraries in Hospitals for the Insane in the United States, 1810–1861," *Libraries and Culture* 26 (Summer 1991): 511–31.

20.   The most useful account of these seagoing libraries is contained in *Books Afloat and Ashore: A History of Books, Libraries, and Reading Among Seamen during the Age of Sail* by Harry R. Skallerup (Hamden, Conn.: Archon Books, 1974).

21.   Several sources mention this concern about the effects of the use of alcohol. Temperance movements are discussed in detail in Ian R. Tyrrell's book, *Sobering Up: From Temperance to Prohibition in Antebellum America, 1800–1860* (Westport, Conn.: Greenwood Press, 1979).

22.   Changes in the attitudes concerning aid for the elderly in one city are discussed in Carole Haber's "The Old Folks at Home: The Development of Institutionalized Care for the Aged in Nineteenth-Century Philadelphia," *Pennsylvania Magazine of History and Biography* 101 (Apr. 1977): 240–57. There may have been similar changes in other places.

Chapter 8

Libraries Belonging to Governmental Agencies

Before 1876, each American library of any kind was likely to serve only persons in a fairly small geographic area. The limited means of communication and travel made it desirable for users to go to the library and return in a short time. So it was to be expected that there would be far more government libraries serving local communities than ones serving larger geographical units. Table 8.1 makes this clear. Even the state and federal territorial libraries were primarily designed to serve persons who lived, temporarily or permanently, at the various capital cities. (For example, the daily hours of service of state libraries were sometimes extended while the legislatures were in session.)

LOCAL GOVERNMENTS

Free Public Libraries. In this study, the term *public library* will be used in a sense that was not yet common before 1876 but that is widely used today. It will indicate a library that (1) was supported mainly by a unit of local government and (2) was available without charge to a large part of the population in a small geographical area. The term *public library* was often more broadly used before 1876 to mean any collection available (free or for a fee) to a group of persons larger than a single family. Thus, any library belonging to a college, a society, or a government was considered to be a public library. For the purposes of the present study, it has seemed appropriate to use the more recent, more restrictive definition given above.

The free public libraries that existed in the United States before 1876 can be divided into two distinct groups: (1) ordinary public libraries established by local governments and (2) township libraries established by state governments but intended for at least partial support and control by local officials. In this study, the ordinary public libraries will be considered first for two reasons: (1) They have a longer history, going back to colonial times and continuing to the

Table 8.1
Libraries Belonging to Governmental Units and Quasi-Governmental Units

	Northeast	South	Middle West	Far West	All U.S.
Local governments					
Free public libraries	282	12	1,659	2	1,955
(township and ordinary libraries)					
Free public (religious) libraries	5	3	0	0	8
Law libraries	57	2	5	1	65
Prison libraries	12	0	1	0	13
Other libraries	5	1	4	1	11
Total	361	18	1,669	4	2,052
State and territorial governments					
State and territorial libraries	9	17	12	12	50
Law libraries	19	13	7	3	42
Prison libraries	22	8	22	3	55
Other libraries	6	0	9	0	15
Total	56	38	50	18	162
Federal government					
General and miscellaneous libraries	2	11	0	1	14
Engineering and scientific libraries	0	12	0	0	12
Law libraries	0	9	1	0	10
Military libraries	1	5	0	1	7
Other libraries	0	4	1	0	5
Total	3	41	2	2	48
Kinds of government uncertain	10	0	2	0	12
(prison libraries)					
Total (all government libraries)	430	97	1,723	24	2,274
Quasi-governmental units	19	54	31	45	149
(military post libraries)					
Total	449	151	1,754	69	2,423

present. Township libraries appeared in the 1830s and enthusiasm for them had begun to wane by the time of the Civil War. (2) The ordinary free public libraries more clearly fit our concept of a local public library because the township libraries were in some ways closely related to the school libraries and because the governments of the two midwestern states where they existed in large numbers had more control over them than do state governments today.

Not all of the public libraries other than township libraries conformed completely with the definition given above. In regard to libraries, as with other social agencies that existed before 1876, Americans occasionally exercised some freedom in the way in which they combined elements to meet their objectives. A general collection could be freely available yet supported to some extent by a voluntary organization. Or, a government could operate the library yet charge a small fee for its use. Also, there could be restrictions as to the age or race of the users.

The ordinary public libraries that appeared before 1876 resembled the social libraries discussed in chapter 5. The support of public libraries came from users in the form of taxes paid to local or state governments in much the same way that support for the social libraries came from members of the library societies, whose annual dues had sometimes been called taxes.

One indication of the similarity between public libraries and social libraries is the ease with which some social libraries were converted into public libraries. When the members of a library society lost interest in their collection, they often turned it over to the town government, which converted it to a public library by supporting it financially and opening it to the citizens of the town. In the present study, the public library is considered to have been founded when the town government took over, even though the present-day library officials may emphasize the close relationship to the antecedent social library by claiming the latter's founding date as their own.

Even though public libraries resembled social libraries, they were considered to be a distinct type of library and were beginning to appear in substantial numbers by 1876 despite the continuing popularity of the library societies. Jesse Shera has thoroughly analyzed the causes for the rise of public libraries in New England before 1855. He examined various conditions that existed there. Among them were: (1) communities with resources greater than those needed for the usual governmental functions, (2) local pride in small towns as well as in larger centers of population, and (3) a concern for educational materials beyond those available in elementary schools.[1] Many of the public libraries that were founded before 1876 were located either in New England or in areas where Yankee influence was significant, so what Shera said is applicable to public libraries as a whole.

If the establishment of public libraries before 1876 can be considered a movement, it was one that was mostly confined to New England. Of 403 total public libraries (other than township libraries), New England was home to 253. And much of the moving had occurred in Massachusetts. The total of 172 in that state was about six times as many as in any other state. Even though in the East North Central sub-region, township libraries greatly outnumbered other public libraries, the total number of ordinary public libraries (eighty-nine) was greater than in any other sub-region outside of New England. Only thirty-four could be identified in the Middle Atlantic states, and the six other sub-regions combined had only twenty-seven.

In examining the changes in the rate of founding of the strict social libraries, in chapter 5, we looked at the average number appearing in each year. By the 1790s it was around twenty to twenty-five. The average fluctuated in the nineteenth century until the Civil War, then rose noticeably; for the ten-year period from 1866 through 1876 it averaged more than forty per year. The average for public libraries was less than one per year before the 1840s. In the 1850s it rose to about eight per year. In the ten-year period from 1866 through 1875 it was higher, but had risen to an average of only twenty per year. If the rate of founding is an indication of the relative enthusiasm for public libraries, the people of New England still were more enthusiastic in the postwar years than other Americans. Of the 193 founding dates that could be discovered for the years from 1866 through 1875, 134 were for New England libraries. Of course there were some libraries for which founding dates could not be discovered. By 1875, the number of free public libraries known to exist in the entire United States was 343, of which 150 were in New England.

Eight of the free public libraries included in the totals given above did not fit one part of the usual definition of a public library because they were on a special topic: religion. It is difficult to be sure exactly how many should be considered religious public libraries because it is usually not possible to determine what part of each collection was on religion and what part was on other topics. Also, in some cases, town officials seem to have shared control of the library with church officers.

We can be sure about two characteristics of the libraries that were specialized in this way. Each consisted of books given by an individual or a group to a community to establish a library, and the gifts were made early in the period. Five of them were founded in the British colonies before the Revolution and the last was founded in 1827. The Rev. Thomas Bray or his associates were responsible, wholly or in part, for the founding of four of the earliest ones, although for two of those, persons living outside of the towns may have been included among the intended users. This kind of library did not continue. For only two of them was there evidence that they still existed after about 1830.

The township libraries outnumbered the other public libraries four to one, and all but one of them were located in two Midwestern states, Michigan (with 620) and Indiana (with 939). A library was established in the township of Peabody, Kansas, in 1874 or 1875, with the aid of E. F. Peabody of Boston, who provided the collection together with funds for its maintenance.[2]

In the present study, the township libraries of Michigan and Indiana have been included with ordinary public libraries for two reasons: (1) Even though they were established by state governments, state officials tried, with varying degrees of success, to persuade local governments to maintain them. (2) They were clearly intended for the public; in some instances, most of the books were of the kinds that only adults would want to read.[3] Township libraries appeared earlier in Michigan than in Indiana. The Michigan constitution of 1835 provided that the legislature should establish at least one library in each township and that the library should be supported by persons in return for their exemption from military duty and by fines collected in each county for any breach of the penal laws. Sometimes local officials used these funds for library purposes, but sometimes they failed to do so.[4]

The founding dates for only forty-five of the Michigan libraries were available in the sources used for this study. The earliest known date was 1839; a few were still being created after the Civil War. Information about the number in existence at various times is also incomplete. The available annual reports of the Michigan Superintendent of Public Instruction indicate that in 1845 there were approximately two hundred; by 1850 there were three hundred; in 1855, close to four hundred, and in 1860, close to two hundred. Several reports of the Superintendent of Public Instruction in the 1870s give the exact figure of 207; only fifty-six individual libraries could be identified as existing in 1875. The decrease of Michigan libraries in later years seems to have been partly caused by indifference of township residents, but it also was partly caused by laws passed to encourage township officers to distribute the books among each township's school districts to make them more accessible in rural areas.

The history of Indiana township libraries is quite different. They did not appear until the mid-1850s. The books were bought, assembled, and shipped to the township officials from the state's office of the Superintendent of Public Instruction. Almost all of the 939 known collections were distributed in a three-year period: in 1854, 597 were established; in 1855, 197; and in 1856, 138. For seven others, the date of distribution is not known. As in Michigan, people seem to have been enthusiastic at first but lost interest when new books were not added. Only twenty-five libraries were identified as existing in 1875, but there must have been considerably more than that.[5]

The annual reports of the superintendents of public instruction in Michigan and Indiana show that a few very well-intentioned men tried hard, by establishing township libraries, to provide well-selected reading matter for the citizens of those two states. The reports show that these state officials were disappointed when they did not have the cooperation of the members of the state legislatures, the officials of local governments, and the people.

Law Libraries. In addition to public libraries intended for all citizens, many local governments maintained collections on special subjects, intended for the use of particular groups. Most of these were law libraries, to be used by government officials and lawyers who had business with courts. These were sometimes called court libraries, but most seem to have been called county law libraries.

For this study, a total of only sixty-five law collections belonging to local governments could be identified. However, the actual number was far greater than that: there were a total of 203 law collections, which had to be placed in chapter 10 with other libraries of unknown ownership. For reasons mentioned in that chapter, it seems likely that many of these were owned by town or county governments.

The freedom that Americans exercised in establishing and operating various kinds of libraries was a freedom that was often employed in regard to law libraries. A local government could share responsibility with a bar association in various ways as they jointly supported and managed a collection. However, it is unlikely that many had the arrangement that existed in Dubuque, Iowa, during the 1840s, whereby, in the days when court was in session, each lawyer was required to move his books into the courtroom for the use of all the other lawyers.[6]

Of the sixty-five law libraries owned by local governments that have been considered in this study, fifty-seven were in the Northeast, twenty-one of those in New York and twenty-two in Pennsylvania; no other state had more than eight. However, it is likely that many other collections existed in the South and the Middle West.

The law libraries owned by local governments (usually county governments) began to appear in the 1790s; the ones that could be identified were founded at an average rate of less than one per year until 1865 when six appeared. Twenty were established during the ten-year span from 1866 through 1875. No founding dates for 1826 through 1835 were discovered; this hiatus may have been due to chance, but that was a period when lawyers and government officials were less popular than usual. Once established (before 1826 or after 1835), a county law library was likely to continue functioning. All but two of the sixty-five collections still existed in 1875.

Libraries in Prisons and Reformatories. Most libraries in prisons or reformatories were to be found in state institutions. However, thirteen collections could be identified that clearly belonged to cities or counties. Twelve of these were in the Northeast. They all served medium or larger units of government; eight were in Boston, New York City, Brooklyn (still a separate city in 1875), or Philadelphia. The only one outside of the Northeast was in the St. Louis, Missouri, jail. City and county governments did not deserve all the credit for establishing and maintaining these libraries. Generous individuals or voluntary organizations often contributed books or funds for purchasing books.[7] It could not always be determined whether a library was in a prison maintained by a state or by a local government. Ten of the twelve collections with uncertain ownership were in the Northeast; the only libraries located elsewhere were one in Michigan and one in Wisconsin.

The only collection that clearly was established before 1840 was the one in the Boston House of Reformation for Juvenile Offenders, which, in the 1870s, reported a founding date of 1827. All thirteen of the prison libraries belonging to local governments still existed in 1875—as were all twelve of the ones that might have belonged either to local or state governments. In the part of chapter 7 about libraries in asylums, it was mentioned that eight collections in houses of refuge may have served establishments that were similar to reformatories. Any of these may have been operated by local governments.

Other Libraries. Apparently, the work of officials in only a few departments in city governments required the establishment of their own book collections before 1876. All eleven that could be discovered were to be found in cities or larger towns: five of them in the Northeast, four in the Middle West, one in the South, and one in the Far West.

Seven libraries were operated by city boards of education, four of them established in the 1850s and the other three from 1863 through 1872. The collections seem to have been general in content and were mainly intended for teachers' use. Several were replaced by public libraries, intended for the public. The only one that still existed in 1875 belonged to the New York City Board of Education. The other four libraries serving departments within city governments all appeared after the Civil War. In Boston, the City Engineers' Department established one in 1869, and the Bureau of Statistics and Labor in that city opened one in 1874. Libraries for Boards of Health in Baltimore and New York City were established in 1873, although one source dates the library in the latter city from 1870.

Local governments seem to have had few of the kinds of libraries that were sometimes owned by governments and sometimes by other organizations, mentioned in chapter 7. There seems to be no record of a college or professional school operated by a town or city before 1876. Only four hospital libraries were controlled by local governments, although nine more were in hospitals that may have belonged to towns or cities. Only six asylum libraries are known to have been operated by local governments, but there was a very large number (seventy-six) whose ownership could not be determined.

STATE AND TERRITORIAL GOVERNMENTS

State and Territorial Libraries. When the British colonies became states at the time of the Revolution, it was natural for Americans to attach importance to the government of each state. Later, western territories were created, and they, like the earlier colonies, turned into states, although the boundaries of a new state might be somewhat different from those of the territory from which it was formed.[8]

In a few of the early colonies, government officials had collections available for their use. The earliest may have been two that were mentioned in chapter 2. Pennsylvania's Assembly Library in Philadelphia, which some sources date from 1745, may have been first. A short-lived "Trust Library," containing mainly religious books, was sent from the mother country to the government of the Georgia colony in the 1750s. However, it apparently was not much like the collections that territorial and state governments established later in Georgia and elsewhere.

By 1875 every state or territory had a government library. Even Hawaii, which was not yet a part of the United States, established one in 1851. In 1875, Alaska did not yet have territorial status. The area now occupied by that state was administered by the U.S. Army; a library in the barracks at Sitka did not have a purpose similar to the ones at the capitals of states and territories.

It is hard to be certain about the date of founding of several of the state libraries because, occasionally, books were held in one or more offices for some time and only gradually came to be organized into what could reasonably be called a library. The result of this situation is that, for nineteen of the forty-eight states for which founding dates are on record, different sources give dates that vary by three or more years. (When two sources disagree by only one or two years, one source may be considering the date when the library was authorized and the other may be considering the date when the collection was first made available for use by state or territorial officials and legislators.)

By accepting the dates reported by the sources that seem most reliable, (usually the national surveys, based on answers to questionnaires), it is possible to discover a general pattern for the times and regions where state and territorial libraries were established. The country seems to have been divided into two large areas: (1) the states east of the Mississippi River, and (2) the states west of the Mississippi. This generalization is possible: By about 1850, most of the states east of the Mississippi River had state libraries, but only a few states or territories west of that river had them.

For the most part, western states and territories acquired libraries early in their history. At the times when some of the western territories were being organized, the U.S. Congress aided them by providing books or money (in some cases $5,000, in others, $2,500) for a library.[9] Later, when statehood was attained, this collection became the state library. We have already seen how state officials provided libraries for local communities; here is an example of provision by federal officials of libraries for individual territories within the Union.

The number of state or territorial libraries increased steadily before 1876 because, when a library was once established, it almost always held on to the end of the period—indeed, up to the present day. The longevity of state libraries is perhaps an illustration of the general rule that a library will have a better chance of survival if it is attached to an agency, which also lives a long while.

In the earlier years, the main purpose of most territorial or state libraries was to provide law books, but, typically, collections also contained other books. By 1876, in a few states, the law books were not in the state library but were controlled by the Supreme Court. In other states, the proportion of law books varied from one-sixth to two-thirds of the collection.[10] If these law libraries were considered to be separate from the state libraries, they are included in this chapter's section about various kinds of state-owned library collections other than state libraries. Before 1876, the use of state and territorial libraries was sometimes, in theory, restricted to state officials and legislators; however, circulation records remaining for several collections show that they were often used by other persons as well.

Law Libraries. We have seen that most or all state and territorial libraries contained subjects on the law as well as other books. However, in most states, governments operated separate law libraries, intended for the use of courts. A few had names that implied a larger group of users than just persons connected with courts; occasionally the title might be "state law library" rather than "superior court library" or "district court library."

Forty-two law libraries belonging to state governments could be identified for this study, but there probably were considerably more, because, as mentioned in connection with law libraries owned by local governments, the large number (203) of law libraries of unknown ownership must have included some operated by state governments. Almost half of the law collections owned by states (nineteen) were in the Northeast and of those northeastern libraries, sixteen were in a single state, New York. No other state had more than four. The ones outside of the Northeast were mostly to be found in two areas, thirteen in the South and seven in the East North Central states. Only three were located elsewhere.

Few law collections owned by states were established before the 1830s. From that decade through 1875 they appeared irregularly; there was no marked tendency for the rate of founding to significantly increase or decrease. The number in existence at any one time increased slowly but fairly regularly; available records include twenty-six that existed in 1875.

Libraries in Prisons and Reformatories. By the 1820s and 1830s, Americans were beginning to be concerned about the welfare of prisoners as well as other unfortunate persons. Prison libraries were considered to be one way to make the inmates' lives more bearable—and to inculcate the moral principles that had been lacking in those lives. State officials seemed to share this concern. Of the total of eighty-one prison libraries that could be identified for the years before 1876, fifty-five were located in state prisons and reformatories, and there were twelve more that may or may not have been in establishments operated by state governments. The ones that definitely were in state institutions were distributed widely across the country in thirty states; in each of sixteen of those states only one library was found, and no state had more than four.

In the Northeast, only three libraries appeared in state prisons before 1840 and only two after 1860. All Northeastern states had them by 1853 except Vermont, where 1865 is the earliest founding date in the available records. Outside of the Northeast, only one, in Kentucky, was established before 1840, but thirteen were founded after 1860. For the country as a whole, forty-eight still existed in 1875. As with prison libraries controlled by local governments, if more information were available about the libraries with unknown ownership, one or more of these totals might be higher.

Responses from officials in thirty-five state prisons to a questionnaire about their libraries were published in the U.S. Bureau of Education's report, *Public Libraries in the United States of America*, in 1876. Replies from twelve included no information about the sources of funds for "increase of library," but twenty-two reported income received from the state. One listed "earnings of prison" and seven reported income from "visitors' fees." None reported other sources, but any or all of them may have accepted gifts.[11] The list of their answers was accompanied by a note that told that prison officials often reported the founding date for the library as the year in which state support began, whereas a library actually existed earlier.

Other Libraries. For the most part, it seems as though administrative divisions within state governments, like departments in city governments, had not reached a stage of development by 1875 that made libraries a necessity. A total of only fifteen collections could be discovered in various state boards or departments. Six of these were in the Northeast and nine in the Middle West.

The number of libraries owned by each kind of department was so small that differences in the numbers are not significant. Six collections belonged to state boards of agriculture, three to boards of health, three to departments concerned with some branch of science, two to boards of education, and one (in Pennsylvania) to a board of charities.

The chronological pattern displayed by founding dates was roughly the same as the pattern for libraries in departments within city governments. The earliest is 1848 when one was established in the office of the Superintendent of Public Instruction in Madison, Wisconsin; five more appeared before the Civil War. In 1875, all but one of the total fifteen still existed.

THE FEDERAL GOVERNMENT

Of the libraries in the kinds of agencies that were typically to be found only in governmental bodies, the federal government controlled very few; only forty-eight collections could be identified in all the various departments and bureaus. One other group of libraries might be included here: the military post libraries. The reasons for considering them separately as quasi-government collections are given in the next section of this chapter.

The most distinctive characteristic of the federal libraries was their geographic location: thirty-nine of them were in Washington, D.C. Five more were scattered along the eastern seaboard from Florida to New Hampshire. Of the other four, two were in the Middle West and two on the Pacific coast. These libraries began to appear at about the same time that the federal government was being formed. At least five libraries were founded before the government moved to the District of Columbia in 1800. For this study, they are considered as District libraries, partly because of the difficulty of determining exactly where they were before 1800. The library belonging to the Department of State, for example, is usually considered the oldest, dating from 1789. It moved with the government from New York City to Philadelphia and then, on several occasions, briefly to Trenton, New Jersey, because of outbreaks of yellow fever in Philadelphia.[12]

After the government moved to the District of Columbia, very few new libraries were founded before the 1830s, and even in later years the number of new ones was never very large in any decade. Five existed in 1800. New libraries appeared from time to time: some of them were merged with others or just disappeared from the available records before 1876; however, of the forty-eight federal libraries, forty-two were still in existence in 1875.

For the purposes of this study it has seemed useful to consider the libraries of the federal government in five groups: (1) libraries containing general and miscellaneous collections, (2) engineering and scientific libraries, (3) law libraries, (4) military libraries, and (5) libraries on other subjects.

General and Miscellaneous Libraries. Fourteen libraries have been considered as general or miscellaneous. Each of these is known to have had books on a variety of subjects or to have had a collection whose subject matter could not be determined. It might have been appropriate to place here any library with a substantial accumulation of *documents* because, by the end of the period, several federal agencies had begun to publish documents that were reports and surveys on a wide variety of subjects.

By far the largest and most significant federal library was the Library of Congress. It is usually considered to have been founded in 1802. By 1876 it had approximately three hundred thousand volumes and was much larger than any other government library—in fact, it had one of the two largest collections in the country, being of about the same size as the Boston Public Library. By 1876, reports on the size of the Library of Congress varied, depending on whether three special collections were included: copyright deposits, a collection for the use of the Supreme Court, and the library of the Smithsonian Institution; most of the Smithsonian books had been on deposit at the Library of Congress since 1866. Other libraries included in this group were collections in the Department of State, the Treasury, and the Post Office. Among the smaller libraries were one in the Executive Mansion and two in U.S. mints, one of them in Philadelphia and the other in San Francisco.

Engineering and Scientific Libraries. Collections began to appear in bureaus and offices with scientific or engineering concerns, beginning in the 1830s. There were at least twelve of these in existence by 1875, of which six belonged to agencies that were directly concerned with navigation in some way. Apparently, the earliest belonged to the Coast Survey and was founded in 1832. Others included collections in possession of the Nautical Almanac Office, the Lighthouse Board, and the Hydrographic Office. The only one concerned with science in general was the collection in the Smithsonian Institution, established by the well-known librarian, Charles Coffin Jewett. That collection had reached a total of about forty thousand volumes when, in 1866, most of it was deposited in the Library of Congress, where it continued to grow.

Law Libraries. Each of at least ten libraries maintained by the federal government contained a substantial amount of legal literature. Both the House of Representatives and the Senate had their own libraries. The one belonging to the House was established in 1789 and had reached a total of about one hundred thousand volumes by 1875. Sources disagree about the date of founding for the Senate library; by 1875 it had only about twenty-five thousand volumes.

Of course federal courts had collections. The Supreme Court had to depend on the law department of the Library of Congress during most of the period, but federal courts away from Washington had their own. Collections belonging to only two of these district courts have appeared in available records: one at Wilmington, Delaware, and one at Springfield, Illinois. However, federal courts must have held some of the large number of court libraries (more than two hundred) for which ownership could not be determined. In Washington, the most significant law library belonging to an executive department was probably the Attorney General's library, founded in 1831 and containing about twelve thousand volumes in 1875.

Military Libraries. Only four of the federal libraries located in Washington seem to have been primarily concerned with military subjects. The largest of these was the one in the War Department, dating from 1799; it contained about thirteen thousand volumes in 1875. Other military libraries—for example that of the Army's Signal Corps and the Navy's Ordnance Bureau—may have been similar to the ones considered in this study to be scientific or engineering collections.

Outside of Washington, the only military libraries that could be discovered were at navy yards in Portsmouth, New Hampshire; Pensacola, Florida; and San

Francisco, California. Some of the books at navy yards were used in the training of officers, but parts of some collections may have resembled the collections in military garrisons, considered at the end of this chapter.

Other Libraries. A few libraries on other subjects deserve special mention. A small library had existed in the Navy's Bureau of Medicine and Surgery by 1875, but a much more prosperous one had grown up in the office of the Surgeon General of the Army. It was founded early in the nineteenth century but had fewer than two thousand volumes in 1865 when its management became part of the duties of the Assistant Surgeon General, John Shaw Billings. By 1875 it had forty thousand volumes and Billings correctly saw it as "an excellent foundation for a national medical library."[13]

Two other libraries were organized after the Civil War and were much smaller than the Surgeon General's library in 1875 but were destined to grow into significant collections. One serving the Department of Agriculture had reached seven thousand volumes by 1875, and one in the Bureau of Education had about four thousand five hundred volumes at that time. A library in a federal prison has been identified for this study, at Leavenworth, Kansas, established in 1869. Another library, on Alcatraz Island in California, was serving both prisoners and soldiers stationed there by 1875; it has been counted as a garrison library in the next part of this chapter.

REGIONAL DIFFERENCES

In the discussion in chapter 7, summarizing regional differences in the distribution of libraries belonging to institutions of higher education, hospitals, and asylums, no distinction was made between the ones owned by governmental bodies and ones owned by other institutions. Of the total of 1,081 libraries in that section (in Table 7.1), only 155 clearly belonged to governments. Expressed in percentages, 34.2 percent of those government libraries were in the Northeast, 27.7 percent in the South, 31 percent in the Middle West, and 7.1 percent in the Far West.

For the regional distribution of the kinds of libraries ordinarily established only by governments, we must take into consideration a situation that existed in no other groups of libraries in the United States before 1876: the presence of large numbers of a single kind in a relatively small area. The township libraries in Michigan and Indiana made up 68.1 percent of all of the government libraries considered in this section. It is tempting to look at both the regional differences as they actually existed and the imaginary situation that would have existed if the township libraries had not been bestowed on local communities by the kindness of state officials.

The Northeast had 18.9 percent of all of the government libraries (excluding the quasi-governmental libraries at military posts); if township libraries had been excluded, the Northeast had 60.2 percent of the libraries. The strength of that part of the country was mainly caused by the presence of 287 local public libraries, of which 172 were in a single state, Massachusetts.

In the South there were few local public libraries; as for libraries owned by state governments, the respectable showing of that region was caused at least partly because all states and territories had libraries at the seats of their governments, and there were a few more states in the South than in any other region. The South had far more federal libraries than elsewhere because the District of Columbia had thirty-nine out of the total forty-eight in the entire country.

The main feature of the government libraries in the Middle West was, of course, the presence of 1,559 township libraries in Michigan and Indiana. No proof has been discovered that would indicate that having township libraries inhibited the founding of other public libraries in those two states. Excluding township libraries, the East North Central sub-region had forty-nine local public libraries, more than in any other sub-region except New England.

The Far West presented no surprises in regard to government libraries; twelve out of the twenty-four that could be identified were the usual state or territorial libraries.

LIBRARIES AT MILITARY POSTS

Almost all of the many libraries at military posts were those that were "encouraged and aided by the General Government, but mainly supported by their beneficiaries and by the benevolence of societies and individuals" according to the editors of the U.S. Bureau of Education's *Public Libraries in the United States of America*, published in 1876.[14] The way in which the federal government encouraged and aided the libraries at military posts was by means of an army regulation established in 1820 which provided that the officers of any post could levy a tax on the sutler (the concessionaire who sold various provisions to the men); among the permissible expenditures were books for a library.[15] The role of the federal government was significant during much of the history of these libraries, but during the Civil War, two organizations—the U.S. Christian Commission and the Military Post Library Association—were mainly responsible for establishing and supporting them. After the war, the Military Post Library Association continued to help them.[16]

In 1850 it was reported that these libraries had been formed "at most, if not at all, the military posts occupied by our army."[17] Diaries and letters indicate that the libraries were popular with the officers, the men, and often the families of the soldiers. The libraries continued to be heavily used during and after the war. Two surveys that were mainly concerned with sanitary conditions at army posts, one made in 1870 and one in 1875, included information about libraries at individual garrisons.[18] The combination of concern about hospital facilities, the ventilation of sleeping quarters, and latrines with a concern about library facilities may seem puzzling to us, but it may have seemed appropriate to the young author of both reports, the Assistant Surgeon General, John Shaw Billings. His duties involved both developing ways to maintain the health of the military forces as well as the managing of the headquarters library, mentioned in the section of this chapter about collections belonging to the U.S. Government. Billings was to become well-known, not only as a librarian (particularly as the first head of the New York Public Library) but also as a leader in the public health field.

The earliest post library in available records was one at Sackets Harbor on Lake Ontario in New York, established in 1816. This library may have been similar to the libraries formed by military societies at about the same time; they have been considered, in this study, with other social libraries on particular subjects. Of the 149 post libraries that could be identified, founding dates were discovered for only thirty-five, so almost nothing can be said about the chronological pattern for the establishment of the entire group; only ten had dates before the end of the Civil War.

As to the number in existence at any one time, little can be said before the dates of the surveys made in 1870 and 1875; in 1870, at least ninety-seven existed and, in 1875, eight-one. These figures may represent substantially all of the ones in the post-war period; the editors of the Bureau of Education's 1876 report, *Public Libraries in the United States of America*, received replies concerning only seventy-eight garrison and regimental libraries.[19] (At a few posts, one or more regiments had their own libraries, which they could take with them if they were transferred to another post.)

Geographically, the distribution seems to have been quite different from that for any other kind of library. Because most of the information has been obtained from the 1870 and 1875 surveys, it is likely that the apparent distribution mainly represents the situation that existed just after the Civil War. There were only nineteen in the Northeast, with few in any single state except New York. At least five of the eleven in that state were at garrisons in or near New York harbor.

The only states in the South Atlantic area to have more than three libraries apiece in garrisons were Maryland with ten, and Virginia with six. Fort McHenry, at Baltimore, had three regimental libraries in addition to a post library, and Fort Washington, on the Potomac a few miles below the city of Washington, had three company libraries in addition to its post library. Four of the Virginia collections were at camps in the Hampton Roads area.

Only six garrison libraries could be identified in the East South Central sub-region. The total of twenty-one in the West South Central area was mainly composed of collections at forts in Texas, where there were sixteen libraries. No records concerning libraries that were located at Confederate military establishments could be identified for this study.

It was in the West that libraries at military posts made up a much higher proportion of all libraries than elsewhere. It must be remembered that just after the Civil War, the whites still felt the need for armed protection as they moved west into the lands that they had taken from the Native Americans. The number of post libraries in the east North Central sub-region was not large—only seven—but there were twenty-four in the West North Central and thirty-two in the Mountain states. On the Pacific Coast there were thirteen. Nowhere was there a large collection, and according to Billings' two surveys, the quality of the holdings varied, but there can be no doubt that they were valued in these posts where, sometimes, there was little contact with the white man's world.[20]

NOTES

1. Jesse H. Shera, *Foundations of the Public Library: The Origins of the Public Library Movement in New England, 1629–1855* (Chicago: University of Chicago Press, 1949), 200–44.

2. Allen Gardiner, *Kansas Public Libraries from Abilene to Zenda, a Concise History* (Topeka, Kans.: State Library of Kansas, 1982), 3.

3. Helen Merrill Wilcox, "School District Public Libraries—A Step in Popular Education in the Nineteenth Century with Emphasis on the Period from 1820–1850," (Master's study, Drexel Institute of Technology, 1953).

4. L. M. Miller's *Legislative History of Township Libraries in the State of Michigan from 1835 to 1901, Printed by Order of the Board of the Library Commissioners* (Lansing, Mich.: Robert Smith Printing Co., 1902) provides general information about these libraries. Some of the annual reports of the Michigan Superintendent of Public Instruction from 1837 through 1875 contain more detailed information; twenty-nine of these could be examined for the present study.

5. Several sources contain information about the Indiana township libraries. *A History of Education in Indiana*, by Richard G. Boone (New York: R. Appleton, 1892), on pp. 339–45 provides a judicious review of their history. Several annual reports of the Indiana Superintendent of Public Instruction, beginning with the one for 1852, include details about their distribution to townships.

6. Christine A. Brock, "Law Libraries and Librarians: A Revisionist History, or More Than You Ever Wanted to Know," *Law Library Journal* 67 (Aug. 1974): 338.

7. "Libraries in Prisons and Reformatories," pp. 218–29, in U.S. Bureau of Education, *Public Libraries in the United States of America: Special Report*, Part 1 is mainly about state prisons but refers to a few others.

8. A good short history of state libraries is the chapter "The Historical Development of State Library Agencies," by Wayne A. Wiegand, pp. 1–16 in *State Library Services and Issues: Facing Future Challenges*, ed. by Charles R. McClure (Norwood, N.J.: Ablex Publishing Corp., 1986).

9. Apparently, the role of the federal government in the creation of territorial libraries has never been studied in detail. Congress appropriated money or gave books for at least ten libraries, but in recent correspondence, state library officials in three of those states report no records indicating that their territorial libraries received the gifts.

10. Henry A. Homes, "State and Territorial Libraries," p. 296 in U.S. Bureau of Education, *Public Libraries in the United States of America: Special Report*, Part 1.

11. "Libraries in Prisons and Reformatories," U.S. Bureau of Education, *Public Libraries*, 228–29.

12. Arthur B. Berthold, "The Library of the Department of State," *Library Quarterly* 28 (Jan. 1958): 28.

13. J. S. Billings, "Medical Libraries in the United States" p. 175 in U.S. Bureau of Education, *Public Libraries*.

14. U.S. Bureau of Education, *Public Libraries*, 273.

15. *American State Papers; Military Affairs*, vol. 2 (Washington, D.C.: Gales and Seaton, 1834), 218.

16. David Kaser's *Books and Libraries in Camp and Battle: The Civil War Experience* (Westport, Conn.: Greenwood Press, 1984) discusses post libraries and other agencies that provided reading matter for soldiers during the war.

17. Charles C. Jewett, *Appendix to the Report of the Board of Regents of the Smithsonian Institution, Containing a Report on the Public Libraries of the United States of America, January 1, 1850*, p. 188.

18. U.S. War Department, Surgeon General's Office, *A Report on Barracks and*

Hospitals, with Descriptions of Military Posts, Circular no. 4 (Washington, D.C.: Government Printing Office, 1870), and U.S. War Department, Surgeon General's Office, *A Report on the Hygiene of the United States Army, with Descriptions of Military Posts*, Circular no. 8 (Washington, D.C.: Government Printing Office, 1875). According to a letter to me from Peter B. Hurtle of the National Library of Medicine, October 21, 1991, Billings was the author of both reports.

19. U.S. Bureau of Education, 274.

20. The most useful study of these libraries is contained in the first part of Miller J. Stewart's, "A Touch of Civilization: Culture and Education in the Frontier Army," *Nebraska History* 65 (Summer 1984): 257–82.

Chapter 9

Libraries Belonging to Business Firms and Individuals

Most of this chapter is about libraries maintained by firms or individuals who either charged users a fee or provided reading rooms, usually without charge, for customers who came for other purposes. A few other libraries considered in this chapter were ones that were provided for the benefit of employees or were helpful in the conduct of the owner's business. At the end of the chapter a very few collections are mentioned that were owned by individuals who opened them for the free use of the public. All of these kinds of libraries are shown in Table 9.1.

Commercial Circulating Libraries. The provision of reading matter by all of the libraries considered in this study existed partly because Americans were willing to spend the necessary money to acquire and make available the materials in the collections. It was to be expected that some persons would undertake to provide these materials for a fee, so the commercial circulating library flourished from colonial times through 1875.[1] The user did not have to make the substantial investment and pay the annual "taxes" normally required of members of library societies, nor did he or she have to support the collection through taxes paid to state or local governments. Usually, the borrower rented only the books that he or she wanted, paying the fees monthly, quarterly, or annually.

David Kaser, in his excellent history of the American commercial circulating library, *A Book for a Sixpence*, points out that people rented books for a fee for hundreds of years before this country was settled by Europeans. Commercial libraries were well established in Britain before they came to the American colonies around 1760.[2]

Most of the commercial circulating libraries contained general collections, perhaps with a higher percentage of popular titles than were to be found in the social libraries. At any rate, both kinds were able to flourish; towns often had several of each. Like social libraries and public libraries, commercial libraries

Table 9.1
Libraries Belonging to Business Firms and Individuals

	Northeast	South	Middle West	Far West	All U.S.
Commercial circulating libraries	405	72	72	15	564
Public reading rooms in commercial establishments	20	16	16	5	57
Libraries for the benefit of employees of factories and railroads	25	0	3	1	29
Other libraries in businesses	3	0	3	1	7
Public libraries belonging to individuals	2	0	2	2	6
Total	455	88	96	24	663

were most frequently found in the Northeast—more in new England (262) than in the Middle Atlantic states (144). As with social libraries (the strict kind) and public libraries, Massachusetts had more than any other American state. Of the 123 commercial circulating libraries in Massachusetts, Boston had forty-six, more than any other American city. The six states with the most libraries were in the Northeast, as were the four cities with the most. Although Boston had more than any other, New York City had forty-two; Providence, Rhode Island had thirty; and Philadelphia had twenty-seven.

It was not surprising that the South Atlantic states had forty-nine out of the seventy-two in the South. New Orleans had half of all those in the rest of the South; its total of twelve was more than in any other southern city except Baltimore and more than in any Midwestern city. The names of six of the proprietors of the libraries in New Orleans were French and six were British or German in origin.

Most of the commercial circulating libraries were short-lived. Many were operated as side-lines by bookstore owners who, if their libraries ceased to show a profit, could easily discontinue them and transfer their stock to the bookstore.

Chapters 5 and 6 discussed libraries intended for women. The advertisements for several of the circulating libraries tried to appeal to women readers, and as Kaser mentions, in the earliest years of the nineteenth century several were operated by women, making those ladies America's first female librarians.

The earliest commercial circulating library in the colonies is considered to be the one established in 1762 in Annapolis, Maryland, by William Rind. His was not successful, but a few other individuals in the colonies continued to try to operate them. After the Revolution, the number of libraries getting started increased somewhat, but from the 1790s through the 1850s there was little change—an average of almost exactly two per year. Kaser reports that the chief reason for their lack of success around the middle of the century was the availability of very cheap books. After the Civil War, entrepreneurs were not discouraged: the ten-year span from 1866 through 1875 saw 109 come into existence, far more than in any pre-war decade. The result was that in 1875 there were at least 141 of them, more than twice as many as at any of the five-year measuring points before the war.

Public Reading Rooms in Commercial Establishments. Some proprietors of hotels, taverns, and coffeehouses tried to attract patrons by providing space for them to sit and read. A few bookstores and newspaper offices had reading rooms. Most of the reading matter was current newspapers and periodicals but sometimes there were books, as well.

David Kaser has studied these kinds of establishments and states that they had one advantage over some other libraries; the others often were just reading material collections and did not provide any convenient space for the patron to sit while using the library.[3] Even though these reading rooms provided a service that some other libraries did not supply, the life of many seems to have been short. For only twenty-two out of the total fifty-five is there evidence that the room continued for more than a year. Of course, information about this kind of enterprise was not often included in contemporary lists of libraries, so it is possible that some of the other thirty-three lasted for several years.

The total number of the reading rooms identified for this study is so small that the discovery of a few more might require a change in any statement about their geographic distribution. Of the nineteen known to have existed in the Northeast, nine were in New England (all of them in Rhode Island), and ten in the Middle Atlantic states. The fifteen in the South were more than might have been expected, when compared with the total of only sixteen for the Middle West. Everywhere, they were most likely to be found in larger towns or cities.

Information about founding dates is available for only twenty-two of the rooms. No record of a date in the eighteenth century was discovered. The earliest date that was found for the establishment of any in the nineteenth century was for one maintained from 1808 to 1812 by William S. Haskell, who was editor of the Wilmington, North Carolina *Gazette*; however, a few others had existed before Haskell opened his room.

Not only was the life of individual reading rooms short; the life of the group of enterprises as a whole was short. Only a few were founded before the 1830s, when five new ones appeared. For the 1840s, eight founding dates were discovered, but only four for all the years from 1850 to the end of the period; the last one was established in 1867. There is no proof that any reading room existed at any of the five-year marking dates from 1855 through 1875. During those later years, several other kinds of libraries were supplying popular materials together with space in which they could be read, so the reading rooms established in connection with commercial enterprises may have seemed less attractive.

Libraries for the Benefit of Employees of Factories and Railroads. It is not surprising that libraries provided by industrial firms for their employees were started in New England. The earliest was established in a cotton mill in Massachusetts around 1820, and at least five others existed in cotton mills before 1876. By the 1820s, social libraries were quite popular in New England, but many people could not afford to use them. The mill girls who flocked to the larger towns and cities in the 1820s and 1830s were enthusiastic readers, so mill owners began to provide libraries, often expecting each user to contribute a small part of the cost of maintaining the collections.[4]

It was not long before these libraries could be found in a variety of establishments: at least four in iron and steel works, and some for employees of shoe manufacturers and others. A few of the collections in later years may have contained books useful in the work of the plant; however, five that were provided for railroad employees seem to contain books that were general in subject matter.

Even in those later years, a solid majority of the libraries were in New England. Of the twenty-nine discovered for the entire country before 1876, eleven were in Massachusetts and ten more were in other New England states. The three in the Middle West were all in the East North Central states, and the only western one was provided for employees of a mine in Arizona owned by Samuel Colt, the inventor of the revolver. Several of these company libraries had fairly long lives: thirteen of the ones in the Northeast still existed in 1875 as were the three in the Middle West.

Other Libraries in Businesses. The collections grouped as *other,* unlike the libraries for employees described above, seem to have been formed to aid directly in the work of the firms that owned them. It is quite likely that many more such libraries existed but did not appear in the sources used for this study. However, one reason that the number is so small may be that industry in the United States simply had not developed to the stage where a collection of books could help in conducting business. We have already noted that libraries for young businessmen and artisans (mechanics) usually had few books on commercial or technical subjects.

Of the seven libraries that were owned by commercial firms and that seem to have been intended to aid in the conduct of business, two were libraries owned by law firms and two more were law libraries owned by other kinds of businesses. All four of those collections were established from 1863 to 1873. A bank in Philadelphia had a library in 1811, a drug manufacturing firm in Cincinnati started one in 1864, and a "directory office" in Boston established one in 1846. Records do not show what that collection contained.

Public Libraries belonging to Individuals. We have already seen that several kinds of societies as well as several kinds of governmental bodies established libraries that were intended for free public use. There were, in addition, a few benevolent individuals who permitted others to use their books without paying a fee. Perhaps these libraries should not be considered along with others whose owners expected a return; however, they do not seem to fit better in any other category in this chapter.

Only six such libraries are listed in Table 9.1, and very little information about them has been discovered. Another library, which has been considered in this study to be a collection for mechanics and apprentices, could have been included here and is far better known than any of the six. In the 1850s, Colonel James Anderson of Allegheny, Pennsylvania, allowed working boys to come to his home on Saturdays to borrow books from his private collection. Soon, he added more books and established a library for mechanics and apprentices in a separate building. One of the boys, Andrew Carnegie, an avid reader, was so impressed with Anderson's generosity that, later, when he was able, he helped many towns and cities to provide free public libraries for their citizens.[5]

The six free libraries maintained by individuals exhibit nothing significant in their geographic distribution: two in New England, two in the East North Central states, and two on the west coast. The earliest was in New England; it dated from about 1800 and was owned by Dr. Benjamin Vaughan who settled in Hallowell, Maine, in 1797. In that year or soon thereafter he opened his private library to the public for its free use once a week.[6] The other five were established from the 1840s into the 1870s.

REGIONAL DIFFERENCES

Leaving the public libraries owned by individuals out of our calculations, the commercial circulating libraries constituted 85.8 percent of all the libraries that were included in this section. If the public reading rooms are added to the circulating libraries, the percentage intended for the use of persons other than employees rises to 94.5. It is clear that before 1876, American businessmen were mainly interested in providing reading matter for other persons and saw little use in maintaining collections directly on the subject of business or for the use of employees.

The pattern for the regional distribution of libraries operated by businesses is somewhat different from the pattern for any other major group considered in this study. The Northeast had 68.9 percent of the libraries owned by businesses (that is, of the libraries in Table 9.1 exclusive of the public libraries belonging to individuals). If the collections in chapters 5 through 7 that clearly belonged to voluntary associations are considered together, the Northeast had only 56.8 percent. If we consider only the strict social libraries, whose contents were somewhat like those in the commercial circulating libraries, and which were very popular in the Northeast, that region had only 62.2 percent while it had 71.8 percent of the commercial circulating libraries.

The difference between the percentage of commercial circulating libraries in the Northeast and the percentage of strict social libraries in that region may not be significant. However, these general libraries, operated for profit, seem to have appeared more frequently in larger towns and cities; during much of the period larger places were more prevalent there.

NOTES

1. The term *circulating library* ordinarily meant one that was owned by an individual or a firm who charged a fee for the use of books. However, as I have explained earlier, I

have added the word *commercial* for libraries maintained for profit because social libraries were sometimes called circulating libraries; their books always circulated.

2. David Kaser, *A Book for a Sixpence: The Circulating Library in America* (Pittsburgh, Pa.: Beta Phi Mu, 1980).

3. David Kaser, "Coffee House to Stock Exchange: A Natural History of the Reading Room" in *Milestones to the Present: Papers from Library History Seminar V*. Edited by Harold Goldstein (Syracuse, N.Y.: Gaylord Professional Publications, 1978), 238–54.

4. These libraries have been described in Elfrieda B. McCauley's "The New England Mill Girls: Feminine Influence in the Development of Public Libraries in New England, 1820–1860" (D.L.S. diss., Columbia University, 1971).

5. Andrew Carnegie, *Autobiography of Andrew Carnegie*, Popular Edition (Boston: Houghton Mifflin Company, 1920), 47 and Joseph Frazier Wall, *Andrew Carnegie* (New York: Oxford University Press, 1970), 107–8.

6. Eva H. Chadbourne, "Early Social Libraries in Maine," *Bulletin of the Maine Library Association* 31 (Feb. 1970): 5.

Chapter 10

Libraries of Uncertain Ownership

The main part of the present study is based on the examination of records concerning individual libraries and involves, if possible, (1) what the purpose of each library was, (2) whether some kind of voluntary association, governmental body, or business firm owned the library, and (3) what the subject matter of its collection was. We have already encountered a few kinds of libraries—mainly those in hospitals and asylums—that may have been operated by a voluntary organization or may have been controlled by some government agency. There were still others for which it was not possible to determine exactly what their purpose was or whether they were owned by a voluntary organization or a government body. For some of these, however, the subject matter of the books was clear.

Most of the libraries of uncertain ownership (shown in Table 10.1) were mentioned only in manuscript schedules sent to Washington during the censuses of 1850, 1860, and 1870. Almost always, the location of each library was given by the person taking the census, who placed it in some broad category such as *court library* or *circulating and subscription library*, but the library was not named. By comparing the manuscript census schedule with other records of libraries for a particular location, it was possible to determine whether the library in the census record could have been one that was already known. If that library could not have been, it was included in the group of libraries of uncertain ownership.

Of the total of 242 libraries in the *uncertain* group, 231 were mentioned only on the returns sent to Washington for one or more of the three censuses mentioned above. And of these 231 libraries, 213 were to be found only in returns for the 1870 census. The manuscript census returns for only ten states were examined; if more could have been seen, the numbers probably would have been much larger.[1]

The tables concerning libraries, which were printed in the volumes for the three censuses, were examined but were not used for this study, mainly because

Table 10.1
Libraries of Uncertain Ownership

	Northeast	South	Middle West	Far West	All U.S.
Law (mostly "court libraries")	3	157	46	1	207
Other	7	0	27	1	35
Total	10	157	73	2	242

they give only the total, for each state, of the libraries in each broad category. It was not possible to learn which of the ones in those tables were already known to me because the individual libraries' locations were not given. The eleven libraries of unknown ownership that were not found on a census manuscript return were ones for which some other source made it clear that they were among the kinds included in this study, but the source did not indicate exactly which kind and did not indicate whether they were operated by voluntary organizations or by government bodies.

The regional distribution of the libraries of unknown ownership as shown in Table 10.1 is not significant because it is so heavily dependent on information obtained from the manuscript reports of census takers for only ten states. Even though all four regions were represented, the number of states from each region varied greatly. One state was in the Northeast, five in the South, two in the Middle West, and two in the Far West.

It is clear from Table 10.1 that census takers were able to learn about several law collections that did not appear in other lists of libraries. Census returns for legal libraries never indicated whether the collection was owned by some government agency, by a bar association, by a law library association, or by a law firm. Therefore, any legal library that was clearly not mentioned by any other source had to be placed in this *uncertain* group.

The thirty-five libraries listed as *other* in Table 10.1 were almost all either social libraries, commercial circulating libraries, or free public libraries. Even if we knew how each library was classified by the census taker, we might be unsure as to what kind it really was. The director of the 1870 census reported, in the printed volume, that "differences in classification adopted by assistant or deputy marshals have caused some apparent discrepancies" in some columns in his table.[2]

NOTES

1. The reasons for choosing the ten states are given in the part of chapter 1 about sources.

2. U.S. Superintendent of the Census, *Ninth Census*, vol. 1, *The Statistics of the Population of the United States, 1870* (Washington, D.C.: Government Printing Office, 1872), 473.

Chapter 11

Subject Matter of the Collections

In chapters 4 through 10, libraries have been considered in terms of the various groups who established and maintained them. To some extent, this arrangement has resulted in combining those libraries that contained books on the same subject. However, there have been numerous situations where books on a particular subject have been considered in two or more places—medical collections, for example, in medical schools, medical societies, and hospitals.

Therefore, by way of summarizing, it may be well to consider as a kind all collections on the same subject. This has been possible for almost all libraries: there is sufficient information available to be fairly certain about the subject matter of the books in 9,973 out of the 10,032 libraries in the study. The 9,973 with subject matter considered to be fairly certain includes one group about which little is known: 294 libraries belonged to agricultural societies, classed here under agriculture, but which in some cases may have contained a considerable number of general books.

In this chapter, most of the kinds will be considered in order of size, the kind with the largest number of libraries first. The only exceptions are for two kinds of collections: the collections intended to contain both religious and secular books (the YMCA libraries) are the ones that had predominantly religious books, and the collections that were usually intended to contain both law books and general books (the state or territorial libraries) are placed just below other law collections. Libraries of uncertain subject matter are placed at the end in Table 11.1.

GENERAL

In a country with many small towns whose citizens felt that a general education was beneficial, it is not surprising that men—and sometimes women—established and maintained many collections each of which included

Table 11.1
Subject Matter of the Collections

	Northeast	South	Middle West	Far West	All U.S.
General	3,150	1,000	3,187	335	7,672
Religion	413	152	113	54	732
Religion and general (YMCA)	98	37	46	8	189
Law	126	204	94	10	434
Law and general (state and territorial)	9	17	12	12	50
Agriculture	156	30	149	21	356
Medicine	82	29	40	4	155
Science and engineering	82	19	29	11	141
History	51	14	21	8	94
Literature	37	8	9	3	57
Commerce	14	7	5	4	30
Military affairs	8	10	1	1	20
Music	11	4	5	0	20
Education	5	1	5	1	12
Art	8	0	1	1	10
Charities	1	0	0	0	1
Miscellaneous or Unknown Subjects	24	2	32	1	59
Total	4,274	1,534	3,749	474	10,032

books on a variety of subjects. Of the 9,973 libraries whose subject matter could be determined, 7,672 appear to have been general in content. Voluntary associations that maintained libraries were responsible for 4,789 of them (62.4 percent of all general libraries). One kind of library was dominant among those held by voluntary groups: there were 2,463 strict social libraries owned by associations of persons of no particular age or gender and that had the maintenance of a library as their main purpose. They constituted 32.1 percent of all the general libraries.

Governmental units were responsible for most of the general libraries that were not held by voluntary groups, a total of 2,154 (28.1 percent of all of the general collections). Of these, 1,955 were public libraries intended for people in local communities, sometimes financed entirely by local governments but sometimes deriving part of their support from state governments. Most of the 729 other general libraries were owned by commercial firms. Of these, 564 were circulating libraries, which charged fees.

As might be expected, the geographical distribution of general libraries was not much different from the distribution of all libraries in the main part of this study. The Northeast had 41.1 percent of the general collections and 42.6 percent of all libraries; the Middle West had 41.6 percent of the general collections and 37.4 percent of all libraries. Within the Northeast, one kind of library in one sub-region was mainly responsible for the region's good showing: the available records include 1,170 strict social libraries in New England, far more than any other kind in either New England or the Middle Atlantic states. The 1,559 township libraries established by the state governments of Michigan and Indiana made up approximately half of all the general libraries in the Middle West. The South had 13.0 percent of the general libraries, and the Far West had 4.4 percent. The percentages for those two regions were not far below their percentages for all libraries in the study, 15.2 and 4.7.

RELIGION

Considering the attitudes of many Americans before 1876, it is not surprising that the libraries containing religious books were more numerous than libraries on any other topic. The total of 732 for religion is noticeably higher than the total for any other subject, if the 189 YMCA collections, which deliberately contained some secular books, are not included. Churches and various kinds of religious associations held 590 of the collections; however, it has become clear that there were many church libraries that are not in the records[1], and the number of Sunday school libraries, not included in the main part of this study, was very large. Almost all of the collections not held by churches or other religious associations were held by theological seminaries (a total of 133).

The regional distribution of book collections about religion is quite different from the distribution of all libraries in the study. However, the sources concerning church libraries for some parts of the country are clearly poorer than the records for other parts, so the regional distribution shown in Table 11.1 probably does not accurately represent the actual situation.

LAW

We have already seen that legal literature was important in a country where new governments were constantly being formed and where the settlement of new areas frequently involved legal questions about land ownership. It is clear that the 434 law collections in the records used for this study were only a fraction of the ones that existed; manuscript reports used for the 1870 census were the only sources of information about 188 of those, where they were called *court libraries*. Eighty-seven of these were in various towns in Tennessee,[2] fifty-eight in Louisiana, and forty-two in Michigan.

The regional distribution of law libraries shown in Table 11.1 probably is not representative of the actual situation. Because so much depended on manuscript census records, which were available for only a few states, it seems almost certain that, if information from returns for other states had been used, the pattern would have been noticeably different. One unusual aspect of the figures—the large number of law collections in the South—may come close to representing the actual situation there; that region had 47 percent of the law libraries in the available records and 45.2 percent of those in the printed volume for the 1870 census.

AGRICULTURE

Of the 356 collections listed under agriculture, 294 belonged to agricultural societies or farmers' clubs, which also may have owned general books. If the members were like those of several other occupational groups, they may have felt that the amount of useful literature on their subject was limited and that a wide variety of books was not only useful but also enjoyable. The geographic distribution of farmers' collections was not noticeably different from the distribution of all libraries—perhaps somewhat fewer in the South and somewhat more in the Middle West.

MEDICINE

There can be no doubt about the purposes of the persons who established medical libraries and how libraries were used. Clearly, the collections were formed by physicians for themselves or for future physicians. About half were in medical schools (81 out of 155). Medical societies owned thirty-seven; twenty-five were for hospital staffs. The available records do not tell whether seventeen other hospital libraries contained medical books; they are not counted here. A few were held by societies formed explicitly for the purpose of having medical collections, and a few more were to be found in government agencies.

The Northeast had a somewhat higher percentage of the medical libraries than it had of all libraries (52.9 percent of the ones about medicine versus 42.5 percent of all libraries). This predominance was mainly caused by the relatively large number of collections belonging to medical societies both in New England (fifteen) and in the Middle Atlantic states (eleven) out of a total of thirty-seven for the entire country.

SCIENCE AND ENGINEERING

Libraries on science and engineering have been combined because, for some of them, it has been impossible to know whether the science books in their collections were about pure science or whether they were about applications of science. However, we can be sure that most libraries were formed by groups of laymen who had an avocational interest in science. Of the 141 collections related to science or engineering, 98 were held by societies, of which 69 were clearly concerned with science; only 6 were owned by engineering societies. However, of the twenty-four collections in colleges that specialized in science or engineering, at least fourteen were in institutions that emphasized engineering. The other ten libraries were either in scientific schools or belonged to museums or botanical gardens attached to colleges.

The tendency of scientific and engineering libraries to gather in the Northeast (58.2 percent of the total for the United States) seems to have been partly caused by the tendency of societies with these interests to cluster in larger cities. Twenty-four of the organizations that had these libraries were located in one of three cities: Boston, New York, or Philadelphia.

HISTORY

Almost all of the collections concerned with history belonged to historical societies. The societies having libraries existed in all parts of the country, even in areas where the historical period was short, but about half of the total of ninety-four were located in Northeastern towns or cities (twenty-four in New England and twenty-four in the Middle Atlantic states).

OTHER SUBJECTS

There were 150 libraries of the last seven kinds listed in Table 11.1 (excluding those whose subject matter is unknown). Of these, approximately two-thirds (107) were owned by societies whose main purposes were not to establish libraries. The societies of this kind owned more than half of the collections on these topics: literature, commerce, music, and art.

Twenty libraries considered to be military were almost evenly divided among three kinds: (1) seven in military colleges, (2) seven in various agencies of the federal government, and (3) six owned by military societies. Some or all of the last group may have been largely general in content, similar to those held by garrison libraries—all or most of which seem to have been general. All of the ones classified as education libraries were operated by federal, state, or local governmental agencies. Several of these, owned by boards of education, may have largely consisted of general books for teachers and students.

LIBRARIES ON PARTICULAR SUBJECTS COMPARED WITH GENERAL LIBRARIES

The regional distribution of the general libraries, shown at the top of Table 11.1, was somewhat different from the distribution of the rest of the libraries of known subject matter, taken as a whole. For the general libraries, the percentage distribution for the four major regions is given earlier in this chapter. The specialized collections were distributed in this way: the Northeast had 47.8 percent, which was 6.7 percent higher than its percentage of the general libraries. There may have been two main reasons for this difference: (1) the Northeast had more large towns and cities where there were more likely to be enough persons with special interests to support libraries. (2) The Middle West had a very large number of public (township) libraries with general collections, reducing the percentages for other regions.

The South had 23.1 percent of the subject-specialized collections and only 13 percent of the general collections. Part of this difference may have been caused by the large amount of information available about court libraries in a few southern states.

The Middle West had only 23 percent of the subject-related libraries and 41.6 percent of the general libraries. This difference seems to have been largely caused by the reasons mentioned above for the difference in percentages for the Northeast.

The Far West had 6 percent of the libraries on particular subjects and only 4.4 percent of the general libraries. Because the total number of libraries there was so small, it may be unwise to draw conclusions about the reasons for this difference. Table 11.1 shows that libraries on no one single subject account for the good showing of the Far West. Indeed, if those figures are converted to percentages, ten of the fifteen subjects have more than 4.4 percent of the general collections in the region.

This relatively good showing for special subjects in libraries of the Far West may be partly caused by the situation in California. That state had 55.3 percent of all the libraries in the thirteen states of the region. It had 58 percent of all collections on special subjects and 54.3 percent of all general collections.

One kind of speculation is frequently necessary in a study like this: What are likely to be the differences between the situation indicated by the information available from the study's records and the situation that actually existed before 1876? The review of the subject matter of collections provides the basis for one such speculation: Sometimes, collections that might be considered to be specialized actually were not, whereas the records do indicate that very few if any of the collections considered to be general could have actually been specialized. We have already noticed Americans' strong belief in the value of general knowledge; perhaps that belief was stronger than the records indicate. Perhaps this notion can be tested in the future as scholars examine more of the printed catalogs that still exist for some libraries.

NOTES

1. On p. 475 of volume 1 of the U.S. Superintendent of the Census, *Ninth Census, The Statistics of the Population of the United States, 1870,* the total number of church libraries is given as 4,478. However, the manuscript returns for that census indicate that some of these may have been private libraries owned by pastors.

2. Of the eighty-seven court libraries mentioned in the manuscript reports for Tennessee, somehow only three found their way into the table on page 474 of volume 1 of the printed 1870 census as "court or law" libraries for that state.

Chapter 12

Private Libraries, School Libraries, and Sunday School Libraries

Chapter 1 gave reasons for omitting three kinds of libraries from the main part of this study. All three existed in large numbers in America before 1876, but not enough information is available about individual libraries to permit comparison with the kinds mentioned in chapters 1 through 11. However, an idea as to the prevalence of these three types can be obtained by examining actual counts and estimates reported in surveys compiled before 1876. In chapter 12, each of the three kinds will be considered separately, and then they will be considered as a group.

PRIVATE LIBRARIES

Of course, private libraries in the hands of persons who influenced the direction of American thought and life were of some significance for the history of culture in this country. And the presence of many thousands of small libraries, owned and used by Americans of lesser stature, may be of more significance than we realize.

Before 1876, the compilers of lists of libraries varied in their attitudes toward private collections. Usually these persons omitted them, but they sometimes included them—often with reluctance. Charles C. Jewett, who was responsible for the earliest extensive list that attempted to include various kinds of libraries, wrote: "My investigations have not been limited to the *public* libraries, though I have not felt at liberty to make detailed statements respecting private collections. In one sense they are public libraries. Almost without exception, access to them is freely allowed to all persons who wish to use them for research." In later remarks he makes clear that he has in mind larger collections formed by "scholars."[1]

The compilers of the 1850 census gathered information about some of the private collections that numbered more than one thousand volumes apiece, but they decided not to publish any figures because their data were incomplete.[2] In the 1860 census, 8,149 private libraries were recorded, and in the 1870 census, 108,800.[3] The director of the 1870 census felt that the actual number was perhaps two or three hundred thousand libraries but also gave several reasons why, in his opinion, statistics about private libraries were of little value and should never have been collected in the first place. That census was the only one of the three to give the number of private libraries in each state. However, the published figures for some states were so surprising that the director called them "ludicrously disproportionate."[4] Apparently, census takers in some states were much more diligent than those in other states in this aspect of their work. The editors of the U.S. Bureau of Education's *Public Libraries in the United States of America*, in 1876, decided against collecting information about private libraries, quoting at length from the objections printed in the 1870 census.[5]

SCHOOL LIBRARIES

Unlike private libraries, school libraries were considered to belong to the large class of public libraries and, indeed, might often have been public in the narrower sense of being available at no charge to adults as well as children. However, they existed in such large numbers that authors seldom attempted to report in any detail when and where they existed. The editors of *Public Libraries in the United States of America* devoted most of a chapter to school libraries, mainly telling which legislatures had authorized them at various times.[6]

Most of the legislation had, as its purpose, the creation of libraries in common (elementary) schools. For various reasons, these libraries were often short-lived. Sometimes they weakened and died for the same reasons as did other libraries created by one group of people for the benefit of another group: the unwillingness of the recipients (in this case, the parents) to contribute to the support of the collection. Even so, a substantial number existed at various times.

In secondary schools, libraries were more successful. Most of these institutions were known as "academies" and were privately controlled. Usually, they provided a liberal arts education, but often included training for teaching or business. Some were for boys only, some for girls, and some were coeducational.

Sometimes the compilers of statistics considered the libraries in elementary and secondary schools together, and sometimes they distinguished between the two groups. And sometimes it is not clear whether they were reporting only common schools or were including collections belonging to academies. The first attempt to gather information on a nationwide basis was the census for 1850, which reported a total of 12,067 school libraries for the entire country; 10,802 of those were in New York State.[7] Charles C. Jewett, at about the same time, reported numbers for only a few states. His figures include some estimates; for five states they total about 9,700, of which 8,070 were in New York. For academies, he had figures only for New York, where there were 157 libraries, apparently not included in his other total for that state.[8]

The census of 1860 reported 10,558 school libraries; according to it, there were only 6,321 libraries in New York; Ohio was next with 1,996. William J.

Rhees, writing in 1859, reported that Ohio had 6,437 school libraries.[9] Even though the number of these libraries in various states rose and fell, this precipitous decline in about a year was surely due in part to an error in reporting.

In the 1870 census, figures for school libraries were combined with college libraries. The total given there for both kinds was 14,375.[10] Evidence from other sources indicated the existence of only approximately 580 college libraries in 1870, so it seems likely that there were at least thirteen thousand school libraries at that time. As in earlier years, New York State had far more than did any other state. For school and college libraries combined, its reported figure was 9,879 and other sources reported only 57 college libraries; therefore that state seems to have had well over half of all of the school libraries in the country. The Bureau of Education's *Public Libraries in the United States of America* for 1876 makes no attempt to give the number of libraries in common schools, but states that 826 secondary schools reported libraries and that "there are doubtless many such libraries not reported."[11]

SUNDAY SCHOOL LIBRARIES

The situation of Sunday school libraries is somewhat like the situation of libraries in elementary schools: very large numbers and very few attempts made before 1876 to determine the number that existed at particular times. Most Sunday schools were operated by churches—one school per church—but a church could maintain more than one school, and some schools were operated by religious organizations other than churches. Sunday school libraries were considered to be separate from church libraries. Often, the privilege of borrowing from the Sunday school library was granted only to children whose attendance records were good.

Sunday schools and their libraries have been discussed by several twentieth century historians.[12] The libraries contained both religious and secular material and were popular with children for two reasons: (1) The stories in some of the books were exciting, and (2) in some communities, these were the only libraries available. Two of the writers who tried to collect information about them before 1876 felt that they were beneficial in forming the moral atmosphere in the country.[13]

The 1850 census listed 1,988 Sunday school libraries, a figure that William J. Rhees, a few years later, considered "hardly worth noticing, as [it is] so manifestly incorrect." He quoted, instead, some rather complicated reasoning presented by Frederick A. Packard of the American Sunday-school Union, which resulted in an estimate of 40,000 libraries.[14] The 1860 Census listed only 6,205, but the 1870 census included a total of 33,580.[15] The Bureau of Education's *Public Libraries in the United States of America* for 1876 did not include them in its tables. Its editors wrote: "Indeed, no systematic effort was made to gather the statistics of such libraries, which are almost as numerous as the churches in the country."[16]

Even though the figures in the three censuses are subject to serious question, they may give a rough indication of the distribution of Sunday school libraries among the four regions of the country. In 1850, the Northeast was credited with 61.7 percent; 63.2 percent in 1860, and only 36 percent in 1870. Figures for the South were 10.5 percent in 1850, 7.3 percent in 1860, and 21.3 percent in 1870. The percentages for the Middle West were 27.8 in 1850, 29.0 in 1860, and 41.1 in 1870. The Far West received almost no credit: none in 1850, only 0.5 percent in 1860, and 1.6 percent in 1870. For all libraries in the main part of this study (chapters 3 through 11), the Far West had 4.7 percent. We can only speculate about its lack of Sunday school libraries. Was there less interest in religious matters there or just fewer children in communities where mining was the main industry and men had often left their families in the East?

THE PREVALENCE OF PRIVATE LIBRARIES, SCHOOL LIBRARIES, AND SUNDAY SCHOOL LIBRARIES

The statements reported in this chapter about the three kinds of libraries omitted from the main part of this study would indicate that the total number of libraries in private hands, schools, and Sunday schools before 1876 was much larger than the total number of other libraries. Chapters 1 through 11 are based on records concerning only about ten thousand libraries that could be individually identified. There were more than a hundred and fifty thousand of the three kinds of libraries considered in chapter 12, and the total could have been twice that many. Of these three kinds, at least a hundred thousand were private libraries, but all surveys reported substantial numbers of school and Sunday school libraries. It is clear that very many Americans, before 1876, felt that organized collections of books should be available to children as well as adults.

NOTES

1. U .S. Smithsonian Institution, *Fourth Annual Report of the Board of Regents of the Smithsonian Institution to the Senate and House of Representatives, 1849* (Washington, D.C.: Printers to the Senate, 1850), 38, and *Appendix to the Report of the Board of Regents of the Smithsonian Institution, Containing a Report on the Public Libraries of the United States of America, January 1, 1850*, by Charles C. Jewett (Washington, D.C.: Printed for the Senate, 1850), 3.

2. U.S. Superintendent of the Census, *Statistical View of the United States, Being a Compendium of the Seventh Census*, by J. D. B. DeBow (Washington, D.C.: Beverley Tucker, Senate Printer, 1854), 159.

3. *Statistics of the United States in 1860, Eighth Census* (Washington, D.C.: Government Printing Office, 1866), 502, and *Ninth Census, vol. 1, The Statistics of the Population of the United States* (Washington, D.C.: Government Printing Office, 1872). In the latter volume, the total is given as 108,800 in the table on p. 475 and as 107,673 in the text on p. 472.

4. Ninth Census, vol. 1, The Statistics of the Population of the United States, 472–73.

5. U.S. Bureau of Education, *Public Libraries in the United States of America: Special Report*. Part 1. (Washington, D.C.: Government Printing Office, 1876), xvii.

6. U.S. Bureau of Education, *Public Libraries*, pp. 38–58, "School and Asylum

Libraries: Common School Libraries."

7. The number of school libraries reported for each state in 1850 is presented most conveniently on page 477 of *Ninth Census, vol. 1, The Statistics of the Population of the United States*, "Libraries, Other than Private, 1850."

8. Smithsonian Institution, *Fourth Annual Report*, p. 40, and its *Appendix*, pp. 10, 15, 48, 100–05, and 185. The total for Michigan, on p. 40 of the main report, seems to be corrected on p. 185 of the appendix.

9. *Statistics of the United States in 1860, Eighth Census*, p. 505, and William J. Rhees, *Manual of Public Libraries, Institutions, and Societies, in the United States and British Provinces of North America* (Philadelphia: J. B. Lippincott, 1859), 570.

10. *Ninth Census, vol. 1, The Statistics of the Population of the United States*, p. 475.

11. U.S. Bureau of Education, *Public Libraries*, p. 58.

12. For example: Sunday School: the Formation of an American Institution, 1790–1880, by Anne M. Boylan (New Haven, Conn.: Yale University Press, 1988) and "The Sunday-School Library in the Nineteenth Century," by F. Allen Briggs, Library Quarterly 31 (Apr., 1961): 166–77.

13. Charles C. Jewett in *Fourth Annual Report of the Smithsonian Institution*, p. 40, and William J. Rhees, in his *Manual of Public Libraries, Institutions, and Societies*, 1859, p. 578.

14. "Libraries, Other than Private, 1850," p. 477 in *Ninth Census, vol. 1, The Statistics of the Population of the United States*, and Rhees, *Manual of Public Libraries, Institutions, and Societies*, 1859, pp. 579–80.

15. *Statistics of the United States in 1860, Eighth Census*, p. 505, and *Ninth Census, vol. 1, The Statistics of the Population of the United States*, p. 475.

16. U.S. Bureau of Education, *Public Libraries*, p. 1011.

Afterword

The main part of this book (chapters 1 through 11) is based on information that I have been able to gather over the last fifty years concerning approximately 10,000 libraries that existed in the American colonies and the United States before 1876, far more collections than any other student of American library history has considered. It is likely that many others existed, and that some of my conclusions about the significance of libraries in American life might have been different if I could have learned about those other collections. However, the main conclusions, based on the characteristics of 10,000 libraries, have not been very different from the ones that I drew some years ago when I was aware of only 6,000. Therefore, I would like to think that if I—or someone else—were to discover information about a few thousand more, there might be noticeably different conclusions about only a few particular kinds of libraries, or libraries in a particular part of the country.

Everything in this book can be considered as an indication of attitudes. Most of the collections of books were assembled because small groups of persons were willing to spend money in order to provide themselves or others with information or with the basis for the exercise of their imaginations. Occasionally, units of government established libraries but, unless the users agreed about the value of those collections, those libraries often withered and died.

Librarians existed throughout the period, but there is little evidence that they had any influence on the life of the collections in their care until about the middle of the nineteenth century. Persons who might be considered as "laymen" simply gathered and made use of whatever kinds of books they wanted.

Glossary

This list of kinds of libraries includes definitions of terms used before 1876, terms used by recent writers on American library history (sometimes because of failure to understand earlier terminology), and terms used in a special sense in this study.

Academy library. Almost always the library of a secondary school, so not included in the main part of this study unless it was the library of a military academy that gave college-level work. See the headings *School library* and *Military academy library.*

Agricultural and mechanical college library. The library of a college that emphasized agriculture and engineering. In this study, these colleges have been considered as agricultural colleges.

Agricultural library belonging to a state government. A few state boards of agriculture had libraries, beginning in the 1850s.

Agricultural social library. A library belonging to a group that was organized to establish a library about agriculture.

Agricultural society library. A library owned by a society formed because its members were interested in agriculture. Some of these were called farmers' clubs.

Antiquarian society library. In this study, such a library is considered as a *Historical society library.*

Apprentices' library. A library for the use of apprentices, usually planned and supervised by older businessmen or employees and usually containing a general collection of books. Often open to others besides apprentices. Similar to a *Mechanics' library* or a *Workingmen's library* but counted separately in this study.

Art museum library. A small number of these existed, mainly after the Civil War. In this study they have been considered as art society libraries.

Art society library. A library belonging to a society formed because of its members' interest in art. A very few of these existed, mainly after the Civil War. In this study art museum libraries are included with them.

Association library. See *Society library.*

Asylum library. The term *asylum* was widely used for any institution where handicapped or disadvantaged children or adults lived and were cared for. Many were maintained by charitable societies; others were operated by federal, state, or local governments.

Atheneum library (formerly spelled *athenaeum*). Atheneums were societies, partly social and partly cultural. Their libraries were like social libraries because both kinds were general and because the operation of a library was often one of the main objects of the atheneum. If the atheneum library differed, it was because it might put more emphasis on current journals and newspapers.

Bar association library. A library belonging to a group of lawyers whose association was not formed for the primary purpose of maintaining a library. See also *Social law library.*

Board of trade library. A library owned by an association of merchants whose main purpose was the regulation of trade or the promotion of commerce. In this study, libraries of the similar organizations known as merchants' exchanges and chambers of commerce are included with board of trade libraries.

Book club library. Members of some book clubs exchanged the books they read. If there is evidence that they collected a library, it is included with the libraries maintained by literary societies and reading clubs.

Bray libraries. The libraries sent from England to Church of England parishes, mostly in Maryland beginning around 1700 through the efforts of Thomas Bray, have been considered in this study as *church libraries.*

Business college library. Some schools for instruction in business skills owned libraries beginning in the 1840s. These libraries have been included in the study although it is possible that their institutions did not offer work at the college level.

Chamber of commerce library. A few such libraries existed; in this study, they are grouped with libraries belonging to boards of trade and merchants' exchanges.

Church library. A library maintained by a particular church in a particular town or city. In this study, the term is considered as separate from a *sunday school library* and from any library owned by a group of churches or by some other religious association, which is considered as a *religious society library.*

Circulating library. Originally, any library from which books could be taken home. The term was used to designate two main types: a *commercial circulating library,* operated for profit, and a *social library,* operated for the benefit of its users. In recent years, historians have usually limited the term to mean what is called in this study a *commercial circulating library.*

Club library. The term *club* began to be common in the 1850s to denote a society, usually with a social rather than a subject interest. In this study, a library belonging to such an organization has been considered as a *society library.*

College library. A library belonging to an institution of higher education. In this study, the term *college* alone means a liberal arts college; a more specialized college is distinguished as a *medical college,* a *law school,* a *theological seminary,* or by any other appropriate phrase.

College literary society library. See *College student society library.*

College student society library. A library belonging to a society of students in an institution of higher education. These societies, often called literary societies, held meetings for social and educational purposes and typically owned general collections of books. A few such societies, mainly in theological seminaries, had libraries containing books on religion. Collections on other special subjects were rare.

Commercial circulating library. A library owned by an individual or firm and containing books that were circulated to individuals for a fee. The fee was usually in the form of a subscription, payable monthly, quarterly, or annually. The collections were almost always general and popular in nature.

Commercial college library. See *Business college library.*

Convent library. A few convent libraries were discovered, apparently controlled by

Roman Catholic organizations; they are counted as church libraries in this study.

County law library. This kind of library seems to have usually been the library owned by the county bar association. Therefore, in this study, such a library is considered as one belonging to a bar association unless information indicates that it was not.

County library. This term had no generally accepted meaning, and was rare outside of Indiana, where a county library was a social library that had been established with funds from a special tax. In this study, it has been considered as a *Government-aided social library.*

Court library. Many local, state, and federal courts had libraries. In this study, libraries belonging to each of these three forms of government are combined with other legal collections and considered as *Law libraries.*

Dentistry library. A small number of dental libraries existed. In this study they have been included with medical libraries.

Education library. A few state governments operated libraries that were on the subject of education or were intended for educational professionals, beginning in the 1850s. The libraries operated by a few city boards of education at about the same time may have had an educational emphasis, but several of them clearly were general in content.

Elementary school library. A library in a school containing only the lower grades. These libraries are not included in the main part of this study but are discussed in a general way in chapter 12.

Engineering college library. See *Scientific or engineering college library.*

Engineering society library. A small number of civil and mining engineers' societies had libraries, beginning in the 1850s. See *Scientific or engineering society library.*

Farmers' club library. See *Agricultural society library.*

Federal government library. See *United States government library.*

Female college library. A library belonging to a college for women.

Female library. A term that was used synonymously with *Ladies' library.*

Fire company library. A library owned by a volunteer fire company. These existed mainly in larger cities and were general in content.

Foreign language library. A library collected by a group of people speaking a language other than English. Almost all of them were operated by German immigrant groups; see *German social library*, *German society library*, and *Musical society library.*

Fraternal organization library. A library belonging to a lodge of the Masons, the Independent Order of Odd Fellows, or other fraternal group. In this study, a library belonging to a German-speaking fraternal group is considered as a *German society library*, and the small number of Masonic college libraries are included with other college libraries.

Garrison library. A library at a military post, usually general in nature.

German social library. A term used in this study to include any library formed by German-speaking people if it was like other social libraries in organization.

German society library. A term used in this study to include any library belonging to a society of German-speaking people if the society was formed for some purpose other than the maintenance of a library. However, collections belonging to German singing societies have been grouped with those of other musical societies.

Government library. Many of the libraries in this study were operated by federal, state, or local units of government. See such headings as *Agricultural library belonging to a state government*, *County library*, *Court library*, *Public library*, *School district library*, *State library*, *Territorial library*, and *Township library.*

Government-aided social library. A *Social library* with some support from a unit of government. A few existed in Indiana (see *County library*), Massachusetts, and elsewhere.

Health, state board library. A few state boards of health had libraries after the Civil War.

High school library. A library in a school containing the upper grades, of less than college level. Libraries in elementary and secondary schools are not included in the main part of this study but are discussed in a general way in chapter 12.

Historical social library. A library belonging to a society whose main purpose was to form a library on historical subjects. Very few of these existed.

Historical society library. A library belonging to a society formed because of the members' interest in history.

Horticultural society library. In this study, such a library is considered as an *Agricultural society library.*

Hospital library. A library in a hospital, whether intended for the patients or the medical staff. In this study, the patients' libraries are considered separately from the medical libraries because of the difference in subject matter. A library in a mental hospital is considered as an *Asylum library.*

Hotel reading room. Hotels sometimes maintained reading rooms containing a few books, current journals, and newspapers. In this study, such a room is included as a *Reading room in a commercial enterprise.*

House of refuge library. A library in a home for unfortunate persons: unwed mothers, juvenile delinquents, or others. Considered as an *Asylum library* in this study.

I.O.O.F. library. A library belonging to a lodge of the Independent Order of Odd Fellows. See *Fraternal organization library.*

Industrial school for boys library. It is not always clear whether such a library belonged to a reformatory or to some other kind of school. If it seemed to belong to a reform school, it is included in the main part of this study as a *Prison library*, but if it seemed to belong to another kind of school, it is considered in chapter 12. Only a few libraries in industrial schools were discovered.

Insane asylum library. See *Asylum library.*

Institute library. The word *institute* alone does not help to identify the type of library because some *institutes* were schools, some were societies, and some were charitable enterprises. The word seems to imply only that the agency was in some way educational, charitable, or cultural.

Juvenile social library. A library for children, organized by children or their elders. A few such libraries existed, mainly in New England after about 1790.

Ladies' library. See *Ladies' social library* and *Ladies' society library.*

Ladies' social library. A library formed by women and intended for their use. It was established by an association that was organized in order to maintain the library. These collections were general in content and existed mainly in New England and the state of Michigan.

Ladies' society library. A library belonging to a women's society that did not have the maintenance of a library as its main purpose. Collections belonging to women's sewing clubs and literary societies are included here.

Land grant college library. See *Agricultural and mechanical college library.*

Law library. There were several kinds of libraries containing mainly or entirely law books. See *Bar association library, County law library, Law school library, State law library*, and *State library.*

Law school library. The library of a law school has been included in the study if the school was independent or if its library was reported as separate from that of the college or university with which the school was connected.

Library association. The same as a *Library society.*

Library society. If preceded by a place name, this phrase ordinarily meant a *Social library.*

Literary society library. A library belonging to a society made up of persons interested in literature. However, because that term was often used broadly, the collection could have been general in subject matter.

Lyceum library. A lyceum was an organization made up of people who met together to debate and to listen to lectures and who usually established a general library. If there is evidence that a lyceum had a library, it is included in this study. If a lyceum's main emphasis was its library, its purpose was almost the same as that of a *Social library*.

Lyceum of natural history library. This term occurred occasionally; in this study it is considered as a *Scientific or engineering society library*.

Maclure library. The name sometimes given to any *Workingmen's library* established with the help of funds provided in William Maclure's will.

Manufacturers' library. A term that was used to mean a library maintained in a factory by its owner, for the use of employees, who were sometimes called *manufacturers*. Such a library was more often called a *Mill library*.

Masonic college library. A few liberal arts colleges were supported by the Masons. In this study, their libraries have been included with those of other college libraries.

Masonic library. A library operated by and for a lodge of Masons. See *Fraternal organization library*.

Mechanics' library. A library for artisans. These libraries usually contained general collections and were similar to *Apprentices' libraries* and *Workingmen's libraries*.

Mechanics' society library. A phrase occasionally used; in this study, considered as a *Mechanics' library*.

Medical college library. A library belonging to a school that trained physicians.

Medical social library. A library belonging to a society whose main purpose was to form a library of medical books. Very few of these existed.

Medical society library. A library owned by a society of physicians whose main purpose was not to maintain a library.

Mental hospital library. A few libraries seem to have existed in institutions for the mentally ill, which were hospitals rather than asylums. However, the number was so small and the distinction so vague that each of them has been included in this study as an *Asylum library*.

Mercantile library. A library formed for the use of clerks in business firms. Ordinarily formed by the clerks themselves and ordinarily general in content.

Merchants' exchange library. See *Board of trade library*.

Military academy library. The library belonging to a secondary school or college in which the main emphasis was on military topics. If the academy seems to have been of college grade, its library is included in this study as a *Military college library*.

Military college library. The library belonging to a school of college grade in which the main emphasis was on military topics. There seems to have been a very small number of such libraries.

Military post library. See *Garrison library*.

Military social library. A term used in this study for a *Social library* formed by military personnel. Only rarely was a military library clearly of this type; if its ownership and operation is doubtful it has been considered as a *Garrison library*.

Mill library. A library maintained in a factory by its owner, for the use of employees. Sometimes a small fee was charged. Such a library was more often found in New England than elsewhere.

Mining library. A very few libraries were on the subject of mining. In this study, they have been included with libraries on science and engineering.

Mission library. In this study, any library belonging to a Catholic mission has been considered as a *Church library*. Most of these libraries were in California.

Missionary society library. A few libraries belonging to (mostly Protestant) missionary societies were discovered. Each of them is included in this study as a *Religious society library*.

Musical society library. A library belonging to a society formed because of its members' interest in music. Several of these were established by German-speaking persons.

Officers' library. If a library used by military officers was clearly owned and operated by a group of officers who formed a library society, it is considered in this study as a *Military social library*. Otherwise, it is considered as a *Garrison library*.

Orphanage library. See *Asylum library*.

Patients' library in a hospital. In this study, such a library has been considered as separate from a medical library in a hospital. See *Hospital library*.

Penitentiary library. See *Prison library*.

Pharmacy library. In this study, the very few pharmacy libraries have been considered as medical libraries.

Polytechnic institute library. In this study, each of these libraries has been considered as a *Scientific or engineering college library*.

Post library. A library at a military post. See *Garrison library*.

Prison library. A library for the use of prison inmates. In this study, reform school libraries are included with prison libraries.

Proprietary library. A term that was never in general use in the nineteenth century. It was used interchangeably with the term *Subscription library* by Edward Edwards in his book *Memoirs of Libraries*, published in 1859. Apparently, the two terms were both used to describe social libraries until 1912 when Charles K. Bolton published a pamphlet, *Proprietary and Subscription Libraries* and began to employ the term *Proprietary library* if the users of the collection owned stock in it; he employed the term *Subscription library* for one in which the users paid annual fees. Writers since his day have accepted his idea, apparently ignorant of the fact that, for many social libraries, the proprietors were called subscribers and paid an annual fee. They sometimes permitted others to use the collection for a fee. The term *Proprietary library* is not used in the present study.

Public library. Before 1876, this term was ordinarily used to mean any library other than one owned by an individual for his or her own use. In that sense, it would include every library in the main part of this study. But in this study it is used in its more recent sense to mean a library, usually general in content, which was almost always owned by a local government and was open to most or all of the citizens without charge. No distinction is made as to means of financial support: whether by taxation or through the gifts of individuals. Also see *Religious library belonging to a town*.

Public library owned by a religious group. A few libraries were owned by churches or religious societies and were clearly open to the public without charge. Because of the difficulty of determining the exact content and conditions of use of libraries owned by churches and other religious groups, each of these free libraries has been considered in this study as either a *Church library* or a *Religious society library*, depending on its ownership.

Public library owned by an individual. A very few libraries were owned by individuals who generously opened them for public use without charge. They are considered separately in this study.

Railroad library. A library intended for the use of the employees of a railroad. Similar to a *Mill library*.

Reading club library. Members of reading clubs may have just exchanged the books they read. If there is evidence that they collected a library, it is included in this study and considered as a *Literary society library*.

Reading room. If there is evidence that library materials were available in a reading room, it has been included in this study. Sometimes the term *library and reading room* was used to distinguish a library from others for which no reading space was provided.

Reading room in a commercial enterprise. In this study, reading rooms maintained by hotels, taverns, newspaper offices, and other businesses have been grouped together. Usually, library materials were available to customers at no extra cost.

Reform school library. In this study, the library of a reform school is considered as a *Prison library.*

Religious college society library. This term is used in this study to include two kinds of libraries: 1) a library that had a religious emphasis and was owned by a society made up of students in a liberal arts college, and 2) any library owned by a society of students in a theological seminary. Apparently, all or almost all of these latter societies were religious in nature.

Religious historical society library. A few denominations had historical societies, such as the Presbyterian Historical Society in Philadelphia. A library belonging to such a society has been considered in this study as a *Religious society library.*

Religious library belonging to a town. A very few libraries, religious in content, were operated by towns as free public libraries during the eighteenth century and the early decades of the nineteenth century. These have been considered separately in this study.

Religious social library. A library formed by a group of people who associated themselves together to acquire and use a religious library. See also *Church library* and *Religious society library.*

Religious society library. In this study, this term is used for any library established by a religious group other than a Young Men's Christian Association, a church, or a Sunday school if the group was not organized for the purpose of establishing a library. If the group was formed to establish a library, its library has been considered as a *Religious social library.*

Saloon reading room. Saloons sometimes maintained reading rooms as added attractions for their customers. In this study, such a room is included as a *Reading room in a commercial enterprise.*

School district library. There were many school district libraries. Most of them were very small, and they are seldom listed separately in early national lists. Even though they were often used by adults, they are considered in this study as school libraries, so are not included in the main part. They are included with other school libraries in chapter 12.

School library. The term is used in this study to mean a library belonging to an educational institution of less than college grade. There were many of these but they were often very small, and it has been impossible to obtain information about some of them. They are not included in the main part of the study but are discussed in chapter 12.

Scientific or engineering college library. In this study, libraries belonging to scientific and engineering colleges have been considered together because it has often been difficult to determine how much emphasis was placed on science and how much on engineering.

Scientific or engineering library owned by a government. The federal government maintained several of these, mainly concerned with navigation. State and local governments had very few.

Scientific or engineering society library. The library of a society formed because of its members' interest in science or engineering. In this study, a *Medical society library* or an *Agricultural society library* is not considered as one belonging to a scientific society.

Secondary school library. A library in a school containing the upper grades, below college level. These libraries are not included in the main part of this study but are discussed in chapter 12.

Seminary library. The term was used for two kinds of libraries before 1876. Unless it was preceded by the term *theological* or a similar word, a seminary library belonged to a school of less than college grade and is not included in the main part of this study. See *School library.* If it was a *Theological seminary library* it is included.

Sewing circle library. A few libraries, presumably operated by women, used this phrase in their names. In this study such a library is considered as a *Ladies' society library.*

Social historical library. See *Historical social library.*

Social law library. A library operated by a society whose main purpose was to form a library of legal books. Different from a *Bar association library.*

Social library. This term has been used in various ways by different writers. In this study, if it is used without modification, it means a library owned by an association formed to establish and operate a library intended for its members' use. Usually, the members subscribed for stock in order to purchase the initial collection, which was general in subject matter. Then they were assessed a smaller sum (a "tax") each year to keep up the collection. If the members were drawn from a distinct part of the population or had a distinct subject interest, their library has been considered separately; for example, a *Ladies' social library* or a *Social law library.* If the membership and collection were general in nature, and the maintenance of a library was one of several purposes of a group, it has been considered as a *Society library.*

Social medical library. See *Medical social library.*

Social religious library. See *Religious social library.*

Social theological library. See *Religious social library.*

Society library. In this study, the terms *society* and *association* are considered as having the same meaning. If a place name preceded the phrase *library society* it is considered as a *Social library.* When the word *society* occurs without a place name, it is considered as a library belonging to an association formed because of its members' subject interest, that is, an association that was not formed primarily to operate a library. For these associations, see the name for the kind of society, for example *Bar association library* or *Historical society library.* A few societies seem to have been general in interest; others had a subject interest so specialized that a separate category for them did not seem worthwhile, and for some it has been impossible to determine the main subject interest. These general or miscellaneous societies have been considered as a single group; examples are the library of the stage drivers of Canandaigua, New York, the Tennessee Society for the Diffusion of Knowledge, and the Chess and Literary Association of Shasta, California.

State board of education library. See *Education library.*

State board of health library. See *Health, state board library.*

State law library. A collection of law books belonging to a state court or other state agency. In this study, such a library is considered as different from a *State library,* which typically contained law books and books on general subjects.

State library. The term was used before 1876 to mean the library maintained by the state government at the capital of the state, intended for the use of state officials. Typically, the library was divided into two parts: one for law books and one for general books.

Strict social library. A term used in this study for a *Social library* organized and used by a society made up of people whose main purpose was to gather and read a general or miscellaneous collection of books.

Subscription library. This term has been used by some modern writers to mean a *Social library* in which the users did not own the collection, but paid an annual fee, in contrast to a *Proprietary library,* which was owned by the users. Actually, in a typical library, the proprietors paid annual fees. Sometimes, they permitted others to use the library for a fee. The term *Subscription library* is not used in this study. See the term *Proprietary library* in this glossary.

Sunday school library. An American Sunday school, in the early part of the nineteenth century, was sometimes operated by an individual church and sometimes cooperatively by several churches, mainly to teach religion. Very many existed; usually, their libraries were small. They are not included in the main part of this study, but are discussed in chapter 12.

Supreme court library. In this study, the library of the United States Supreme Court is included with other federal law libraries and the libraries of state supreme courts are included with other law libraries belonging to the states.

Tavern reading room. Some taverns maintained reading rooms, with a few books, current journals, and newspapers. In this study, such a room is included as a *Reading room in a commercial enterprise.*

Temperance library. In this study, a temperance library is considered as a religious library. If it was operated by a church it is considered as a *Church library*, and if by some other organization, as a *Religious society library.*

Territorial library. Several of the territories had libraries at the seats of government. Because such a library became a state library when the territory achieved statehood, no distinction has been made in this study, and it is considered as a *State library* even while it served the territorial government.

Theological public library. See *Public library owned by a religious group.*

Theological seminary library. A library belonging to an institution of college grade or higher, intended for the training of clergymen.

Theological seminary student society library. In this study, any library belonging to a society of students in a theological seminary is considered as a *Religious college society library.*

Township library. A public library for a township, which is a division of a county in the Middle West. Most of these libraries were established by the state governments in Michigan and Indiana, beginning in the 1840s. Sometimes they have been considered as school libraries, but they were intended for adults, as well, and are included in the main part of this study.

United States government library. Some federal libraries were general or miscellaneous, as for example the Library of Congress and the library in the Executive Mansion. A few were on engineering or scientific subjects, and a few others consisted mainly of law books. The total number of federal libraries was not large.

University library. There were several university libraries before 1876, but the university, in the present sense of the word, was so rare that each of them has been considered as a *College library.*

Women's library. See *Ladies' library* and *Ladies' society library.*

Workingmen's library. A library for the use of laborers. Most of these collections were in Indiana and most were established with the aid of funds left in the will of William Maclure. Similar in purpose to a *Mechanics' library* or *Apprentices' library.*

Young men's association library. A library established by young men who belonged to an organization that had been formed for some purpose other than the maintenance of a library. In this study, collections belonging to Young Men's Christian Associations are considered separately.

Young Men's Christian Association library. A library belonging to a YMCA. These libraries normally contained both religious and general materials.

Young men's library association. An association formed by young men for the purpose of maintaining a library.

Youth's library. A name that was sometimes used for a *Juvenile social library.*

Selected Bibliography

Bixby, Mrs. A. F. and Mrs. A. Howell, eds. *Historical Sketches of the Ladies' Library Associations of the State of Michigan.* Adrian, Mich.: Times and Expositor Steam Print, 1876.

Bode, Carl. *The American Lyceum: Town Meeting of the Mind.* Carbondale and Edwardsville, Ill.: Southern Illinois University Press, 1968.

Boone, Richard G. *A History of Education in Indiana.* New York: R. Appleton, 1892.

Boyd, William Douglas, Jr. "Books for Young Businessmen: Mercantile Libraries in the United States, 1820–1865." Ph.D. diss., Indiana University, 1975.

Bremner, Robert H. *The Public Good: Philanthropy and Welfare in the Civil War Era.* New York: Knopf, 1980.

Brown, Richard D. *Knowledge is Power: The Diffusion of Information in Early America, 1700–1865.* New York: Oxford University Press, 1989.

Burke, Colin B. *American Collegiate Populations: A Test of the Traditional View.* New York: New York University Press, 1982.

Dunn, Jacob Piatt. *The Libraries of Indiana.* Indianapolis: Wm. B. Burford, 1893.

Harding, Thomas S. *College Literary Societies: Their Contribution to Higher Education in the United States, 1815–1876.* New York: Pageant Press International, 1971.

Held, Ray E. *Public Libraries in California, 1849–1878.* Berkeley, Calif.: University of California Press, 1963.

Kaser, David. *A Book for a Sixpence: The Circulating Library in America.* Pittsburgh, Pa.: Beta Phi Mu, 1980.

——. *Books and Libraries in Camp and Battle: The Civil War Experience.* Westport, Conn.: Greenwood Press, 1984.

Laugher, Charles T. *Thomas Bray's Grand Design: Libraries of the Church of England in America, 1695–1785.* Chicago: American Library Association, 1973.

Miller, L. M. *Legislative History of Township Libraries in the State of Michigan from 1835 to 1901, Printed by Order of the Board of the Library Commissioners.* Lansing, Mich.: Robert Smith Printing Co., 1902.

Rhees, William J. *Manual of Public Libraries, Institutions, and Societies in the United States and British Provinces of North America.* Philadelphia: J. B. Lippincott, 1859.

Shera, Jesse H. *Foundations of the Public Library: The Origins of the Public Library*

Movement in New England, 1629–1855. Chicago: University of Chicago Press, 1949.

Singerman, Robert. *American Library Book Catalogues, 1801–1875: A National Bibliography.* Occasional Papers, No. 203/204, April 1996. Urbana-Champaign, Ill.: Graduate School of Library and Information Science, University of Illinois, 1996.

Skallerup, Harry R. *Books Afloat and Ashore: A History of Books, Libraries, and Reading Among Seamen during the Age of Sail.* Hamden, Conn.: Archon Books, 1974.

Stewart, Miller J. "A Touch of Civilization: Culture and Education in the Frontier Army." *Nebraska History* 65 (Summer 1984): 257–82.

Tewksbury, Donald G. *The Founding of American Colleges and Universities before the Civil War.* Hamden, Conn.: Archon Books, 1965.

Thompson, C. Seymour. *Evolution of the American Public Library, 1653–1876.* Washington, D.C.: Scarecrow, 1952.

U.S. Bureau of Education. *Public Libraries in the United States of America: Special Report.* 2 vols. Washington, D.C.: Government Printing Office, 1876.

——. *Report of the Commissioner of Education for the Year 1884–85.* Washington, D.C.: Government Printing Office, 1886.

U.S. Bureau of the Census. *Historical Statistics of the United States, Colonial Times to 1970.* Washington, D.C.: Government Printing Office, 1975.

U.S. Commissioner of Agriculture. *Report of the Commissioner of Agriculture for the Year 1867.* 40th Cong., 2d sess., 1868. H. Exec. Doc. 40.

U.S. Patent Office. *Report of the Commissioner of Patents for the Year 1858. Agriculture.* 35th Cong., 2d sess., 1859, S. Exec. Doc. 47.

U.S. Smithsonian Institution. *Fourth Annual Report of the Board of Regents of the Smithsonian Institution to the Senate and House of Representatives, 1849.* Washington, D.C.: Printers to the Senate, 1850 and *Appendix to the Report of the Board of Regents of the Smithsonian Institution, Containing a Report on the Public Libraries of the United States of America, January 1, 1850,* by Charles C. Jewett. Washington, D.C.: Printed for the Senate, 1850.

U.S. Superintendent of the Census. *The Seventh Census of the United States: 1850.* Washington, D.C.: Robert Armstrong, Public Printer, 1853.

——. *Statistical View of the United States, Being a Compendium of the Seventh Census,* by J. D. B. DeBow. Washington, D.C.: Beverley Tucker, Senate Printer, 1854.

——. *Statistics of the United States in 1860, Eighth Census.* Washington, D.C.: Government Printing Office, 1866.

——. *Ninth Census, vol. 1, The Statistics of the Population of the United States, 1870.* Washington, D.C.: Government Printing Office, 1872.

U.S. War Department, Surgeon General's Office. *A Report on Barracks and Hospitals, with Descriptions of Military Posts.* Circular no. 4. Washington, D.C.: Government Printing Office, 1870.

——. *A Report on the Hygiene of the United States Army, with Descriptions of Military Posts.* Circular no. 8. Washington, D.C.: Government Printing Office, 1875.

Wiegand, Wayne A. "The Historical Development of State Library Agencies." In *State Library Services and Issues: Facing Future Challenges,* ed. by Charles R. McClure, 1–16. Norwood, N.J.: Ablex Publishing Corp., 1986.

Zboray, Ronald John. *A Fictive People: Antebellum Economic Development and the American Reading Public.* New York: Oxford University Press, 1993.

Index

About the Author

HAYNES McMULLEN is Emeritus Professor of Library Science, University of North Carolina at Chapel Hill.